A Better Bargain

Mobilizing Employers and Workers to Grow America's Middle Class

Martin Manley

First Edition: September, 2019

Book Design by Andy Meaden meadencreative.com

Cover Art © Shutterstock/durantelallera

Author Photo by Luigi Semenzato

ISBN 978-1-7333155-0-0 Hardback

ISBN 978-1-7333155-1-7 Paperback

ISBN 978-1-7333155-2-4 eBook

Published by Reputation Networks Venture Publishing
www.reputationnetworks.com

Library of Congress Preassigned Control Number:

Manley, Martin

A Better Bargain: Mobilizing Employers and Workers to Grow America's Middle Class / Martin Manley

1st ed.

Includes bibliographical references and index.

1. Economic Policy. 2. Political Economy. 3. Income Inequality.

To Anno Saxenian and Steve Manley (1958-1979).

Advance praise for *A Better Bargain*

"Income inequality threatens our country. We need more than new policies – we need new institutions devoted to preserving middle class incomes. Marty Manley brings his unusual understanding of both Silicon Valley startups and labor unions to outline an innovative approach to organizing companies as well as workers. A Better Bargain *is a powerful, provocative read."*

Tim O'Reilly
Founder and CEO, O'Reilly Media

"To rebuild our middle class, Americans need effective labor unions. In this provocative and important book, Marty Manley describes 21stcentury labor organizations that can grow without corporate interference and a new approach to income bargaining that can help America's lowest paid workers once again earn larger raises."

Robert Reich
Former US Secretary of Labor
Chancellor's Professor of Public Policy, UC Berkeley
Author, *The Common Good and Saving Capitalism for the Many, Not the Few*

"There is no more important debate in the 2020 elections than how to strengthen the ability of American workers to organize unions and bargain their own pay. Marty Manley has kicked off this debate with reforms that deserve wide readership and discussion."

Leo Gerard
President, United Steelworkers

"Marty Manley argues not only for modern labor unions, but for employer organizations that can help strengthen labor markets. I hope that this book gets widespread attention during the 2020 election."

James Bessen
Founder, Bestinfo
Lecturer, Boston University School of Law
Author, *Learning by Doing: The Real Connection Between Innovation, Wages, and Wealth*

Contents

Preface

Lupe Martinez never meant to make me into a union man. Lupe was a skilled cook at the beachfront restaurant where I waited tables after graduating from college at the University of California.

College had been first-rate, demanding, and virtually free. I had fled to the experimental campus at Santa Cruz from the postwar Los Angeles suburbs, where my pharmacist dad and school teacher mom raised four children on a street with thirty-two houses and sixty kids. The guy next door ran the liquor store and next to him was a plumber. When college got boring, I took a year and a half off, worked a minimum wage job in a small factory for six months, and saved enough to spend four months traveling in Europe and North Africa. It was a massively different time.

Late one evening, we were closing the restaurant and my manager asked me to escort a routine drunk out the door. Lupe was taking a cigarette break in the darkened parking lot. When he saw the patron suddenly threaten me with a large knife, he rushed over, howling and swinging his belt. Confronted with a dervish in kitchen whites, the drunk went pale and stumbled to the beach unhurt. Lupe and I were still laughing when our grim-faced boss appeared and fired Lupe on the spot.

A Better Bargain: Mobilizing Employers and Workers to Grow America's Middle Class is the result of the unlikely career that followed. We avenged Lupe's firing by organizing a union at the Dream Inn. The next decade took me from restaurant to hospital workers, to the technology companies that were fast replacing the orchards of Santa Clara County. Hoping to use the local defense industry as a base for organizing "high tech", I became a machinist in a Sunnyvale defense plant. One of my leaflets denounced Apple's brash young CEO as "nonunion Jobs".

A decade with organized labor convinced me that unions needed a much deeper understanding of business strategy, operations, and finance. I decided to study business and joined McKinsey & Co. in San Francisco. Eventually, I left McKinsey to focus exclusively on helping unions adapt to an increasingly global economy, often by enabling workers to become partial, reluctant owners of their troubled enterprises.

In 1992, I met with Secretary of Labor nominee Robert Reich and advocated the creation of a new federal agency modeled after the successful Agricultural Extension Service. With backing from Reich, President Clinton nominated me to create and lead the Office of the American Workplace as Assistant US Secretary of Labor. Following Senate confirmation, I visited workplaces around the country and met with thousands of workers and hundreds of union leaders and managers.

I left Washington to guide a large hospital restructuring at Kaiser Permanente—both the nation's most union-dependent private sector employer and a model of labor-backed, prepaid group health care. Then the Internet boomed. I started Alibris in my living room and served as CEO over the next decade. We built the company into an early example of "long-tail" e-commerce. *The New York Times* praised Alibris for building "a mighty brand on the spines of old books." Deloitte named the company to its Technology Fast 500 and awarded Alibris a coveted place on its list of North America Fast 50 high-growth companies. Initially, we supplied Amazon. Eventually, they crushed us.

A Better Bargain is concerned, above all, with the steady erosion of the American middle class and the democratic values that it nourished. It reflects not only my experience building, unionizing, and advising American workplaces, but also my belief in the pride, dignity, and responsibility that comes with well-paid work. It argues that preserving a vital middle class requires a form of income bargaining that can preserve competitive businesses, strengthen civil society, and once again award larger pay raises to those who earn the least. It is designed to provoke a sharp debate about how to rebuild America's vital middle class not only among labor activists, educators, and business leaders, but among policymakers, regulators, and social entrepreneurs as well.

Oakland, California

August, 2019

"Well, in our country," said Alice, still panting a little, "you'd generally get to somewhere else—if you run very fast for a long time, as we've been doing."

"A slow sort of country!" said the Queen.

"Now here, you see, it takes all the running you can do, to keep in the same place. If you want to get somewhere else, you must run at least twice as fast as that!"

Lewis Carroll
Alice's Adventures in Wonderland & Through the Looking-Glass, 1865

Introduction: Racing the Red Queen

In 2013, Americans were furious. As they dusted themselves off from the worst of the financial crisis, they knew that homeowners had paid a much higher price than bankers and rating agencies. Like a receding tide, the crisis left exposed a grating set of financial inequities. It now cost too much to move to cities with higher wages. College debt had exploded as college wages remained stuck. Many workers, especially those with below-median incomes, concluded that the field was tilted and institutions rigged against them. They came to sympathize with Alice—*...it takes all the running you can do, to keep in the same place. If you want to get somewhere else, you must run at least twice as fast as that!*

President Barack Obama believed that wages for workers without college degrees had flatlined for fifty years, and wages for men without college degrees had fallen. Worse, he noticed that wage stagnation had begun to animate American culture and politics. Like nearly every American president, Obama believed the middle class to be the home to the nation's democratic ideals. He knew that without rising real incomes, families could not deliver a higher standard of living to their children. Citizens would define their interests narrowly. Politics would turn tribal and zero-sum.

Obama declared income inequality "the defining challenge of our time". Unfortunately, he had no clear picture of what had caused income to stagnate or why high earners had captured virtually all of the income growth. Worse, he had no idea what to do about it.

His challenge set off a flurry of economists, sociologists, policy analysts, pundits, journalists, and politicians who tried to understand why American income stagnated and polarized. Many looked back to the "The Great Compression", Paul Krugman's term for the years from 1947 to 1973 when American income inequality actually shrank. It is difficult to imagine today, but during those years pay grew faster for workers who earned the least, not for those who already had the most.[1] During this simpler time, markets were less global, products less specialized, and workers less diverse. An autoworker could buy a home, save for retirement, and send his (less often, her) kid to college. That kid could save enough from a minimum wage job to bum around Europe.

In 2016, voters backed populist leaders who reflected their suspicion of self-serving institutions. The left looked to the state to tax income and wealth, raise minimum wages, and consider universal basic incomes. The right turned reflexively to market solutions and in some cases to nativist explanations for wage stagnation. Almost nobody looked to reform and repair America's employer associations, labor unions, and vocational training that had helped sustain the Great Compression in a different industrial era.

The Argument

Economists have a hard time explaining wages, but observably there are three reasons that workers get a raise. The first is because they produce more and managers share some of the surplus, especially with workers who have essential skills. The second reason pay goes up is if lawmakers require it. The third is because employers bargain higher wages. *A Better Bargain* argues that the first is necessary but not sufficient for more equitable pay increases. The second, legislating pay, can help those at the bottom but cannot restore broad-based income growth. Income bargaining by groups of workers offers the most flexibility and the strongest guarantee of broad-based pay raises but as currently structured is not an option for most workers—nor is it likely to become one.

Part One considers each of these three approaches. It argues that we cannot invest and grow our way into a better distribution of income because the forces that grow the modern economy—education, technology, and trade—all reward similar skills and traits. By themselves, they cannot create more inclusive income distribution. Private investments to increase productivity and legislated wage minimums both matter, but neither can restart broad-based income growth as reliably as bargains struck privately between organized workers and organized employers.

Part Two describes why our current collective bargaining structure is not merely flawed but fundamentally unworkable. The problem is not only that managers can easily resist unions in their current form; as currently structured, enterprise-based unions impose unacceptable penalties on individual companies. A system of exclusive union representation creates powerful incentives for unions to become highly judicial, leading to much less worker engagement than effective unions need. And allowing unions to create a labor cartel destroyed any hope of that union innovation would be either required or rewarded. To be sure, law-breaking managers bent on union destruction have hurt organized labor, but *A Better Bargain* demonstrates that they succeeded only because unions were already weak, thanks to a design that is deeply incompatible with today's economy.

Part Three describes a revitalized system of income bargaining that can restore middle-class wage growth, labor market standards, and occupational training by rewarding companies instead of penalizing them. The plan meets six important tests:

- It creates labor organizations strong enough to compress income distribution, meaning that below-median workers would once again receive larger raises in percentage terms than those earning above the median. The US can only rebuild a strong middle class with labor market institutions strong enough to steadily compress incomes.
- It minimizes penalties on individual companies by enabling workers to bargain wages for an industry or regional subset of an industry.
- It uses wage subsidies to offer employers a powerful financial incentive to set skill standards, develop talent pipelines, invest in training, and bargain income. Without these incentives to organize industry associations, support training efforts, and bargain seriously with employees, most employers will continue to resist income bargaining in any form.
- It enables workers to create a rich variety of labor and professional associations that are stronger, more innovative, and more adaptable than those built for the New Deal.
- It specifies the rights, regulations, and information disclosure needed to make this approach to income bargaining work. These include the use of federally chartered workplace auditors, bargaining rights that increase with worker support, and the public disclosure of pay brackets in each company.
- With leadership, the approach is politically feasible, a topic discussed in the concluding essay.

This tall order guarantees that *A Better Bargain* will frustrate some readers. Most corporate bosses who accept that businesses require a thriving middle class today pray that economic growth alone will somehow deliver greater income equality. They will prefer to set wages on their own, not in concert with their industry peers—much less in negotiation with labor organizations. *A Better Bargain* challenges business to imagine industry associations that actively shape skill and talent pipelines in local labor markets and, by standardizing wages, reduce pay as a competitive factor. It also proposes a large wage subsidy for companies who do this. Companies in industries that hire large numbers of workers who earn below median pay will find it especially worthwhile to bargain income under the approach outlined here.

Many progressives who share the conclusion that collectively bargaining below median incomes is essential to preserving a strong middle class will encounter a different frustration in these pages. Those accustomed to highly regulated labor unions and loosely regulated employer organizations often find it difficult to imagine the merits of reversing this arrangement. Many union leaders are entirely comfortable with the failed system of exclusive, enterprise representation that has crippled them for decades. Most believe that their path to renewed relevance begins with stronger penalties against lawbreaking employers—a view that is understandable but incomplete. Despite the determination of committed leaders, unions that function as exclusive representatives for workers in a single enterprise cannot grow to relevance in the current economy. Only easy to join, radically diverse, competing labor organizations that can improvise and innovate can become powerful enough to bargain larger pay raises for workers with below-median incomes. If sheer determination were sufficient to restore American unions, 65 percent of private sector workers would belong to unions instead of one-tenth that share.

Finally, scholars and progressive public policy analysts are also more comfortable debating paths to rebuilding unions as they exist today instead of exploring how income bargaining might be organized differently.[2] The scholarship on income bargaining systems tends to evaluate today's organizations or compare unions in different countries, not debate the redesign of core labor market institutions from first principles. *A Better Bargain* is a manifesto for thinking bigger rather than tinkering at the margins.

What Happened?

The nature, extent, and causes of income inequality are the subject of vigorous and useful debates. Readers who are secure in their convictions on the subject can skip to Part One. The problem with stagnant wage growth isn't simple "inequality". Few Americans expect paychecks to be equal or static. Most do expect to participate fully in the nation's economic progress, however. The essence of the American Dream is an expectation that a lifetime of hard work will enable our children to live better than we did.

Is America delivering this dream? At the urging of *New York Times* columnist David Leonhardt, economist Raj Chetty tried to find out. Chetty and his team asked, "What are the odds that a person born at different periods of recent history will earn more than their parents?" This turned out to be an excellent research question, but a tough one. The ability to ask and carefully answer questions like this has made Chetty one of the world's most influential economists in the minds of many of his peers.

In December 2016, Leonhardt reported that they had their answer.

> "It took them months of work, using old Census data to estimate long-ago decades, but they have done it. They've constructed a data set that shows the percentage of American children who earn more money — and less money — than their parents made at the same age.
>
> "The index is deeply alarming. It's a portrait of an economy that disappoints a huge number of people who have heard that they live in a country where life gets better, only to experience something entirely different."[3]

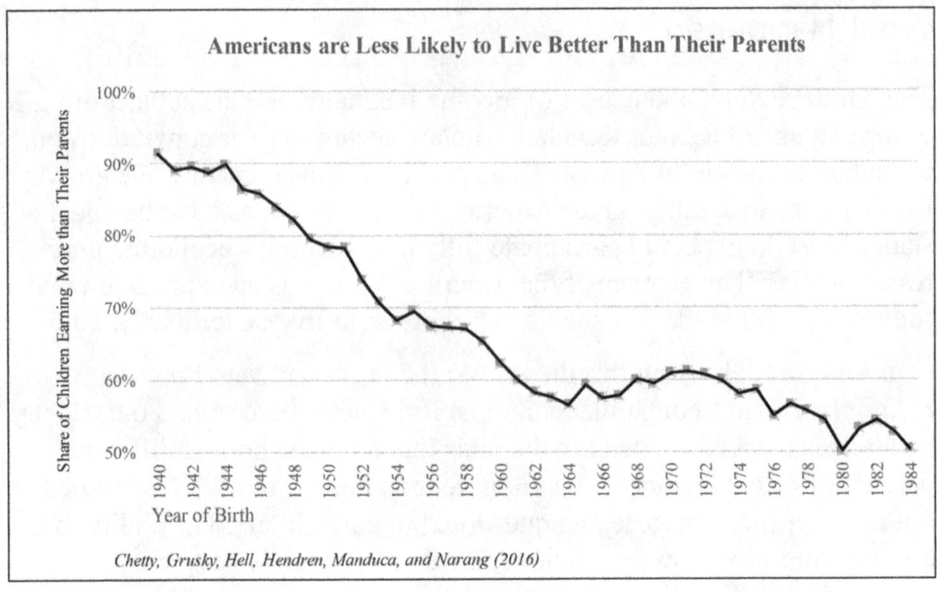

Chetty and his team showed that children born in 1940 had a 92 percent chance of earning more than their parents. Those born twenty years later had a 62 percent of doing so. (The odds of making more than one's parents are naturally the highest for those born poorest and lowest for those born at the top. They determined both distributions and averages.)[4] To those born in 1980 (the latest cohort for which researchers can estimate lifetime incomes), the odds have dropped to 50 percent, meaning that the odds that America honors its promise is now at best a coin toss. Chetty later concluded that Canadians were twice as likely as Americans to realize the American Dream.

Critically, Chetty and his colleagues tested counterfactuals. They asked, "Is the economy growing too slowly? Or is something wrong with the way America distributes income?" Both a faster-growing economy and more inclusive income distribution can raise wages at the bottom. They asked whether it helps the economy more to restore the historic growth rate or the historic distribution of income.

Chetty showed that the overwhelming problem is the manner in which America now distributes income. Paying workers more equitably would give more people a shot at the American Dream than growing the economy faster—although faster growth helps.

Economists Emmanuel Saez and Gabriel Zucman took a different approach than Chetty. They used income tax records to build a database of all US income from 1913 to the present to analyze the exact distribution of national economic growth. They took a broad view of income, including employer-provided health care and pensions (critical, since health care premiums have skyrocketed). They added in the value of food stamps, Medicaid, and other transfer programs. They measured the income of adults, not households or tax filers, so that changes in household composition wouldn't matter. They indexed income using the slower-growing index of income, not of consumer prices. They even reconciled the tax data submitted by individuals and companies with national income accounts—a massive undertaking. As with Chetty's team, this was an especially audacious and arduous analysis. The data that emerged suggest that high earners have captured virtually all of the income growth in recent years.[5]

These findings have caused a howl of protest, generally from analysts with more conservative views than David Leonhardt or Emmanuel Saez. That does not mean that the objections are wrong or politically motivated, however—and it is a mistake to dismiss them out of hand. Much of the debate revolves around two issues.

Should we measure the income of households, income deciles, or individual workers over their lifetimes? First, we need to decide that income is the relevant measure of living standards. For example, does income really capture how technology has improved lives during the past decade? Probably not.[6] After all, nobody is clamoring to return to the 1970s, when it took ten hours of work at average wages to buy a bicycle when it took only four hours in 2015.[7]

Analysts also raise technical concerns about how Chetty and others count income. They worried that he failed to include refundable tax credits, public benefits like food stamps and Medicaid, or health or retirement benefits as income. For this reason, Saez, Chetty and other economists have turned to individual tax records, not census data on household income, and take pains to add back transfer payments, health care premiums, etc.

As people marry less, divorce more, and live longer in less extended families, we end up with more households. Income per household naturally falls. Chetty's team not only documented their assumptions about households and many other things, but they tested the sensitivity of their findings to each assumption, something few scholars do. For example, Chetty's finding that those born in 1980 have only a 50 percent chance of earning more than their parents does not correct for changes in household size over time. Depending on how one corrects Chetty's data for household size, the odds of a child earning more than his or her parent in the most recent cohort increase to 60–67 percent. Saez and Zucman measured individual income, not households or tax filers, for just this reason.

The second way we count people wrong is by relying on income deciles or quintiles. The problem, as economist Russ Roberts points out, is that the composition of income groups changes over time.[8] The people in the top decile today are not the same people as they were a decade ago.

This matters because Americans increasingly think about income groups. Our richest families are now richer than ever. In 1963, families in the fabled top 0.1 percent held 10 percent of America's wealth. By 2012, the 160,000 households in the top tenth of a percent held 22 percent.[9] Elite athletes, musicians, CEOs, and investment bankers all earn vastly more than their counterparts did three or four decades ago. Golden State Warriors ace Steph Curry, who earns about $40 million per year, earns vastly more than LA Lakers celebrity Jerry West did in the 1960s.

For some, this is the full story: the middle class has suffered because the gains from productivity and growth have flowed to the very rich at the expense of the bottom 99.9 percent. In the minds of this group, Marx is grinning. But the top 9.9 percent has also done quite well. Our "upper middle class" holds between 50–60 percent of the pie, a share that has not changed much since 1975. These are our most successful professionals: doctors, lawyers, senior managers, and all except the most elite investment bankers. As of 2016, this group has $1.2–$10 million in net worth. It is predominantly white, intermarries more and at a later age, divorces less, is healthier, has fewer car accidents, and lives longer. Members of this group rarely go to jail. When they do, they serve time in nicer, safer facilities. As a group, it is fiercely self-perpetuating. *The Atlantic* reports, "In America today, the single best predictor of whether an individual will get married, stay married, pursue advanced education, live in a good neighborhood, have an extensive social network, and experience good health is the performance of his or her parents on those same metrics."[10]

Using groups is not always a useful way to describe income, however, because individuals experience rising and falling incomes throughout their lives. About 12 percent of the population will spend a year in the top one percent of incomes at some point in their life. More than half, about 56 percent, spend at least one year in the top 10 percent.[11] Conversely, 54 percent of Americans will experience poverty or near poverty at least once between the ages of 25 and 60. Not surprisingly, those who are young, nonwhite, disabled, female, single, or noncollege grads are at the highest risk.[12] For this reason as well as the problem with households, Saez and Zucman chose to track individual incomes as reported on tax returns—although they expressed some of their findings using income groups. Even more powerfully, other scholars have turned to recent microdata that enables them to assess lifetime income.

Because of swings in individual income and uneven participation rates, it is useful to contrast census income of annual earnings with panel data of lifetime earnings. This analysis requires microdata that has not been available until fairly recently. Even measuring earnings from age 25–55 to avoid most students and retirees requires three decades of data for a single cohort. The best analysis to date looked at 27 such cohorts, born between 1957 and 1983, a period that masked growing income inequality among men with decreasing inequality among women, who entered the labor force in large and permanent numbers for the first time during these years. These analysts concluded that:

> "the lifetime income of the median male worker declined by 10% to 19% (depending on the price deflator we use), beginning with the cohort that turned 25 in 1967 and ending with the cohort that turned 25 in 1983. Perhaps more strikingly, more than three-quarters of the distribution of men experienced no rise in their lifetime income across these cohorts. The only time period during which the lifetime incomes of these men rose is from the 1957 cohort to the 1966 cohort. In contrast, subsequent cohorts of female workers have seen large and very steady gains—on the order of 22% to 33% for the median female worker. However, because these gains started from a very low level of lifetime income for the 1957 cohort, they were not large enough to offset the losses by men."[13]

Analysts often fight over a technical issue when they analyze income: how to deflate it properly. Income needs to be expressed in constant dollars if we are to compare it over time. The US produces two price indexes that let scholars adjust for inflation: the Consumer Price Index (CPI), which measures how much a basket of goods changes in price, and the Personal Consumption Expenditures (PCE), which measures spending as a component of overall economic growth. The CPI counts the increase in the price of bananas and of apples, but it does not account for consumers substituting bananas when the price of apples rises. As a result, since 1959 PCE inflation has averaged 3.3 percent, while CPI has grown 3.8 percent over the same time period.[14] These small differences can produce completely different answers when applied to decades of actual earnings.

Which matters more, income or economic mobility? An implication of counting income deciles instead of individual incomes is that we might confuse growing income volatility with real wage stagnation. If Americans had high incomes some years and low income in other years, inequality based on deciles or quintiles might be illusory, as Roberts and others assert is the case. Those who fare worse today might do better tomorrow. Individual insecurity might be higher, but overall households might be better off than if declining incomes represented permanent losses.

Are polarized American incomes transient or permanent? A 2011 study by the Federal Reserve, the Treasury Department, and two Midwestern universities examined income data from 1987 to 2009 and found that for men, the increase in inequality from lost pay was entirely permanent. For total household income, roughly three-quarters of the increase in income inequality was permanent.[15]

Economists measure economic mobility with a metric known as Intergenerational Earnings Elasticity. (For reasons lost to history, its acronym is IGE, not IEE.) IGE measures how much parental income explains a child's income. In Norway or Denmark, where mobility is high, the IGE is less than 0.15, meaning that kids inherit about 15 percent of their economic destiny. In the UK and the US, the IGE is about 50 percent. A half-century ago, America's IGE was 30 percent.[16] The late Alan Kreuger drew a graph showing that a country's Gini coefficient (a measure of economic equality) and its IGE are straight-line correlated. He dubbed his graph "The Great Gatsby Curve" and it demonstrates that income inequality and economic opportunity are closely linked. Countries rarely achieve one without the other.[17]

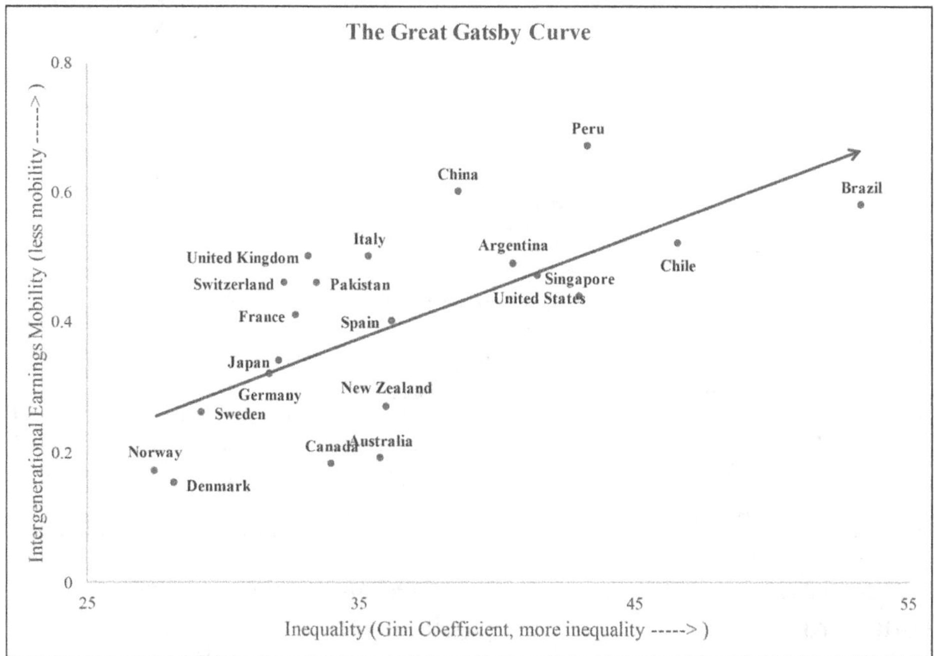

This book focuses on the stagnant and often declining pay of workers earning below-median incomes (even if during some part of their lives, some earned above-median incomes). Sometimes below median workers are referred to as "non-college" workers, since two-thirds of American workers don't have a four-year college degree. This nomenclature too, can make income categories sound more static than they actually are.

In modern economies, most workers with four-year college degrees earn more than non-college workers. A graphic illustration of the difference in earnings growth by educational attainment makes this division so pronounced that conservative journalist Mickey Kaus called it "the most important chart around when it comes to explaining contemporary politics, including Trump."[18]

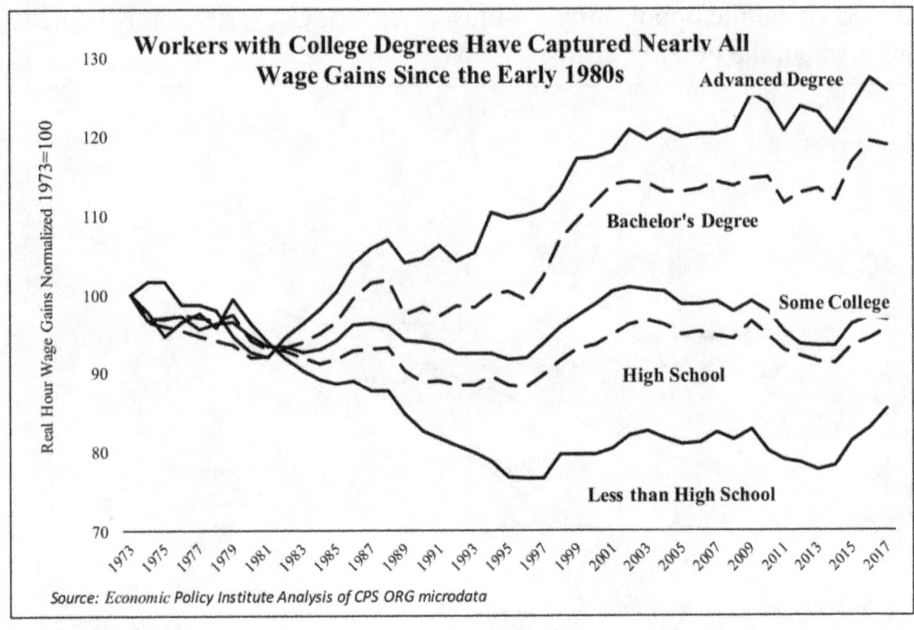

Once again, however, descriptions of median incomes conceal important truths. In 2016, the median pay of a worker over age 25 working full-time with only a high school diploma was about $35,000 per year. Look more closely, however, and 80 percent of high school–only grads earned between $20,000 and $73,000—so 10 percent earned more and 10 percent earned less than this. The equivalent for an employee with some college or an associate degree was about $41,000 and 80 percent earned between $22,000 and $84,000. For college grads without advanced degrees, the median was $60,000. Eighty percent earned between $29,000 and $130,000.[19] As a result, plenty of individual workers with only a high school degree earned more than graduates of a four-year college. As we would expect, educational attainment strongly predicts income but many other factors determine it.[20]

The study of who gets paid what is complex. Disagreements are the norm. Most researchers find increased income polarization and declining income mobility, even though individuals continue to move between quintiles and deciles. The Tax Analysis Office of the US Treasury, however, found that incomes since 1979 had polarized by about half of what Saez and his team found.[21]

Stagnant incomes now feature prominently in American culture and politics because those whose wages stagnated helped elect Donald Trump. In 2016, Trump did not improve much over Mitt Romney's performance four years earlier among whites, women, or men. But he gained 12 points among voters without college degrees and 15 points among whites in this group. Pew declared his 39-point margin over Democrats among white voters without a college degree "the largest among any candidate in exit polls since 1980."[22] Even if income polarization did not directly create the opioid or obesity epidemics, reduce trust in civic institutions, or dig the moat of high housing prices around major US cities, sluggish and uneven paycheck growth amplifies problems that would be easier to solve in an economy that shared its bounty more equitably.

What Changed?

Since the Great Compression, five related trends have made US income distribution less even. Coming chapters treat two of these trends in detail: changes in the impact of education, technology, and global trade on income and the decline of labor unions, which appears to have mattered more than most economists once believed. Three other factors have also hurt the income of below-median workers. First, low-wage service sector jobs have exploded and fewer Americans work, perhaps as a result. Second, America has urbanized and those who move to cities are different from those who do not. Finally, the overall share of national income that goes to paychecks appears to have declined, potentially because technology has enabled fewer firms to dominate almost every industry.

Work has changed profoundly. Nine of the dozen occupations expected to grow fastest over the next decade are variations on "nurse": physical-therapy assistants, home health aides, occupational therapy assistants, nurse practitioners, physical therapists, occupational therapy aides, etc.[23] More than ever, jobs either require specialized skills or they pay poorly. Possibly as a result, fewer Americans work than at any time in modern history. Since the year 2000, the adult population of the US has grown about 18 percent but total paid hours of work have grown by only four percent—a 12 percent drop in paid work per person since the start of the new century. Retiring baby boomers account for a small fraction of this change.[24] The falling US labor participation rate means that more than 22 million Americans of prime working age are now outside the labor force.

The most widely reported measure of unemployment, the Labor Department's U3, excludes this group entirely.

Economists debate the reason for this. Many note that men have been affected more severely than women.[25] The women's employment rate had grown since the sixties, but declined in 2000. Today, job prospects for "prime-age" women (between 25 and 55) have slid back to where they were in the late 1980s. The growing tendency of men and women to select spouses with the same education magnifies wage polarization at the household level.[26]

If the race with the Red Queen has set women back, it has crushed most men without a four-year college degree. Their median pay has not risen since 1980. Perhaps as a result, fewer men now work. In 1970, 93 percent of prime-age men were in the workforce—either working or seeking work. Today, one in five is unemployed, in prison, or on disability. Men under thirty without college degrees live at home longer than their fathers did. They are less likely to marry and more likely to be addicted to opioids and video games. They are also much more likely to go to prison: an astounding one of every eight American men has a felony conviction on his resume.[27]

Urbanization, the steady migration of humans from the countryside to the city, has transformed the lives of working people more than any factor in the past two centuries. It now matters enormously where you live. Because modern growth industries like software, finance, biotech, federal programs, and entertainment tend to cluster geographically, American income has stratified regionally. Moreover, those who migrate are unlike those who do not. They are less likely to be white, religious, or culturally conservative. The relative economic stagnation of rural areas widens the cultural and political gap between urban and rural Americans.[28]

Both the extent and nature of urban migration have changed. During the Great Compression, about 20 percent of all households moved each year. High school–only graduates moved the most often and moved the furthest.[29] Today, only 11 percent of households move each year and college graduates are twice as likely to undertake long-distance moves, whereas high school–only grads move more often within their home county.[30] Because affordable cities have grown slowly while most high-growth cities have failed to build enough housing to keep up with demand, housing in prosperous cities has become a substantial tax on those seeking higher incomes. College graduates in these cities earn more, but they lose about a quarter of their pay advantage to higher housing costs.[31] The housing penalty for most workers without a college degree is high enough to make moving impossible.[32]

Reduced geographic mobility hurts Americans in small towns especially hard. Data from the 100 largest metropolitan areas shows that large regions recovered from the recession almost twice as fast as 182 small towns. Income grew 50 percent faster and the labor participation rate shrank only half as much. Partly as a result of reduced geographic mobility, workers hang on to jobs longer, reducing "labor market fluidity" and limiting opportunities for young people.[33]

A growing population used to help distressed regions recover. It no longer does. A report by the Economic Innovation Group noted that not only has US population growth has fallen to an 80-year low, but we add about 900,000 fewer people each year than we did in the early 2000s. The last decade marks the first time in the past century that the United States has experienced low population growth and low prime working-age growth on a sustained basis at the same time.

These unfavorable demographic trends are becoming the rule, not the exception. Only 14 percent of US counties tend to grow faster than the economy as a whole—86 percent now grow more slowly. By 2037, two-thirds of US counties will contain fewer prime working-age adults than they did in 1997, even though the country will add 24.1 million prime working-age adults and 98.8 million people in total over that same period. Educated families leave, so the fastest-shrinking counties have educational attainment equal to Mexico today or the United States in 1978. Population losses reduce housing values, the local tax base, productivity, and the rate of startups. For good reason, many compare the American industrial heartland to Japan in the 1990s, which experienced at least one decade of lost growth.

This is the worst of all worlds for hard-hit regions and fosters a zero-sum, often white nationalist mindset receptive to populist rhetoric scapegoating immigrants, minorities, and urban elites who dwell in multicultural cities. Combined with an electoral system designed to favor low-density states, this change enabled an alarmingly corrupt populist demagogue to capture the Republican Party and the White House.

Stagnant regions tend to experience slow rates of worker churn. Workers are understandably reluctant to quit jobs when it appears they will have trouble securing another one. At least one high-growth company looks at this as a business problem and pays its workers to quit. Zappos had a policy of paying an employee $1,000 to quit. The policy seemed to help retain motivated people and encourage those who were ambivalent about their work to leave. When Amazon bought Zappos, they adopted the policy and expanded it. Each year after the holiday rush, Amazon offers full-time employees $1,000 per year of service up to $5,000 to quit. They like fluidity enough in their internal labor market that they help their least satisfied people to leave to open up jobs for others.

The result is employees who are highly committed, even when they are not especially well-paid. Sandi Dolan, a customer service rep at Zappos, recalled working for employers where "I wasn't even allowed to take a break with someone if they were a different pay grade than I was." She knows that she would be paid well to leave Zappos, but she likes a job with health insurance and a retirement plan. She especially likes working for a business that holds events, demos, and scavenger hunts to encourage employees to get to know people throughout the company. Even though she thinks she could earn more elsewhere, Sandi told *The New York Times*, "I haven't looked for a job since I stepped foot in here. I don't plan on it."[34]

Not only has the nature of work and location changed, but the American economy appears to divert a smaller fraction of its overall income to paychecks than it once did. The share of our national income that goes to wages has dropped, although both the math and the meaning of this change is fraught. The math is tough because attempts to account for depreciation (which reduces capital and thus raises the capital share), volatile housing and commodities, intellectual property, and small business owners' income all tend to gum the calculations. The meaning is unclear because, at worst, counting the labor share of income reflects a 19th-century mindset with interchangeable workers toiling in capital-intensive factories. In an economy where intangible capital matters more and more, it means less than it once did to label some factors "capital income" and others "labor income".

So why do economists try to calculate the labor share of national income? The main reason is that for generations the labor share has been a mysterious and totemic constant, a bit like the speed of light for a physicist. About two-thirds of national income always went to wages. Nobody could explain why. John Maynard Keynes declared the constant "a bit of a miracle."

The debate over the labor share of national income is not only subject to category errors, but it is heavily affected by boom and bust cycles in commodity industries and by accounting rules that depreciate software and intellectual assets more rapidly than buildings or factories. Neither of these things have anything to do with wages. Moreover, families eat their incomes, not their "share of national income." As he often does, Nobel economist Robert Solow clarifies:

> "Would you rather live in a society in which the real wage was rising rapidly but the labor share was falling (because productivity was increasing even faster), or one in which the real wage was stagnating, along with productivity, so the labor share was unchanging?
>
> "The first is surely better on narrowly economic grounds: you eat your wage, not your share of national income. But there could be political and social advantages to the second option. If a small class of owners of wealth—and it is small—comes to collect a growing share of the national income, it is likely to dominate the society in other ways as well. This dichotomy need not arise, but it is good to be clear."[35]

Most national income analysts conclude that labor began losing its share of national income as the Great Compression came to an end in the 1970s. Although the matter isn't fully settled, most economists, the Federal Reserve Bank, and the White House conclude that labor's share of national income has declined.[36]

Analysts have offered a smorgasbord of explanations. Global trade made labor cheaper.[37] Or perhaps it made capital cheaper, so technology substituted for workers more easily.[38] Or exploding housing prices in certain cities made the capital share artificially high.[39] Or accounting for intellectual property explains the apparent growth of the capital share of income.[40] Or it is due to problems categorizing income for small business owners, which is sort of capital and sort of labor.[41]

The McKinsey Global Institute (MGI) analyzed the contribution of these factors to the drop in the labor share across a dozen industrial sectors that account for most of the decline. They found that increased profits from rapidly rising real estate and commodity prices (often from Chinese demand) explained about a third of the decrease in the labor share of income. Increased depreciation and the shift to intangible and intellectual capital explained another quarter (higher depreciation reduces the amount of capital firms deploy, which increases the capital share of income, especially in pharma, technology, and information services). Industry consolidation and reduced competition contributed to about a fifth of the decline. Automation, which substitutes capital for labor, accounted for another 12 percent. The decline of union contracts was, perhaps not surprisingly, found to be a small effect (11 percent) in part because so few private sector workers were unionized in the period under review.[42]

MGI's work, along with that of several other scholars, confirms that "superstar" firms have reduced competition, and may have discouraged startups (an aging population affects startup rates as well). Beneath it all, digital technologies may be reducing competition. In sector after sector, the top three or four firms control more of the market than they have in the past. Thanks to reduced competition, the strongest companies are more profitable today than they were in the past. One prominent team investigated superstar firms across a variety of industries and found that they generate higher profits using less labor (put another way, as top companies have become more productive, labor has failed to claim its traditional share of income). As a result, the labor share of income has fallen. The researchers applied a series of technical tests and found strong support for a superstar firm thesis in every sector of the economy.[43] Crucially, they linked superstar firms to the drop in the labor share of income, not to income polarization.

MGI researched 5,750 firms with revenues in excess of $1 billion in every region and sector including global banks, manufacturing companies, consumer branded goods, and tech firms. They declared as superstars those firms in the top 10 percent of industry profitability. They made several valuable findings. Superstars tended to be larger, more globalized, and more productive than median companies. They benefit more from intangible investments (software, data, brands, partnerships, and training).

They invest two to three times more in R&D than their peers and rely much more on M&A for growth. MGI also found that a company's location and sector accounted for most of its success.

MGI found that superstar firms capture 80 percent of the profits among billion-dollar revenue companies—a number 60 percent larger than it was twenty years ago. Amazingly, however, bottom-decile firms ("zombies") destroyed 50 percent more value than they did twenty years ago. Even more remarkably, this terrain is highly contested, not stable, and monopolized. Nearly half of all superstar firms fell out of the top 10 percent during two business cycles. Of these, 40 percent end up zombies, members of the bottom 10 percent. Some firms rose the other way—zombies who rose from the dead to the top decile. The overall life expectancy of superstars and zombies has not changed.[44]

But why did superstars emerge in the first place? MGI suggests that adoption of digital technologies contributes to increased industry concentration. MGI surveyed companies in dozens of sectors around the world. They determined that early and rapid adopters of digital technologies often placed a substantial distance between themselves and their rivals. These companies enjoyed increased returns not only to capital but to talent as well. MGI concluded that:

> The pronounced gap between the digital "haves" and "have-mores" is a major factor shaping competition at all levels of the economy. The companies leading the charge are winning the battle for market share and profit growth; some are reshaping entire industries to their own advantage. Workers with the most sophisticated digital skills are in such high demand that they command wages far above the national average. Meanwhile, there is a growing opportunity cost for the organizations and individuals that fall behind…

MGI found that software-intensive sectors such as media, professional services, and finance have seen profit margins grow by two to three times more than those in less digitized sectors. Sectors affected by software or other digital technologies are not only developing a winner-take-all dynamic, but they can more easily absorb or squash startups that may threaten their dominance.[45] In Silicon Valley, venture capitalists use a PlayStation term to describe the dangerous shoals around established behemoths. They warn entrepreneurs to stay out of "Killzones".

The rise of superstars may increase the capital share by reducing the number of startups. Unfortunately, the US starts far fewer new businesses than it once did. Startups are fashionable, but only 8 percent of all US firms are startups (new companies that have survived three years).[46] In 1978, 15 percent of American firms were startups. Standard economic theory insists that to encourage startups to challenge incumbents, countries should cut business taxes and reduce regulations that restrict startups.

Sweden tried this recently. Today, twenty Swedes start companies per thousand employees compared with five per thousand in the United States.[47] According to the OECD, Stockholm produces more billion-dollar tech companies per capita than any region in the world except Silicon Valley.[48] Startups helped Sweden's economy grew at a rate of four percent in 2015 and three percent in 2016. Even if comparisons between a homogeneous country the size of Los Angeles County with the United States are limited, they are provocative. If Sweden can undertake a systematic effort to reduce barriers to entrepreneurship while preserving a robust safety net and preventing income polarization, it should tempt American states or large cities to try something similar.

Despite hundreds of books and academic papers, we have indicators but no definitive explanation as to why below median income growth has stagnated and why top earners now capture such a large share of income growth. As a group, economists find themselves groping the proverbial elephant. They surface essential truths but struggle to connect them to a larger picture. Some treat this as weakness or failure, but it is the natural limitation of trying to fit observable facts to hypotheses or models. Economics isn't chemistry, which draws deductive conclusions from repeatable experiments. There is a built-in tendency to "overfit" inductive data and overstate confidence in modeled results. That researchers can't agree on what has caused wages to stagnate is the unavoidable byproduct of professional pachyderm poking.

About the Book

Regardless of their favored diagnosis, researchers tend to prescribe similar therapies to limit wage polarization. Most advocate investment to improve productivity and hope that equitable pay raises will somehow follow. A few argue for higher minimum wages or a basic income and hope that productivity will somehow catch up. A third group advocates for stronger collective bargaining and hopes that the public benefit of these bargains will somehow exceed their private costs. Not only is each of these designs unreliable, but some can and have made the problem worse.

A Better Bargain is a book of political economy. It starts with a foundational respect for the economic laws of gravity: the ability of markets to aggregate information and allocate scarce resources, the power of incentives, and the value of specialization and trade. It accepts the need of modern markets for property rights, enforceable contracts, macroeconomic stability, and prudent regulation.

That said, *A Better Bargain* treats markets as social constructions, not divine ones. Labor markets, the primary concern here, are embedded in non-market institutions that establish the "rules of the game". Labor market institutions, especially privately organized employer and labor associations, are creatures of government policies. When the policies that enable these institutions fail to adapt to changes in the underlying economy, they weaken markets they once strengthened. This is fundamentally a political problem, not an economic one. For this reason, political questions accompany nearly every imaginable economic discussion involving labor markets.

Income in America is complex, in part because our work is exceptionally varied. We work in global enterprises, small nonprofits, hopeful startups, government agencies, and family businesses. Our friends and neighbors dedicate themselves to agriculture, biotech, and hospitality. Or energy, health care, dry cleaning, education, financial services, fast food, law enforcement, personal training, or manufacturing. We work as employees, temps, consultants, tenured faculty, owners, gig workers, and freelancers. The day's work may be common as mud or comically specialized, like the woman who helps giraffes paint pictures to raise money for the Oakland Zoo or the St. Louis attorney who only accepts cases involving malfunctioning garage door openers.[49] This cacophonous market is emergent, protean, and unmanaged. It reliably humbles those brave enough to reform its laws, much less its tacit rules.

Because of this complexity, it is very tempting to simplify problems into nails that yield to familiar analytic hammers. Analysts often reduce workers to one-dimensional maximizers and employers to simple minimizers. In fact, every worker and his or her boss is much more than a pay stub. Those who approach income as an economic problem often neglect the role of political power. Those who treat it as a political problem overlook changes in the economy and the profound way that worsened prospects for workers is embedded in a range of social problems.

Analysts are always tempted to ignore what they can't quantify. Ideas that may prove valuable, like inadequate "soft skills" and weak professional networks among some blue-collar men, are notoriously hard to measure. Others, like the refusal of working families to leave dying regions, may have cultural causes that scholars have not considered like information gaps, working spouses, or cultural anxieties. Cause and effect often blur: that stagnant wages are associated with a host of social and economic evils does not prove that wages are the root of the problem and certainly does not demonstrate that raising wages cure every associated malady.

Likewise, we too often assume that people work for money, not meaning. A book about income may evade the real value of the work many people do by ignoring the human need for work as a source of dignity, recognition, and purpose. The main job of workplace leaders is to create meaning. Those who give work purpose know that money, or at least loyalty, generally follows. *A Better Bargain* assumes that people work for money. It relies more on political and economic explanations than on cultural ones—a potentially serious blind spot.

Likewise, books about institutions and markets chronically downplay the role of individual choices. In the end, people decide the living standard of the worker who earns the least. She may lack skills and present an undistinguished job history. She may come from a war-torn region, a broken family, or a culture that devalues her gender. Her immigrant status or religion may raise the eyebrows of her co-workers. Her fate is nonetheless a moral choice decided by people, not the outcome of an impersonal labor market. For this reason, income bargaining is as much a moral conversation as an economic one. At its best, bargaining forces us to make our choices explicit.

PART ONE

Why Productivity Investments Are Insufficient to Grow Middle-Class Incomes

"The white man knows how to make everything, but he does not know how to distribute it."

Sitting Bull
Stanley Vestal, *Sitting Bull: Champion of the Sioux*
University of Oklahoma Press, 2014

1. The Productivity Seduction

Economists concerned with income stagnation and inequality generally encourage public and private investment in higher education, new technology, and globalization to increase output and lift all boats. Some favor higher minimum wages, social benefits, and perhaps even a universal basic income. Most ignore labor market organizations altogether, often because they seem not to work, although union devotees call for stronger enforcement of the nation's collective bargaining laws.

The next three chapters argue that none of these approaches are sufficient. Chapter One asserts that although higher output is a good thing, almost every known method for improving productivity favors the same educated cognitive elite that already captures most income growth. Chapter Two indicates that legislation has a similar problem: if necessary for those who earn the least, it is inadequate to make pay broadly more equitable. Chapter Three asks whether income bargaining works, even if we had stronger unions and smarter employer associations—or whether pay must always and invariably reflects the demand for and distribution of scarce skills.

"Improve labor productivity" is a trusted and versatile answer to many economic questions. Want higher wages without higher prices or lower profits? Increase productivity! Want to increase tax revenue without increasing the tax rate or cutting spending? Work smarter! There is not even a good counterargument; nobody advocates wasting time, working dumber, or consuming more without producing more.

Any discussion of pay starts with productivity. Paul Krugman makes the first of three cornerstone observations about productivity growth: in the long run, it is "almost everything".[50] Over time, workers can't earn more than they produce just as no group can eat more than it grows or kills. Without productivity growth, living standards cannot rise. To care about pay is to care about productivity.

But an exclusive focus on productivity conceals differences in market power. Sometimes workers help increase output but fail to see an increase in pay. A famous "wedge chart" shows that hourly pay tracked productivity during the Great Compression. Both rose by more than 90 percent. From 1973 to 2015, however, median pay rose 13 percent even though productivity grew by 73 percent.[51]

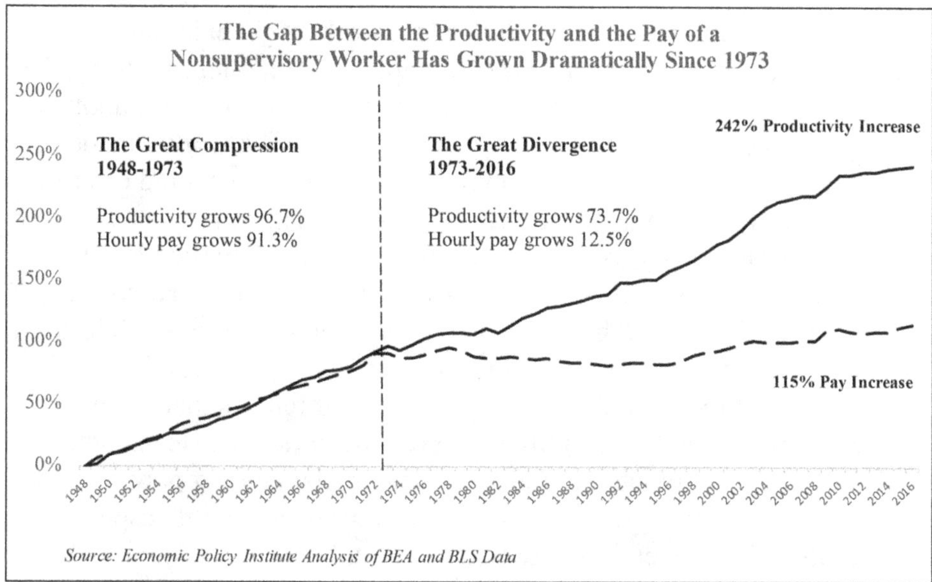

Absent labor market institutions to prevent them from doing so, owners or highly paid workers reliably claim for themselves the fruits of greater productivity. Without labor organizations, investments in education, technology, or trade do little to help those who don't thrive in classrooms to end their maddening race with the Red Queen.

Productivity growth is thus necessary to grow wages but not sufficient to do so. Nor is productivity a useful way to determine individual wages. Managers and economists frequently assert that differences in worker productivity justify differences in pay. Both for individuals and the nation as a whole, however, output affects pay but does not determine it.

Economics lacks a consistent theory of how wages are determined. Most economists write as though wages are prices that emerge from frictionless markets. By this account, employers don't determine wages; they pay the wage that results from the neat intersection of supply and demand. In this case, pay should depend almost entirely on a worker's "human capital", namely his or her education, age, IQ, experience, proven skills, and, in some cases, their professional relationships that together predict their productivity. In detailed studies, however, the Federal Reserve has concluded that these factors explain less than half of the wage variation in the population.[52] The remaining variation is due to employer discretion, regulation, or, in a few cases, to income bargaining.

A popular theory in economics holds that workers get paid their "marginal product", meaning the amount an employer would lose by firing the worker. It makes intuitive sense. If a worker made less than this, another employer could hire him or her away and pay more. If a worker made more, the employer would lose money and other workers would offer to do the job for less. In practice, recent studies find that employers use their market power to set pay as markets become more concentrated.[53] Unskilled work pays less not because it produces less, but because so many people can do the work. The pay of a tenured professor of English history, a real estate agent, a nurse, or a senior manager rarely reflects the careful measurement of their economic output. Instead, it reflects their ability to command higher pay based on their market power (real estate agents), distinctive personal reputation (elite professors), bargaining power (most nurses), or the relative price insensitivity of owners given the responsibility of the job for overall output (executives). None of this has anything to do with the measurable output of individual workers, although this of course constrains pay at some margin.

In short, although productivity matters, it explains neither individual pay nor how companies allocate increased output. Worryingly, however, the gap between the growth of productivity and the growth of pay reflects not only the growing ability of those with top decile incomes to capture productivity gains—it reflects underlying cost problems, a slowing of output, and a delay between technology investment and productivity results. These factors complicate both productivity and pay.

The American economy has a large, under-researched, and undertheorized problem with the explosion of education, health care, and infrastructure costs. American spending per student on K-12 education has doubled in the past fifty years, with no improvement in math, science, or reading scores. Worse, college costs have increased tenfold with no measurable improvement in graduate quality. Health insurance premiums have also increased tenfold so that the US now pays about four times more for health care than citizens of other modern countries with equal or better health outcomes. Even American subway systems cost eight times more than similar subways in other first world countries.[54]

These costs represent productivity declines since consumers pay more for less output. They doubtless contribute to the slowing of annual productivity growth since 2000. Some economic historians, like Northwestern's Robert Gordon, suggest that the problem is secular and long-term. Modern countries don't have as many life-changing inventions like electrical power, modern chemistry, vaccines, airplanes, etc., available to them in the early 21st century as they had in the early 20th century.[55]

Even if productivity does not explain pay or variations in pay, Americans retain a view that investments to increase productivity are an unmitigated good thing. Our living standards grow because we invest in education, technology, and trade. Unfortunately, growing evidence suggests that these investments directly contribute to stagnant incomes for most workers. On the one hand, education, automation, and flows of goods, people, and money clearly improve output, which enables living standards to grow. But each of these forces tends to reward the same group of educated high achievers, mostly from stable, affluent families. The resulting productivity paradox is the focus of this chapter.

Later chapters will explore income bargaining. Today's working families, however, believe that higher incomes come from individual effort, not collective action. As a result, they bet their children's future on America's favorite labor market organization: college.

College Cannot Restart Equitable Income Growth

America entrusts the job of selecting, developing, and certifying human capital to high schools and colleges. These schools purport to credential individual effort and talent independent of family background or circumstance. They don't do this and likely never have.

The case for a college degree is incredibly simple. Graduates earn almost twice as much as high school–only grads and are rarely unemployed. One estimate suggests that it costs the average student who fails to graduate from college a half million dollars in lifetime earnings.[56] Moreover, those with four-year college degrees seem better able to adapt to changing workplace demands than those without a degree.[57]

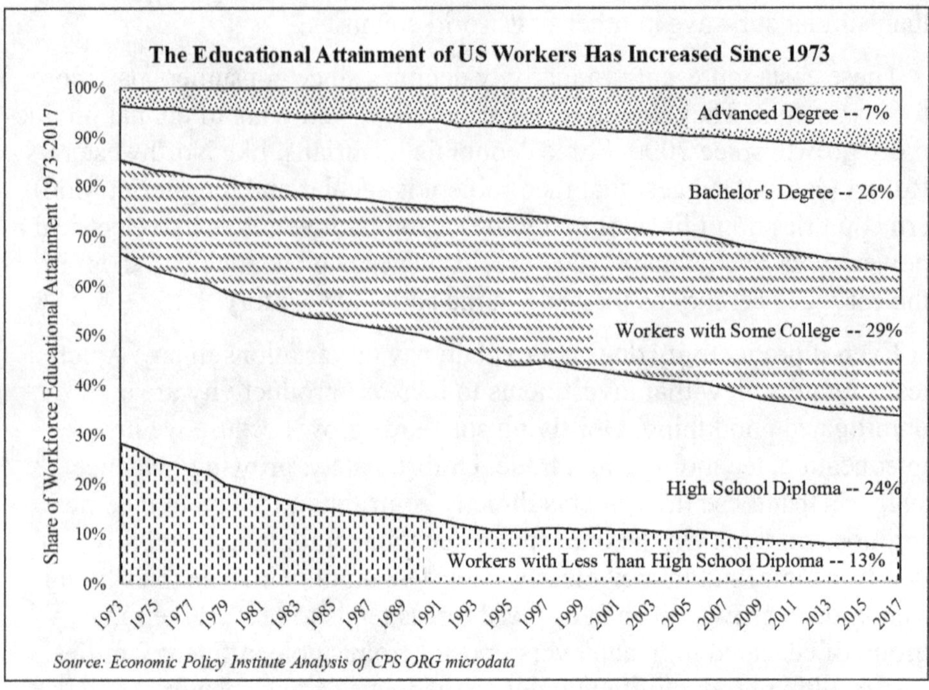

Reality is more complicated. America has carried out an extended debate about whether the value of college is in the skills students acquire or the signals they send employers. Michael Spence shared the 2001 Nobel Prize in Economics for work he did as a grad student showing that much of the value of college isn't discernable occupational skills but rather the signal that a degree sends an employer about conformity, wealth, and intelligence.[58] Those who have long forgotten everything they learned in college often sympathize. Others point to the "sheepskin effect" as evidence for signaling—or the fact that those who earn 80 percent of a college degree earn much less than 80 percent of the paycheck of a person who completes a full degree.[59]

Regardless of the source of value, however, a college degree looks like such a spectacular investment that 70 percent of American high school graduates now enroll in college—a greater share than any other country. Between 2000 and 2014, undergraduate enrollment in the US grew 31 percent from 13.2 to 17.3 million students.[60] The 2007 recession accounted for a small share of this growth.[61]

But the economy rewards diplomas, not enrollment—and only 60 percent of those who enroll in college complete a four-year degree. Worse, graduates are not the students with the most grit or academic ability—they are the ones with parents who can afford to subsidize full-time study. Full-time students are vastly more likely to graduate than those who can only study part-time.

Researchers at the National Center for Education Statistics decided to test whether family wealth or academic talent better predicted who would graduate from college. They divided 15,000 high school sophomores into four groups based on family income. They gave students a battery of math and reading tests to determine whether their economic background or academic aptitude drove college outcomes. Among those who scored in the top quartile on the math test, 74 percent of the wealthiest students graduated with a four-year degree compared with 41 percent in the same quartile from low-income families.[62] Outstanding students from these families had the same graduation rate as below-average (second quartile) students from wealthy families.

The New York Times concluded, "Put bluntly, class trumps ability when it comes to college graduation".[63] Seventy percent of the students in the top 200 colleges come from the top quarter of the income distribution. These students are vastly more likely to complete their bachelor's degree than those who attend local schools and frequently attend part-time.

Graduation rates at elite colleges are high because elite schools not only select strong students from affluent families but also because they invest much more money in each student. During the sixties, colleges invested relatively evenly in students regardless of the status of the school or the academic potential of the student. By 2013, however, America's most selective colleges and universities spent ten times more per student than schools of below-average selectivity. In many cases, these educational investments began well before a student enrolled in college.[64]

Progressives offer an easy answer: increase the public funds for student loans so that college is more affordable. To date, this has made the problem worse because universities promptly raise tuition to absorb increased public funding. As one careful study recently concluded, "…expanded student loan borrowing limits are the largest driving force for the increase in tuition, followed by the rise in the college (wage) premium."[65]

It would be hard to devise a faster way to polarize American earnings than to base pay on college completion and then increase tuition faster than inflation, as the US has done for a half-century. In the name of educational excellence, universities both public and private have become revenue maximizers unbounded by any metrics that gauge the cost-effectiveness of their results. Setting aside the waste of tenured faculty, unreproducible research, and idle summers, the only limit on spending on many college campuses is their ability to grow revenue from tuition, government aid, grants, or donations.

This is tragic. Americans enroll more students and spend twice as much per student on college as citizens of the average OECD country. The share of students enrolled in college is rising in every American demographic group.[66] But if college graduates earn the lion's share of income and if family income strongly predicts graduation rates, then high-income families are making a solid bet. However, lower-income Americans not only earn lower returns on their education investment, but they also take the greatest risk in borrowing to pay for it.[67]

Nobody rigged higher education. But if they had, it would be difficult to design a system more frustrating to middle- and lower-income families. The result is a system that risks helping America become a society with hereditary economic classes like those our founders fled.[68] It is utterly incapable of helping America generate inclusive income growth.

Peter Cappelli at Wharton has researched which families recoup their investment in a college education. He finds incredible variation across colleges. "Looking at the actual return on the costs of attending college, careful analyses suggest that the payoff from many college programs—as much as one in four—is actually negative. Incredibly, the schools seem to add nothing to the market value of the students."[69]

The unpleasant truth about American colleges is that their value to students depends heavily on the college and the degree program. The "college wage premium" (the average earnings of all high school–only graduates divided by the average earnings of all college graduates) conceals this fact. The premium is a ratio that reflects less the growing earnings for college graduates and more the collapsing paychecks for those whose education ends at high school. Moreover, the four-year college wage premium conceals a credentials race. Just as a high school diploma once commanded a wage premium until a four-year college degree upstaged it, recent income gains have gone to those with advanced degrees—a small subset of all college graduates. The growth of the college wage premium conceals a four-year-degree premium that has remained essentially flat for the past decade.[70]

More fundamentally, the college wage premium presumes that differences acquired or revealed by age seventeen don't matter. College applicants and politicians alike presume that every high school student can thrive in college. It has never been true. The average graduate of the average college is nothing like the marginal applicant to the marginal college.

Marginal applicants who struggle to graduate from high school derive fewer benefits from college. They are less prepared (in some high schools, most seniors are not ready for college). The college they attend is more likely to attract inferior teachers and students and to produce below-average results. They are much less likely to graduate. Doubling per-student spending since the early 1970s has helped improve the reading and math scores of both nine and thirteen-year-olds, but scores for seventeen-year-olds have not improved.[71] An *Atlantic* article titled *The War on Stupid People* concludes that "...most Americans aren't smart enough to do something we are told is an essential step toward succeeding in our new, brain-centric economy—namely, get through four years of college with moderately good grades."[72]

Finally, the college wage premium applies to graduates, not applicants. A graduate has persevered, in many cases because they were socialized and financially supported to do so. They have what the Federal Reserve called *Sitzfleisch* (staying power, or the ability to keep the seat of one's pants in the seat of one's chair).[73] But the college wage premium is irrelevant to state colleges that graduate only 15 percent of their students. Citing returns to graduates instead of to enrollees, as many prominent studies do, misleads those deciding whether or not to enroll.[74] Those who leave college before graduating may acquire useful skills, but their earnings more closely resemble high school-only graduates than four-year college grads.

A college degree is valuable to those who get one, even if promoting college cannot restart equitable income growth. College is very valuable to strong students from disadvantaged backgrounds.[75] Research by the

Federal Reserve suggests that children from the poorest fifth of US households are six times more likely to reach the top fifth if they graduate from college.[76] Similar research shows the high impact of helping even marginal students to graduate from solid four-year colleges, especially state universities.[77] Many of these schools are engines of social mobility that are associated with much higher earnings for students who can complete four-year degrees. It's nice to be born rich, but graduating from a good four-year college still makes a massive difference to those who start from behind and learn to thrive in classrooms.

Colleges and universities can't drive broad-based income growth because they don't and can't meet the needs of most of the US population. The strongest colleges are those that make their search for talented students and faculty into a paramount mission. Their commitment to selectivity drives their conduct because selection effects in higher education are like network effects in technology. They are difficult to establish; they create enduring competitive barriers; and they exert a profoundly conservative influence on leadership, for whom creating and sustaining these advantages becomes an overriding strategic focus. These are not institutions that are even remotely equipped to drive broad-based improvements in American incomes.

Underrated Humans and Overdue Robots.

Elon Musk is a restless technologist who has attempted to revolutionize money (PayPal), space exploration (SpaceX), cars (Tesla), electric power (Solar City), AI (Open AI), and underground transport (Hyperloop and the Boring Company). A man prone to impulsive pronouncements, Musk once warned that "Robots will be able to do everything better than us. I mean all of us."

He then attempted to install robots at his Tesla plant, apparently unaware of the intense fights over automation between the United Auto Workers and General Motors that had raged in this same assembly plant when Musk was a child. Less than two years later, Musk emerged from the factory, scarred from his tour through "production hell". He conceded that "excessive automation at Tesla was a mistake. To be precise, my mistake. Humans are underrated."[78]

Musk is not the first person to learn this lesson. Automation has raised fears of technology-induced unemployment for the past two centuries. Underrated workers worry that new inventions will kill more jobs than they create. They fear that those who lose the old jobs will not be able to perform the new ones that arise—a fear made worse by our lack of strong institutions to help labor markets adjust to external shocks. As a result, even when employment rises or remains stable, those who can't "race with the machine" end up in real trouble.

Fear of technological unemployment along with the gee-whiz nature of modern technology helps to obscure America's real economic risk: that technology is improving productivity not too rapidly, but much too slowly. Slow productivity growth makes restarting wage growth vastly more challenging. Ideally, technology can improve every single job in the economy. Will this lead to technology-driven unemployment? It never has.

The fear of technology-induced unemployment is ancient. Five centuries ago, Queen Elizabeth I denied William Lee a patent for an automatic knitting machine, citing her "regard for the poor women and unprotected young maidens" she thought would be "reduced to starvation" (of course, without a patent, mills adopted the device even faster). In the mid-1920s, Secretary of Labor James Davis warned of the coming "end of work". In the 1960s, President Johnson convened a blue-ribbon commission on the impending "crisis of excess leisure" due to technological progress. Today, a cottage industry of pundits (including Elon Musk) warn that work itself is on the verge of extinction.

These fears are understandable to anyone who contemplates the unprecedented range of technologies assaulting the American workplace. Robots now operate more precisely than surgeons; some can stitch closed an incision in the skin of a grape. They read X-rays more accurately than many radiologists and diagnose skin disease better than any single dermatologist. 3-D printing is revolutionizing not only manufacturing, but biotech as computers learn to print proteins.[79] Amazon is deploying tens of thousands of Kiva robots in its 200+ warehouses. They are using facial-recognition technology with demonstrated Orwellian potential to eliminate work now done by 3.4 million cashiers.[80]

Advanced genomics is producing customized medicines that may upend drug production. It is poised to transform farming by developing crops that require less water, insecticide, or fertilizer. Rapid improvements in solar, wind, and battery technology are making energy cheaper, cleaner, and more widely available than believed possible only a decade ago. Advanced chemicals and materials are changing how Americans make semiconductors, cars, clothing, and almost everything else. Drones already do work previously done by airplanes as well as work airplanes could never do. Self-driving and electric cars, buses, and trucks are emerging steadily. Much of this was not clear five years ago—meaning that many technologies that will matter five years from now are not visible today.

Technology is designed to displace work. To the extent that cars become a service, Americans will need fewer than 253 million vehicles or 500 million parking spaces.[81] We can quickly identify at least 4.3 million Americans who earn a living driving, fixing, ticketing, renting, or parking cars. They take home more than $150 billion in pay each year.[82] We imagine that all of this will vanish. And someday, it may.

It is correspondingly difficult to see the businesses, jobs, or crimes that new technologies enable. The smartphone is the innovation of the age, but when Steve Jobs introduced the iPhone in 2007, the King of Silicon Valley himself failed to foresee apps, video, or voice response. He did not imagine that mobile technology would soon mediate friendship, gossip, shopping, dining, banking, housing, dating, or navigation. The greatest technologist of the age did not realize that his device would revolutionize books, games, and movies (he nailed downloaded music, which promptly shifted to streaming services, which Jobs dismissed). Steve would smile to see how his bit of magic transformed transportation and security—and delight at how it is starting to change health care, education, and government services.

It has always been this way. Thomas Edison famously failed to anticipate how consumers would use his inventions. Edison was confident that customers would use the phonograph to listen to religious sermons at home. Music was not among the top ten purposes he imagined for recorded sound.[83] The idea of an entire industry devoted to recording and distributing music was literally beyond imagining. If inventors themselves can't anticipate the commercial impact of their technologies, why suppose that the rest of us can?

Technology has never created unemployment on a large scale. Trucks may become more autonomous, but today the trucking industry suffers a massive shortage of drivers prepared for the "good living but rough life" that the occupation offers.[84] Even when individuals lose their jobs to technology and end up with lower wages, large numbers of jobs don't go extinct. Historian Robert Gordon notes that no invention in the past 250 years of industrialization has ever caused mass unemployment. He cites three useful examples for the present day. Amidst fears that artificial intelligence will destroy white-collar jobs, marketing has seen more AI investment than any other business function.

Nonetheless, marketing analyst jobs have flourished. Since the introduction of the spreadsheet, the economy has needed a million fewer bookkeepers and clerks and 1.5 million more financial analysts. E-commerce and mail-order technologies have eliminated perhaps 100,000 brick-and-mortar retail jobs. They have created about 400,000 new jobs in the process.[85]

Humans frequently misjudge technology. When Washington rescued Detroit in 2008, nobody imagined that the US would ever recover leadership of the global automotive industry. A decade later, many people expect that it will because the technologies crucial to self-driving vehicles are emerging almost entirely in the United States. Critical university research, components like LIDAR processors, simultaneous localization and mapping (SLAM) technologies, automotive operating systems, simulators essential to testing and refining software, HD mapping, vehicles, software security, and Uber/Lyft-type mobility platforms have all emerged primarily in the United States.

Weirdly, many jobs don't disappear despite advancing technology—a fact so mysterious that it moved one of the nation's leading labor economists to ask "Why Are There Still So Many Jobs Left?" David Autor analyzed the comparative advantage of humans and machines. He confirmed that computers substitute for workers in performing routine, codifiable tasks. He also documented how digital tools amplify the comparative advantage of people who supply problem-solving skills, adaptability, and creativity. Autor concluded, "In many cases, machines both substitute for and complement human labor. Focusing only on what is lost misses a central economic mechanism by which automation affects the demand for labor: raising the value of the tasks that workers uniquely supply."[86]

Autor identified four factors that determine whether technology creates or destroys jobs. The first is cost, which determines the feasibility of automation in the first place. Second is whether the technology complements labor or substitutes for it. Third—and by far hardest to see—is whether demand for the automated goods or services (or demand for related, adjacent products and services) goes up or down as costs fall. The final factor is how quickly someone can learn to do the jobs that emerge.

The costs of automation and labor influence the rate that managers substitute one for the other. European companies with higher labor costs can often more easily justify investments to replace labor with machines. For this reason, it isn't hard to find workers in US mills and factories doing jobs that Europeans have automated. Because technology is deeply embedded in work, equipment or new software requires customization, maintenance, and changes in processes to pay off. As a result, the cost of implementing new enterprise software services is often multiples of the cost of the software itself. Managers try to factor in all of these costs, including distraction and opportunity costs, into a decision to invest in automation.

Even when automation is cost-justified, however, it is rarely obvious in advance whether it will complement a particular skill or substitute for it. Many observers expected travel websites to kill off travel agents and for ATMs to eliminate bank tellers. The first prediction was right—the few remaining travel agents have retreated to niches like corporations and cruises. But banks did not lay off their tellers when ATMs automated the work of dispensing cash. They used them to develop new customers and deliver new services. In 1985, the United States had 60,000 automated teller machines and 485,000 bank tellers. In 2002, banks had installed 352,000 ATMs, but employed 527,000 bank tellers.[87] Today, the Bureau of Labor Statistics (BLS) reports 520,500 tellers and expects the number of these jobs to drop only slightly during the next decade.[88]

Sometimes automation relieves production constraints, which allows volume to grow. For example, demand for airline gate agents has been unaffected by self-serve kiosks at airports. McDonald's kiosks increased business so much that the chain hired an average of two more people per restaurant.[89] Likewise, lawyers who worried that AI-driven software to help legal discovery would precipitate a "jobpocalypse" discovered that employment grew as costs fell and legal services expanded into underserved markets.[90] As with smartphones, nobody saw this coming—or could have.

Boston University economic historian James Bessen explains some of the reasons why the impact of technology on jobs is hard to see in advance:

> "Automation reduces the cost of a product or service, and lower prices tend to attract more customers...
>
> "So when demand increases enough in response to lower prices, employment goes up with automation, not down. And this is what has been happening with computer automation overall during the last three decades. It's also what happened during the Industrial Revolution when automation in textiles, steel-making, and a whole range of other industries led to a major increase in manufacturing jobs."[91]

Technology that reduces costs might increase demand for a product or service—or it might not. Technology has reduced farming and construction costs by complementing human labor, but lower costs did not grow these markets. Consumers may buy the same amount of food or buildings even if the cost goes down. Medical procedures or engineering services might be a counterexample. If new technologies reduce the cost of a procedure, a physician may order more of them. In this case, technology may grow employment or have little overall impact. Technology that automates tasks lowers costs, but it eliminates jobs only if demand fails to increase as a result. As the ATM example suggests, this is impossible to see in advance.

Even if a technology does not reduce employment, can it lead to lower pay? Automation can force pay either higher or lower, depending on whether more people can do the remaining work or fewer can. A job only pays well if workers can bargain higher pay, either because they are organized to bargain collectively or able to bargain individually because relatively few people can do the job in question. If technology makes dentists more efficient or if dental hygienists were not prohibited from opening teeth cleaning clinics without a dentist present, the world might need fewer dentists. Or pay for dentists might fall. Or patients might decide to have their teeth cleaned more often.

Consumer tastes and preferences affect how technology influences jobs. For example, computers can reliably fly and route airplanes. Eliminating pilots and many controllers would reduce travel costs and improve safety. But passengers who ride driverless elevators and trains to their gate prefer airplanes with a crisply uniformed human up front.[92] Pilot jobs are safe—except perhaps on cargo flights.

We cannot predict the future course or consequences of technology in large part because the factors that determine how technology affects work or pay are largely emergent. Cost, complementarity, market demand, and skill profiles influence each other. They are the result of cumulative human actions, not of human engineering or design. They produce third, fourth, and tenth order effects that influence each other and are more consequential for job creation than the more obvious first and second order effects. These "butterfly effects" (small changes that lead to large downstream consequences) routinely turn economic prognosticators into fools. As a result, it isn't possible to know much about how technology affects the quantity or quality of the work it automates.

It is as difficult to know when technology will improve productivity as whether it will do so. Fundamental technology innovation is rare: electrification, air flight, the internal combustion engine all transformed twentieth-century America. Advanced robotics, artificial intelligence, CRISPER-enabled gene editing, and the mobile Internet are doing the same for the twenty-first. But technology changes can take a long time to improve productivity because productivity (output per worker) always grows more slowly than capital investment per worker or than living standards (output per person, which jumped when women entered the workforce, for example).[93] This helps explain the "Solow paradox", the widely discussed observation by Robert Solow in the 1990s that "we see computers everywhere except in the productivity statistics. "

The time lag between investment in many technologies and a measurable impact on productivity means that it is difficult to predict when a new technology will affect jobs. Most technology change takes a long time. Electric lighting eventually transformed everyday life, but forty years after Edison demonstrated working lightbulbs in 1882, fewer than 10 percent of American farms had electricity.[94] So too in factories, where an entire generation of managers ignored the potential to electrify individual machines. They replaced parts as machines wore out but still drove them off of centralized power. Subsequent generations had to completely redesign factories and invent new work processes to use electrification to double and triple productivity. The invention of the electric motor was essential, but making it valuable required dozens of less dramatic innovations.[95]

Nonetheless, the prospect of large-scale technological change invariably produces widespread and contagious emotional anxiety. Workers know that even if technology leaves most people better off, the jobs that emerge are often out of their reach. Technologists like to compare these fears to those of the machine-bashing Luddites of 19th-century England. It's a good comparison because in retrospect, these much-maligned weavers had a clear-eyed understanding of their situation. The automation the Luddites feared genuinely did devastate their livelihoods. Most felt small consolation that productivity increases allowed their children and grandchildren to live in unimagined prosperity. Markets don't care much about this problem—only labor market institutions that live outside the job market can advocate for the well-being of workers whose jobs are affected by technology or trade.

Technology can help increase output but cannot, by itself, restore America's middle class. Technology either helps worsen the distribution of pay by further empowering certain highly paid skills or has no effect on how the gains it produces are distributed. Moreover, the gains from technology may be slowing. As noted earlier, America is starting fewer new companies—a big problem for anyone who wants to grow middle-class incomes or preserve health care and Social Security entitlements. This is in part because of demographics. America is aging and young people are creating fewer families and smaller ones. Without immigrants or higher productivity growth from technology, Americans will face pressure to retire later, pay heavily for health care and retirement, or live in towns starved of vital infrastructure investments. Americans who worry about the rise of the robots should instead pray that either robots or poor immigrants arrive soon. It isn't clear who else will bring them food and help them shower in their senior years.

Sovereignty, Democracy, or Globalization: Pick Two

If investing in education and technology are America's two favorite approaches to growing productivity, globalization is third. Economist Dani Rodrik studies globalization and, as the child of a Turkish business owner who benefited from trade protection, he takes its side effects seriously. He has documented not only the benefits of globally integrated capital, product, and labor markets for increasing productivity, but the cost of social disintegration that comes with it as longstanding social arrangements succumb to market pressure. In 2007, he suggested an "impossibility theorem".

Rodrik posited that political democracy, national sovereignty, and deep global economic integration are mutually incompatible. Countries can have two but not all three at the same time.[96] Those that choose democracy and sovereignty, as Rodrik advocates, may not pursue hyper-globalization. Democratic states that wish to integrate deeply into the global economy invariably forfeit national sovereignty to global governments or trade organizations in order to do so. Perhaps worst, those that prefer sovereignty and deep globalization will inevitably be forced to abandon democratic accountability.

The decade that followed has largely validated Rodrik's trilemma. Most countries have chosen to pursue globalization by becoming either less democratic or less sovereign. Even nations with a common history like those in the EU have a hard time pursuing global federalism (reducing national sovereignty with a mix of economic integration plus democratic politics). Likewise, fencing global economic growth around Bretton Woods–style arrangements that limit trade liberalization and impose capital controls has inspired little interest or serious discussion. Notably, however, every democratic country that has increased the share of its economy devoted to global trade has also grown the size of its state safety net programs.[97]

Rodrik recognizes that technology, global trade, and immigration change the employment relationship. Savvy investors and highly trained professionals have the skills and mobility to flourish in global markets. Others do not. Globalization may on balance be valuable, but it always creates losers as well as winners. America has neither the institutions nor the social commitment to require those who win to share their bounty with those left worse off.

World trade has skyrocketed from 39 percent of GDP in 1990 to 58 percent in 2018 (down from a peak of 61 percent).[98] Since 2005, America has doubled its trade in goods and services with other countries.[99] Not only do more capital, services, and merchandise cross borders, more people do too. Worldwide immigration is up 40 percent since 2000. In part, this is due to a refugee crisis from people fleeing Syria, Honduras, and other failed states. Immigration has tested the resilience, generosity, and political culture of the rich nations of the world.[100] Not surprisingly, trade and immigration have become political lightning rods in the United States and much of Europe.

An obvious reason is that the growth of trade and immigration has coincided with stagnant pay for most workers without four-year college degrees. Misplaced nationalism and nativism also play a role. Trade between Chicago and Los Angeles causes Americans almost no political concern, regardless of its impact on jobs or income. Even trade and immigration with Canada is rarely a political issue. But Americans have grown suspicious of trade and immigration with growing Asian or Latin American countries, including Mexico.

Some of this is political expediency. Trade agreements are a soft political target. Alan Blinder and Brad DeLong have pointed out that economists and the politicians they advise often oversell the impact of trade agreements on jobs. These deals rarely create as many jobs as adherents promise nor destroy as many as detractors fear.[101] There is a strong case that even if the US is substantially better off than it would have been without NAFTA, even if the most extravagant claims of those of us who campaigned for the agreement never materialized. Likewise, there appears today little basis for believing that boosting economic liberalization by admitting China into the World Trade Organization will accelerate Chinese political liberalization as most proponents promised.[102]

Even more than trade, immigration has become a lightning rod for global economic integration. There is a strong economic case that the United States needs more low-skilled workers, not fewer.[103] Economists note that immigrants take different jobs than native-born workers, especially agricultural jobs and those that don't require English, like the work done by Congolese refugee Ruhatijuru Sebatutsi of Columbus, Ohio. He works a nine-hour shift pushing meat through cutting machines seven days a week alongside men and women from war-torn Myanmar and the Democratic Republic of Congo. His commute by bus takes four hours round trip. Reflecting on his situation, he told *The New York Times,* "I am so lucky."[104]

As with trade, however, even economists who support increased immigration recognize that it will leave some Americans worse off. The United Nations counts 68.5 million people, a population the size of France, who have been displaced by persecution, conflict, violence, or human rights violations. Two-thirds are fleeing one of five failed states: Syria, Afghanistan, South Sudan, Myanmar, and Somalia. Murder rates in three failing states, El Salvador, Guatemala, and Honduras, are at historic highs. Global demand for relocation will, for the foreseeable future, exceed the absorption capacity of any single country.

Every advanced country will determine sensible limits on unskilled immigrants. A policy of putting American worker interests first would limit unskilled immigration visas based on the long-term needs of the US economy plus the historic commitment to absorb refugees of political repression. When US labor markets have more unfilled jobs than unemployed workers, which is common thanks to long-term demographic trends, we would encourage more workers to legally immigrate. When unemployment rises, governments would restrict visas for those without specialized skills.

It also assumes consistent enforcement using a combination of E-Verify job screening, national or state ID cards, and last-in-first-out deportations. Offering those who have worked, paid taxes, and raised families in the US for more than a decade and have become *de facto* citizens, visas and a straightforward path to citizenship solve a huge piece of the immigration puzzle. Because illegal immigration into the US has plummeted for more than a decade, two-thirds of undocumented families are shadow citizens who have lived in the US for more than ten years.[105]

Discussions of trade and immigration policy are often plagued by localism, nativism, or naïve beliefs that public policies can bring back large numbers of high-paying unskilled manufacturing jobs. Manufacturing jobs have become a shorthand for a time when average families could reliably get ahead. The romantic attachment to manufacturing may be badly informed, but it reflects a deep and authentic desire for secure, well-paying jobs for workers without college degrees.

Many Americans are surprised to learn that the US manufacturing sector has not declined in economic importance. US factories have produced about 12 percent of real GDP every year since data collection began in 1947. But manufacturing has accounted for a lower share of employment every year since 1955 and is now about 12 percent.[106] This story is familiar and hardly unique: since 2011, even China has lost manufacturing jobs.[107] The same thing happened as agriculture became more productive (the well-understood difference is that displaced farmers could move to well-paying factory jobs). Today's displaced workers face a service economy that pays lower wages to workers without specialized skills. Those who benefit from trade and technology provide little transition support for those who got hurt.

The surge of Chinese imports affected some communities differently than America as a whole. Until recently, economists had failed to consider how certain regions manufactured products so similar to those made in China that several companies would be forced to relocate or close at the same time. If only a few towns produced the goods that the US trades with China, increased trade could and did wreck the entire neighborhood. It had a disproportionate effect on towns like Providence and Buffalo that specialized in apparel, footwear, furniture, home electronics, toys, and sports equipment. Washington, D.C., or Houston, in contrast, produced higher value or more diversified goods. They experienced much smaller effects from the growth of trade with China.

In research that rocked the economics profession but surprised nobody in the Midwest, investigators discovered that much of the economic adjustment that models predicted had simply never happened. Recovery from employment shocks in some communities taken much longer than predicted—if it occurred at all.[108] Wages remained low and unemployment high in towns that relied on products that China could easily produce. America's trade with China may have grown the economic pie, but their research showed that it changed the distribution of the slices. It confirmed that America had faced little pressure from labor markets or labor market organizations to transfer some of the gains from trade to those who lost their livelihoods. They also showed that losses extended well beyond the shuttered factory gates because manufacturers support a host of service businesses. As Ron Bloom, President Obama's car and manufacturing czar, memorably put it, "If you get an auto assembly plant, Walmart follows; if you get a Walmart, an auto assembly plant does not follow."

Ergo, communities that lose the assembly plant often lose the Walmart.[109]

Not surprisingly, economic catastrophes have political consequences. Follow-up research by David Autor, who was part of the initial research on hard-hit communities, showed that regions hardest hit by Chinese competition elected more extreme candidates to represent them in Congress.[110] Workers in these communities know that to its eternal shame, American business allocated almost none of its gains from global trade or technology to help those damaged by their decisions. As constructed today, however, neither government, business, nor labor organizations can help workers and communities adjust to technology and trade shocks.

This was never the idea. Even in the theoretical models, trade creates losers as well as winners. Frequently winning has more to do with the fortunes of geography and history, not individual initiative, skill, or effort. Losing out to trade or immigration shouldn't matter since those who win are still much better off after they compensate losers for their losses. But the United States lacks labor market institutions to ensure that winners use a share of their winnings to retire, retrain, relocate, or subsidize the wages of workers injured by these forces.

Investments in higher education, technology, and globalization have not grown incomes equitably, in part because they reward high earners and in part because market forces alone care little for fairness. It should come as no surprise that, in many cases, legislators decided to do something about it.

2. The Lure and the Limits of Mandated Pay

Lawmakers who are frustrated by the failure of labor markets to distribute income equitably can be counted on to legislate. They understandably seek to increase minimum wages, introduce basic income schemes, or use taxes, transfers, and public services to supplement the market income of low-paid workers.

These policies may help alleviate poverty. Unfortunately, they can't rebuild a thriving middle class or restart inclusive income growth. Wage minimums, negative income taxes, public health care options, and vouchers for housing or food make a massive difference to America's lowest paid workers. They have little impact on the median full-time worker who earns between $40,000 and $50,000 per year.[111]

The great virtue of markets is that when kept free of political interference, they generate prices to reflect changes in supply and demand. The instinct to not interfere with markets is thus understandable and reasonable. But labor markets frequently don't behave like markets at all. Modest increases in immigration or minimum wages don't appear to reduce either hours of work or demand for low wage workers.[112] In 2016, Walmart decided to raise the wages of its unskilled workers throughout North America.[113] Commodity markets don't behave that way. Buyers of copper never decide to give sellers 10 percent more than the market-clearing price.

Both the market for people and the market for commodities are socially constructed. (A simple market for wheat futures requires a decision to base the market on soft red winter wheat, a clear definition of what wheat products qualify, and enforceable lending agreements.) Nonetheless, the differences between labor and commodity markets are massive and worth summarizing.

Wages are sticky. People work harder and are more valuable if you pay them more—a ton of copper doesn't and isn't. Commodity markets depend on visible prices, but wages and salaries are opaque. When demand for labor falls, wages don't fall with it. A company can pay a nickel below the going wage and not lose its entire workforce. It can pay a nickel more and not see job applicants swamp the hiring office. The market for wheat futures does not work this way.[114]

Employers enjoy market power. Many large companies enjoy a monopsony, meaning that they have the power to set the going wage in a local market. They can underpay. Or they discover that paying more than the market requires brings them much smarter or more committed workers who are more productive. Or it forces them to automate routine work. Under these conditions, wage minimums or income bargains that force wages up need not reduce an employer's profits. Walmart and Amazon both discovered this when they raised wages unilaterally.

People respond slowly to price signals. When a town loses a doctor, local prices for medical services rise if a new doctor can't be found because growing or attracting a new doctor takes time—usually the local carpenter can't change jobs. Workers can't always retrain to pursue higher-paying opportunities. They have mortgages, working spouses, kids in school, and family commitments. Retraining works unevenly at best, especially as workers get older. Cotton futures don't have these problems.

Hiring is subjective. Unlike buying soybean futures, hiring people is subject to cognitive biases. The best managers unconsciously select employees whose race, gender, height, weight, age, schooling, ethnicity, smoking and drinking habits, religion, sexual orientation, parental or caregiver status, accent, economic background, and hobbies are similar to their own. Hiring distortions are unfair and discriminatory from a legal perspective. Economically, they are wasteful.[115]

Regulations distort labor markets. Immigration, child labor policies, licensure and credentialing requirements, non-compete provisions, taxes, union contracts, minimum wages, mandatory health and retirement benefits, and much else guarantee that labor markets are never frictionless, neoclassical models of intersecting supply and demand.

Discovering the Maximum Minimum Wage

The argument for increasing the minimum wage is simple: it raises incomes for America's lowest paid workers. The economic argument against minimum wages is also simple: mandating high pay discourages hiring, just as aggressive rent controls discourage investment in housing. This is intuitive. The first lesson of shopping is that if the price goes up, people buy less. Or, as only an economist could put it, "demand curves slope downward".

If labor markets were perfectly competitive, an increase in the minimum wage would force employers to either reduce either hours or hire fewer people. However, respected economists have shown that modest increases in the minimum wage don't always produce this result. During the late sixties, Oliver Williamson showed that minimum wages help larger, more productive firms and lead to fewer small or less productive firms.[116] Famous research by David Card and Alan Krueger on the restaurant industry in New Jersey and Pennsylvania concluded that small increases in the Pennsylvania minimum wage had little impact on job creation.[117] This research, along with pioneering research by Michael Reich and colleagues at UC Berkeley has extended the original work has become iconic among progressives because it suggests that few locations experience the anticipated costs associated with higher minimum wages.[118]

When the BLS began collecting the data in 1979, the federal minimum wage bound 13.4 percent of all employees. Today it binds only 2.7 percent.[119] As a result, over forty cities and seven states are phasing in increases to $15 per hour and 29 states representing more than 60 percent of the American population have elected to set a higher minimum wage.

Of course findings that hold at the margin never extend infinitely. Even ardent minimum wage advocates acknowledge that a $75 per hour minimum wage would produce untenable side effects. But there are several under-appreciated reasons that minimum wages can grow higher without triggering undesirable results.

In some cases, especially in restaurants and retail, employers are able to raise prices without suffering significant volume losses.[120] In other cases, higher wages appear to be offset by reduced employee turnover costs or by increased employment in more concentrated (monopsonistic) local labor markets where competition (and thus wage pressure) is less intense.[121]

Other studies have found increases in worker productivity and economic stimulus effects generated by increased worker purchasing power.[122] Finally, minimum wages can lead to increased automation, but this appears to be more common in companies that produce tradable goods, which generally pay higher wages and offshore a great deal of their low-skill work.[123]

Increasingly, the search for the "maximum minimum wage" is a regional one. Ideally it is based on testing and carefully gathered evidence.

A national minimum wage of $15 per hour would be worth $11.80 in San Jose compared with a median-cost town like Dallas, but $19.04 in Beckley, West Virginia. Even within large states, the difference between high- and low-cost towns is often 30–40 percent.[124] One size rarely fits all when it comes to American labor markets.

How should regions determine their maximum minimum wage? The experience of Seattle, the site of the first successful "Fight for Fifteen" campaign, may turn out to be instructive. David Rolf, president of SEIU 775 and a rising star in the labor movement, led an initiative for the city to raise its minimum wage in three phases. To its credit, the city carefully measured the results. Seattle increased the minimum once from $9.47 to $10 or $11 per hour, depending upon business size, a raise of about 10 percent. It then raised the minimum by 18 percent to $13. It recently raised the minimum by 15 percent more to $15.

A flurry of studies followed, most concluding that Seattle had tolerated the first increase without incident. Employers did not cut hours worked or reduce the number of jobs.[125] The results seemed to confirm the Card and Krueger finding that a small increase in minimum wages had little discernible impact on employment.[126] But a detailed analysis of the second increase—to $13 an hour—concluded that employers had reduced worker hours by three percent for every one percent increase in their hourly wage. If true, the second increase cost an average worker $125 in monthly earnings and reversed all gains from the prior wage hike. In other words, researchers concluded that Seattle's second increase forced low-wage workers to give up more in hours than they earned in higher wages.[127] These findings led MIT labor economist David Autor to declare that "if I were a Seattle lawmaker, I would be thinking hard about the $15 an hour phase-in. "

These findings were immediately challenged by Reich and other economists.[128] Sure enough, four months later the oversight group revised its findings based on a more segmented view of the labor market. They concluded that experienced workers who worked at least 700 hours in low-wage jobs earned about $84 per month more. The new minimum wage had not hurt them. However, those who worked fewer hours saw almost no pay increase. The third group, those who had not worked at all before the new wage law, fared the worst because the hiring of new staff had slowed compared with counties adjacent to Seattle without the $13 minimum. Moreover, the higher minimum wage had reduced job turnover rates by 8 percent.

The debate will no doubt continue for several more rounds—as it should. Seattle is a model of increasing the local minimum wage incrementally and gathering the detailed data needed to observe the effects. Analysts will disagree—that's part of the process—but without this analysis, no region will know when it has exceeded its maximum minimum wage and caused paychecks to decline.

Rather than invite a massive political fight each generation, the federal government could instead set the national minimum wage by formula. One approach might be for each metro area to start with a minimum wage that is half of the local average wage for a full-time employee (based on the employer's location, not the employee's residence). A minimum wage formula would provide a consistent, localized, self-adjusting, and in most cases an economically supportable minimum that each region could increase as necessary.

"Fight for the Formula" admittedly lacks the resonance of "Fight for Fifteen", but it would end up helping more workers until their states and counties got around to tailoring their own minimum wage.[129] Determining the maximum minimum wage first by formula, then by local initiative puts a floor under otherwise stagnant incomes. It allows the floor to rise or fall with the fortunes of the region. It allows distressed regions to attract businesses with wages that are lower, but economically sustainable for both employer and employee.[130] It reflects the reality that one minimum wage can't fit everywhere when most workers in West Virginia, Arkansas, and Mississippi earn less than $15 per hour today, while $15 is of little help to workers in New York, San Jose, or San Francisco.[131]

Adjusting income floors regionally can help encourage workers to relocate. Historically, geographic mobility has reduced income polarization; income has grown more rapidly in poor regions than rich ones for more than a century. Until recently, geographic mobility caused regional incomes to converge.

Today, however, janitors in New York City make less money after subtracting for housing costs than they do in the Deep South.[132] Because geographic mobility is reversing, regional income convergence has slowed to a stop over the past three decades. Land use regulations that restrict new construction, reinforce racial and economic segregation, segregate schools both geographically and economically, and drive up housing costs in wealthy areas are a widely suspected culprit. High-cost housing makes it difficult for relocation to help poorer regions catch up with richer ones. For this reason, migration is today more attractive for high-skill, high-income individuals than for lower-income people looking to move up.

Work Platforms and the Gig Economy

Some alternative work arrangements enable companies to circumvent wage minimums. Uber and Lyft pay drivers as contractors not subject to minimum wage laws. Others, like Upwork, pay freelancers for one-time gigs regardless of the hourly pay. Amazon's Mechanical Turk pays workers (who range from women working a few hours each week in India to bored US Army sergeants in Kabul) piece rates for completing a "Human Intelligence Task". Rates vary from a few cents to a few dollars per task, but hourly rates are often low.[133] Critics note that this enables employers to avoid not only minimum wages, but payroll taxes, health benefits, vacation pay, and retirement contributions. It also removes the ability of workers to bargain their pay collectively.

These loopholes matter less than widely believed. Economists have had a tough time agreeing on the magnitude of alternative work arrangements. Inconsistent classifications, data sources, and methodologies have frustrated accurate measurements. Surveys that count all part-time jobs as "alternative work", for example, naturally find a large alternative work economy. Otherwise, the so-called "gig economy" is largely a myth.

Until 2016, the most comprehensive survey of alternative work was the 2005 Contingent Work Survey (CWS) by the BLS, which found that 10.7 percent of all jobs were temp agency work, on-call work, contract work, and independent contract work.[134] In 2016, two prominent labor economists, Lawrence Katz and Alan Krueger, tried to update the CWS using a different dataset—the RAND Corporation American Life Panel. They tried to weight this data the way that CPS had done, but got it wrong. They ended up overestimating the extent of contingent and alternative work.

They found that those performing alternative work rose from 10.1 percent of all workers in February 2005 to 15.8 percent in late 2015—a massive increase.[135] Another study, using data from the General Social

Survey, estimated that freelancing accounted for nearly a third of all new jobs added between 2010 and 2014.[136] In 2018, the Federal Reserve used its Survey of Household Economics and Decision-making to conclude that "Three in ten adults participated in the gig economy in 2017." These estimates all showed an exploding gig economy built around temp agencies and digital work platforms.

In May 2017 the BLS finally updated the Contingent Work Survey. The results confused everybody. The new CWS found that independent contractors, on-call workers, temp agency workers, and workers provided under contract to third parties amounted to 10.1 percent of all jobs—meaning that alternative employment arrangements had *declined* as a share of all jobs since in 2005. The 2005 data appear to be heavily influenced by workers displaced by the Great Recession doing odd jobs to make ends meet. The BLS also noted that self-employment and the holding of multiple jobs have declined steadily since about 1950 and that both the creation and the destruction of traditional jobs have trended down for at least three decades. The new CWS led Katz and Krueger to revise downward their estimates of the gig economy in January 2019 and to carefully document the perils of attempting to reconstruct the CWS from other surveys.[137]

They also showed that the Labor Department does not yet account well for people with multiple jobs. For example, Uber drivers think of themselves as employed by Uber, not as self-employed. Some Airbnb hosts don't see themselves as "working a second job" or as even as "self-employed". Some researchers argue that instead of surveys, the 1099-MISC forms issued to freelance and temporary workers is a better measure.[138] Unfortunately, many housekeepers and babysitters don't receive a 1099, nor do Airbnb hosts or third-party sellers on Amazon or eBay unless they record more than 200 transactions and $20,000 in a year. These discrepancies are large and material and lead to two conclusions. First, a lot of workers have contingent or part-time jobs and always have. Second, we are not especially good at measuring either the size or the growth of alternative work.

The CWS contains a remarkable and often overlooked finding, however. Nearly two-thirds of alternative workers are independent contractors, and almost 80 percent of them prefer this work arrangement. Conversely, a majority of the remaining third are on-call, temp agency, and contract workers, who would prefer traditional employment.[139] Although some alternative work arrangements are designed to help employers avoid minimum wages and other labor costs, the vast majority of these arrangements are a rational response to both employer and employee preferences.

Targeted, Not Universal, Basic Incomes

Minimum wages are not the only way to legislate pay. More recently, some policymakers both left and right have revived the idea of a universal basic income (UBI).[140] Proponents argue that a UBI has two big advantages. One is efficiency. A UBI would be simple to administer and could in principle consolidate many of the 126 separate federal antipoverty programs. Libertarians argue that it could replace Medicaid and other health care programs, disability insurance (SSDI), some 33 federal housing programs, and 21 food or food purchasing assistance programs. It makes sense to simplify and streamline these programs with a UBI or without one. These overlapping programs are held in place by overlapping Congressional committee jurisdictions—a problem that a UBI can't address.

The economic case for a UBI is tenuous. Many UBI advocates hold a dystopian view of future job creation. They have succumbed to the ancient fear that technology will destroy more work than it creates. Like Nobel economist Wassily Leontief, they expect AI to do to workers "what tractors did to plough horses." They argue that work will be so scarce that income needs to be separated from production. Most UBI proponents assume that there is little productive public work that income recipients could perform. Others cite advantages including preserving the market for wages, such as it is, or enhancing the freedom of workers to walk away from abusive employers. Like the efficiency arguments, however, these benefits can be achieved without a UBI.

The fundamental challenge with any UBI is that the universality that makes it simple also makes it expensive. A $10,000 annual check for 215 million working-age Americans is a two-trillion-dollar scheme. An entitlement on this scale would make sense only if productivity growth outstrips job creation for a prolonged period of time and the country has no public services worth funding. Otherwise, public funds should fund public investment and public employment.

Neither condition exists in the United States. Concerns about automation notwithstanding, productivity growth is at generational lows. Job destruction has trended down for forty years. As of 2019, job creation has exceeded job destruction every month for nearly eight years. The need for labor-intensive investments in public infrastructure and services is one of America's few areas of broad political agreement. Moreover, most Americans see the role of the state as helping people to help themselves, not subsidizing idleness. Even with the support of conservative as well as liberal policy wonks, a UBI is a tough political sell.

UBI proponents are addressing a very real political sentiment, but they appear to have the economic and technology arguments backward. During a record period of job growth, the economic case is stronger for more automation than for less. Technology can improve the rate of new company formation, which has fallen for forty years. New technology platforms often enable companies to grow quickly. Uber, for example, built out its global operations in a matter of months thanks to the reach of worldwide smartphones apps hosted by Google and Apple.

The economic case may be thin, but UBI adherents are on to something, in part because technology companies have lost their political immunity. High tech has come to represent income volatility and uncertainty, global elitism, sexually abusive bro culture, monopoly power, and privacy risk. Even those working alongside it in San Francisco or New York resent its impact on gentrification. Most Americans believe that the economy is on the wrong track, presumably because their paychecks don't lie and because they associate technology with economic insecurity. A UBI may be ill-advised, but it speaks directly to these anxieties.

The experience of health care reform illustrates how treacherous the politics of UBI can become. Donald Trump understood the resentment felt by Americans who earn between $40,000 and $70,000 per year who saw their neighbors working less but receiving Medicaid benefits. Medicaid costs less than Obamacare, for which they are required to pay high, if sometimes subsidized, premiums. Under these conditions, a UBI that raised taxes on middle-income families to support payments to lower-income families would add insult to injury.

More fundamentally, the "defining challenge of our time" is to ensure that work and public policy support broad-based income growth. This calls for an opportunity-creation mindset, the embrace of technology, and substantial investment in infrastructure. It demands a commitment to practical workplace training, internships, certificate programs, and abundant training for those who learn best outside of traditional classrooms. No society grows prosperous by retiring productive citizens or by providing income unrelated to work to working-age adults able to work.

In the end, the biggest problem with a UBI is that it is universal. It isn't easy to justify mailing affluent citizens a monthly government check that they neither requested nor need. A Temporary Basic Income targeted to full-time students, new parents, and displaced workers in hard-hit regions would seem more promising.

A four-year Student Basic Income designed to encourage college, vocational training, internships, and apprenticeships might enable students to study full-time and improve college completion rates. For those enrolled in vocational programs, a basic income might subsidize pay during an initial period of low earnings as interns or apprentices. The McKinsey Social Initiative has shown the value of this approach. They have paid over 10,000 students in 31 cities to complete training in occupations that need workers. They place 83 percent of graduates in jobs with local employers.[141]

A Temporary Basic Income could award parents several weeks of basic income upon the birth of a child, which might reduce current penalties on motherhood, especially on lower-income women. (These same markets appear to reward fatherhood irrationally, especially among higher-income men.) Subsidizing both men and women to take several weeks off following the birth of a child might improve outcomes for men, women, and newborns.

Regions where labor force participation by those aged 25-55 falls below a threshold could use a Temporary Basic Income to subsidize relocation and retraining. Individuals could receive a monthly check to support approved retraining. The money would be paid to workers who retrain for a new job, so long as the training program discloses auditable graduation rates, placement rates, and the average income of its graduates so that students can make informed choices.

A Temporary Basic Income can help build a robust market for relocation support. Germany tried something like this. In order to mobilize grassroots support to help workers relocate, they created vouchers to enable a private market for relocation services. They targeted hard-hit communities of displaced workers. Any person or agency could earn money by helping a displaced worker find a job. The payment ranged from €1,500 to €2,500 (then $1,700–$2,800) came partly from the unemployment fund and partly from the hiring employer. The amount paid depended on the duration of each worker's prior unemployment. An agent earned more money by placing the harder cases. The program only paid to help displaced workers from particular distressed regions find employment and excluded workers who already held jobs. Unlike American Trade Adjustment Assistance, the German experiment did not worry about why a person had lost his or her job. To prevent scams, part of the payment came after the worker had been on the job for six months.

Germany conducted a formal evaluation of this program and used a valid control group. Researchers determined that the program promoted mobility, placement, and efficiency. Although it saved money, they concluded that they needed to pay agents a good deal more to place the highest risk workers.[142] (Note that this experiment involved only a relocation and employment bounty, not a wage subsidy, relocation assistance, or income support.)

How should states best counter the powerful forces that polarize income? Finding the local maximum minimum wage, perhaps using a formula, is a start. Well-designed redistribution (taxes including negative income taxes like the EITC) and pre-distribution (wage and income requirements) are a part of every functional labor market, much as central bank monetary controls are important to monetary regimes and financial regulations are essential to capital markets.

In sum, both private investment and public legislation are valuable elements of a national income strategy, but neither can restore equitable income growth. In the modern era, neither markets nor legislatures have demonstrated an ability to preserve a strong middle-class. Neither investments nor laws can adapt as easily to the massive variety of American companies, industries, and regional economies as privately organized workers and employers.

But does income bargaining truly work? America embraced collective bargaining during the Great Compression, but did unions raise pay—or did they represent workers whose pay was going to be higher anyway?

3. Does Income Bargaining Matter?

Economists, sociologists, and historians debate whether institutions or market forces have a greater impact on income. Do unions make a real difference? Or does worker pay increase due to variations in the supply and demand for skills—potentially caused by factors like new technologies and college completion rates? Or are still other forces at work?

The nature of public data means that this debate suffers from "streetlight effects", also known as a "drunkard's search". The bias comes from our tendency to search where data make it easiest. The effect is named for the drunk who drops his keys in the park but searches for them beneath a lamp post "because this is where the light is".

The structure of government data creates the streetlight effect that makes it more likely for researchers to use changes in the demand for skills to explain changes in income. The United States Census Bureau has tracked wages and education consistently since 1940. However, they did not track a household's union affiliation until 1973. Until then, it was easy to correlate higher earnings with skill and difficult to test any correlation with union affiliation.

Most economists search where the light is. Sober or not, they attribute the rise in wage inequality to "skill-biased technical change" (SBTC) and point specifically to the role of new computer technologies. These researchers have often concluded that income bargaining had little if any effect on income distribution. The collapse of unions and growing income inequality are the simple by-product of SBTC.

The Bias of Skill-Biased Technical Change

SBTC occurs when technology suddenly increases the relative productivity of more skilled workers over less skilled ones. Demand for skilled workers goes up, sometimes rapidly, and compensation rises accordingly. SBTC places technological change at the center of the income distribution debate, where it has arguably resided for more than two centuries. (Some historians have suggested that mid-nineteenth -century debates over machinery that emerged in the aftermath of the Industrial Revolution gave birth to economics as a distinct field of study.[143]) An assertion that technology drives changes in income distribution naturally infuriates those who dislike any explanation of income inequality not congenial to a public policy remedy.

Evidence for SBTC is easy to find even without streetlights. Take a quick visit to San Francisco. Observe well-paid engineers with computer science degrees earning twice as much as their equally skilled classmates who studied civil engineering, a skill set less affected by technology. Observe further that CS students who specialized in AI, LIDAR, or SLAM technologies crucial to self-driving cars and other fields attracting massive investment capital now earn two or three times more than those who primarily excel at front or back end software engineering. A sudden demand for new technology-related skills helps some people to command high wages. One group's wage rises, income polarizes—case closed.

Or maybe not. SBTC describes parts of the compensation structure in Silicon Valley. But does it explain why pay has polarized throughout the economy? The explanation has a lot of small problems. The timing is off: periods of increased polarization don't correlate well with periods of increased demand for technical skill. In many cases pay has polarized *within* occupations—not across them. If most people in the same occupation share about the same skills, then SBTC can't explain polarization. SBTC also has less to say about changes in women's pay or about broad-based wage stagnation. Researchers expressed serious reservations about SBTC as a single explanation for changes in US wages starting in the 1980s. As early as 2002, one prominent team concluded:

> "There were many technological innovations in the 1970s, 1980s, and 1990s, and it seems likely that these changes had some effect on relative wages. Rather, we argue that the SBTC hypothesis by itself isn't particularly helpful in organizing or understanding the shifts in the structure of wages that have occurred in the US labor market. Based on our reading of the evidence, we believe it is time to reevaluate the case that SBTC offers a satisfactory explanation for the rise in US wage inequality in the last quarter of the twentieth-century."[144]

The most comprehensive and trusted data available to researchers makes it difficult to test the major competing theory. What if institutions affect labor market outcomes as much as the supply and demand for labor? Because the Census Bureau, which conducts the Current Population Survey (CPS), did not begin asking households whether a union represented the income earner until 1973, analysts were not able to easily figure out whether unions were a significant factor in the Great Compression in the postwar period.

The Surprising Story of How Unions Mattered.

Progressives who despair of income inequality often produce charts showing that reduced income inequality and a stronger middle-class correlates with active labor unions. Sure enough, during the Great Compression, union membership was higher and income inequality was lower. Demonstrating that one of these facts caused the other, however, is much more difficult. Did unions represent more male, skilled, or older workers who would have earned more anyway? Did their members concentrate in higher-paying regions or industries? Proving that unions caused pay increases requires granular data that allows analysts to adjust for variations in skill, education, region, industry, worker age, technology, and more. The analysis requires information on which household members were represented by a union, which became available only well after unions began to decline. Without this data, searchlight effects alone ensure that SBTC will become the prevalent economic explanation for income disparities.

A team at Princeton led by Henry Farber attempted to explain different measures of income inequality: skill premiums, the ratio of the bottom 90 percent of earners to the top 10 percent, Gini coefficients (a widely used single measure of how much income varies in a population), and others. They tested several alternative explanations of different measures of income inequality, including SBTC and the role of labor unions.

They ran smack up against the limitations of CPS data before 1973 but found a clever solution. It turns out that the Gallup Company conducted almost five hundred survey of almost a million households and included extensive questions on demographics and socioeconomic status starting in 1936. As a result, researchers were able to "harmonize" or stitch together the

Current Population Survey and Gallup datasets. Because both Gallup and CPS include the state of residence of the household, the resulting data was robust not only for each year going back to 1936 but for each state as well.

The resulting data has created a new and much more complete picture of why income has stagnated and polarized. Researchers concluded that "unions have had a significant equalizing effect on the income distribution over our long sample period" and helped drive the Great Compression.[145]

Farber and his team demonstrated that labor unions are not mere artifacts of larger market forces. Unions helped to create and sustain an American middle class in the postwar period by increasing the wages of the least skilled workers. Collective bargaining even improved the pay of large numbers of workers who were not in unions, including managers. Moreover, the Princeton data suggests that the image of labor unions as representing primarily skilled and relatively educated workers was incorrect during the Great Compression. Union wages were not higher because unions represented more skilled, often white workers. Until the early 1970s, unions represented more workers who were less skilled. It was the ability of these workers to bargain income collectively that raised their wages by 15–20 percent over their nonunion counterparts.

The research team then looked at states, where union density varies considerably. They showed that the effect of union density on standard measures of income inequality was not only strong but that in many cases union density accounted for changes in income inequality better than changes in skills. Their finding that the erosion of collective bargaining led to wage declines for the middle class mirrors findings that stagnant minimum wages contributed to real wage declines at the bottom.[146]

Surprisingly perhaps, the research contained bad news for America's surviving labor unions. Today's unions affect income distribution less than they once did not only because they are smaller, but because they represent fewer unskilled workers. The researchers found that historically, unions delivered a higher wage premium to less skilled workers—as they must if they are to reduce income polarization. Between 1940 and 1970, when unionization peaked as a share of all workers and income was less polarized, unions were drawing in the least skilled (and least white) workers. Before and after that period, unions were not only smaller, but a higher fraction of their members came from the ranks of high-skill workers. The clear implication is that unions as currently constructed have less of an equalizing effect on income distribution than they did in the middle of the 20th century.

Both economic theory and evidence point increasingly to the critical role of power in labor markets. Markets without income bargaining are increasingly regarded as monopsonistic, meaning dominated by a single buyer—here an employer. These are not competitive markets, which is why pay varies substantially across employers for workers with similar skills (functioning markets don't produce this—workers would change jobs). Increasingly, evidence suggests that the US moved from a labor market based on negotiated wages for below-median workers to one where employers have the power to set wages unilaterally, subject to very limited market discipline. The loss of income bargaining and the weakening ability of labor unions to provide countervailing power looms ever larger in modern explanations of why real wages have stagnated for most working Americans.

Many economists take too narrow a view not only as to whether unions truly mattered but also as to why. Most assume that workers organize unions to capture a share of the economic rents produced by a company. Without question, many workers organize out of economic self-interest, although it is often not the main reason. As James Oppenheim noted in his poem honoring the 1911 textile workers strike in Lawrence, Massachusetts, "Yes, it is bread we fight for, but we fight for roses, too."[147]

The subject is undertheorized and poorly researched, but both history and the experience of many organizers suggests that a desire for respect motivates more organizing than a simple desire for higher wages. The history of labor and civil rights organizing suggests that beyond wages or benefits, many workers gained self-respect and dignity in these struggles. Walter Reuther, Mother Jones, and Cesar Chavez appealed not only to workers' lack of market power but to their need for respect and purpose.

Effective leaders, including good managers, always give purpose and meaning to the work at hand. In tight labor markets like Silicon Valley, money is not enough. Engineers can easily change jobs. What matters is the opportunity to work on something that matters, that changes the world in a way that both justifies a heroic individual effort and creates justified pride if the project or startup succeeds. The privileged life of a modern software engineer would of course be unrecognizable to her great-grandmother who worked in a Lawrence mill—but engineers nonetheless understand that "hearts starve as well as bodies—give us bread, but give us roses."

Unions once enabled hourly workers to advance not only their economic interests but their dignity as well. Collective action by hourly workers gave those involved community, respect, a voice at work, and a purpose. The private income bargains that resulted avoided the one-size-fits-all tendency of state or federal regulations. They were often tailored to reflect the unique challenges facing specific industries and regions. They ensured that winners did not abscond with all of the gains from improved productivity, leaving losers in the lurch. Frequently, bargaining forced capital substitution—it became much easier for employers to justify investing in equipment to increase productivity.

The success of labor unions leaves us a great mystery. If private sector labor unions helped fuel the Great Compression by reducing income polarization, why did they fail so comprehensively in the United States? Unions peaked as a share of all workers in 1955 with a market share, or "density", of 35 percent. They peaked in absolute numbers in 1979 with about 20 million members. Today the economy is three times larger after inflation, but fewer than 15 million Americans belong to unions—the same number as during the Kennedy Administration in 1962. Fewer than seven percent of private sector workers now belong to unions. Although a third of public sector employees belong to unions, private sector union density today is lower than it was in 1935 when federal labor law first protected labor unions.[148]

Some explain union decline by pointing to anti-union "Right-to-Work" initiatives. These are state referendums that effectively measure public support for New Deal labor unions. In 1947, Congress authorized individual states to outlaw any requirement that workers pay dues or fees to the union that represents them. Four states already had these provisions in their state constitutions; eight more passed what came to be known as Right-to-Work laws within the year. During the 1950s, seven more states went Right to Work. Then came Louisiana in 1976, Idaho in 1985, Oklahoma in 2001, Indiana and Michigan in 2012, and West Virginia in 2016. Twenty-six states now have Right-to-Work laws on the books. The recent Supreme Court *Janus* ruling effectively extended Right-to-Work laws to public employees in all fifty states. No state has ever repealed a Right-to-Work law, although several have declined to pass them, including Missouri in 2018.

If labor unions contributed to a thriving middle class, why have they consistently lost Right-to-Work elections and ended up representing a share of US workers that have declined unrelentingly since 1955?

Progressives marshal abundant evidence that companies killed labor unions in cold blood, often with the support of conservative politicians. Businesses point to the unsupportable cost of union agreements and plea that containing unions is a matter of economic self-defense. Oddly, unions appear in some cases to have colluded in their own demise.

So whodunnit? Did unions die due to murder, manslaughter, or suicide? To reimagine income bargaining in an economy that continually places new demands on workers and employers, it is essential to understand exactly where New Deal–style collective bargaining went wrong.

PART TWO

Why New Deal Collective Bargaining Collapsed

"The first principle is that you must not fool yourself—and you are the easiest person to fool."

Nobel Physicist Richard P. Feynman,

Caltech Commencement Address, 1974

4. The High Cost of Enterprise Bargaining

Before envisioning what modern income bargaining might look like, it is useful to assess why collective bargaining strengthened middle-class pay for many years, then failed comprehensively in the United States.

The conventional explanation is straightforward: the combined onslaught of unfavorable industry changes, hostile employers, and conservative Right to Work laws crushed American labor unions. Under closer examination, however, these forces appear to be symptoms of an underlying design failure. The legal framework that gave rise to American unions in 1935 contained fatal defects that forced private sector unions to fight unwinnable battles and restricted their ability to adapt to massive economic and technological change. These defects grow directly out of America's first labor law, the Wagner Act.

The first crippling incentive of the Wagner Act was the requirement that workers form enterprise unions. When unions bargain income for each company, a government agency must decide which unions represent which workers at which companies. Unions must challenge one company at a time to intense industrial combat just to be recognized as legitimate representatives. Worse, a union that bargains with a single company is likely to inadvertently limit the company's growth. Not surprisingly, most employers reciprocate by attempting to restrict union growth. In doing this, employers often violate weakly enforced federal labor laws. Without excusing these violations, it is helpful to inspect the system of income bargaining that creates an unusually powerful incentive for them to do so.

The second federal design error was to award unions exclusive bargaining rights. Exclusivity restricts worker choice, creates a highly litigious form of worker representation, and produces distracting fights over mandatory membership or fees to offset the cost of union representation.

The third design failure was permitting unions to form a cartel to prevent them from competing with each other for members. Until 1955, unions typically fought not only companies—they fought each other. The collapse of private sector unions in the United States coincided precisely with the formation of a labor federation designed to stop competition between unions.

The results of these failures have been tragic. Those who wrote the Wagner Act designed it for an economy of large companies and limited competition. It worked well until the late 1970s, even as unions covered an ever smaller share of the workforce. It thrives today primarily in the public sector—where states imitated the Wagner Ace in order to regulate union formation and bargaining in large public enterprises that face minimal competition. In the process, unions and companies alike have not only been forced to operate in an unworkable system, but most have violated Feynman's first principle and fooled themselves as to the underlying problem.

The balance of this chapter describes how the cost of enterprise bargaining grew as markets became global and more competitive. Chapter Five discusses the adverse consequences of exclusive bargaining. Chapter Six takes up the unwitting role of the AFL-CIO in reducing worker choice and accelerating union decline. Chapter Seven looks at the challenges posed by the unexpected rise of public employee unions.

The United States legalized labor unions under conditions that are unimaginable today. When Franklin Roosevelt took the Presidential oath of office in March of 1933, the economy lay in ruins. That month, the nation experienced the highest unemployment rate in its history at 29 percent of the civilian labor force.[149] The stock market was dead, having lost 80 percent of its 1929 value. Banks had defaulted on depositors in large numbers and half of all home borrowers had defaulted on their mortgages.[150] Millions of men had abandoned their families and taken to wandering from state to state in a futile search for work. Children went to work as adult wages fell below subsistence level. As families disintegrated, crime, prostitution, and alcoholism rose at an alarming rate.[151] As part of legislation designed to promote economic recovery, the United States passed laws to permit workers to organize labor unions.

Roosevelt's National Recovery Act launched an alphabet soup of public programs designed to provide work for the unemployed. Section 7(a) of the act permitted workers to form labor unions to bargain income. The measure provided no way for a union to earn bargaining rights, however, and backfired. By summer, the economy reeled as strikes rose at an alarming rate. Workers fought hard not for pay and benefit improvements, but simply for employers to recognize their union and bargain in good faith.

In the ensuing chaos, industries adopted two approaches to recognizing unions. The Automobile Labor Board bargained with unions according to proportional representation (a dozen unions each spoke for their own members). If there were ten unions with one or two representing a large share of workers and the rest representing skilled trades, the unions involved typically formed a bargaining committee and got to work. Of course, where unions were weak, they made less progress—but in the auto industry, unions typically enjoyed broad support.

Other industries adopted the "Reading Formula"—a method first tested with striking hosiery workers around Reading, Pennsylvania. It provided that an employer would recognize a union that won a secret ballot election. In part because some personalities toxic to the fierce mineworker leader John L. Lewis dominated the Automobile Labor Board, the Reading Formula was widely used to settle strikes for union recognition and became a cornerstone of national labor policy.

It was not enough. In 1934, the US saw 1,856 work stoppages, by far the largest number since World War I. Several of these strikes were politically inspired and brought economic upheaval to Toledo, Minneapolis, Lowell, and especially San Francisco. That year, exasperated longshoremen struck the port. The strike spread from the Bay to other west coast ports and soon became the largest general strike in US history. Federal officials warned Roosevelt that labor revolts were spinning out of control. They not only threatened commerce, but they also imperiled America's ability to respond to the stunning rise of European fascism.[152]

The war clouds gathering over Germany made military readiness a surpassing concern. Desperate for labor stability, Roosevelt used his landslide electoral mandate to sign workplace regulations designed by New York Senator Robert Wagner. When he signed the Wagner Act in July 1935, he made the Reading Formula the law of the land. He created a federal agency, the National Labor Relations Board (NLRB), to enforce a worker's right to organize a union, defined by Wagner as an exclusive, enterprise-based bargaining agent.

Not surprisingly, employers resented this dramatic and adversarial expansion of employee rights and power. They tied up the NLRB with injunctions and lawsuits for almost two years. In 1937, however, the Supreme Court upheld the statute by a five-to-four vote in five related cases.

In the end, most large industrial employers were unionized. Most could pass the cost of a labor union to their customers without penalty. For his part, Roosevelt achieved enough labor peace to prepare the nation for war. By 1941, labor unions were strong and growing. Within two decades of the passing of the Wagner Act, American unions represented 35 percent of private sector workers and used their bargaining power to create and strengthen the nation's middle class. By war's end, union members had achieved the dream of Wobbly songwriter Ralph Chaplin. They brought to birth a new world from the ashes of the old.

The Inevitable Penalty of Enterprise Unions

The Wagner Act, as later modified by the Taft-Hartley Act, created the DNA of American unions. It awards to a single union the monopoly right to bargain with a single employer on behalf of a subset of employees (the federally designated "bargaining unit"). By creating unions that represented some workers in some companies in an industry but not others, the law guaranteed that labor agreements would increase costs for unionized companies above their nonunion competitors. Unionized companies would suffer a competitive disadvantage unless they could increase productivity above their peers or pass on higher costs to customers without losing business. Before the Second World War, most large companies could do this; as the economy became less regulated and more global in the 1980s, most could not.

A unionized company felt the difference immediately. When the cashiers at Joe's grocery store organized a union and bargain higher wages, Joe pays a "union wage premium" which to workers is the benefit of being unionized and for Joe is the penalty. Unless Joe's cashiers become more productive or organize their colleagues in competing stores, their higher paychecks give Joe's nonunion competitors options Joe does not have. These competitors can pass on their savings from lower cashier wages as lower prices to customers, larger profits for owners, or higher salaries to managers.

Even with highly informed labor unions and cooperative employers, enterprise bargaining often turns out to be economically punitive. Smart managers and union leaders who trust each other, share information, and are committed to a productive relationship have a notoriously difficult time finding a wage premium that does not make a business less competitive.

It isn't surprising that American employers have tended to view the whole idea of income bargaining as a hopeless mess. Most bosses develop a simple view, akin to an allergy: income bargaining reduces control, adds cost, and increases complexity—so they oppose it. This outlook may be shortsighted and antisocial, but it is hardly irrational from an employer's perspective.

In 1984, economists Richard Freeman and James Medoff published a landmark study of the economics of labor unions. They tried to measure the costs and benefits of conventional enterprise unions on the companies whose workers they represented. Their book, *What Do Unions Do?,* was immediately heralded as a classic and remains America's most widely cited book on labor economics. Freeman and Medoff argued that unions are a paradox because they confer both benefits and costs:

> "Beneficial to organized workers, almost always; beneficial to the economy, in many ways; but harmful to the bottom line of company balance sheets: this is the paradox of American trade unionism, which underlies some of the ambivalence of our national policies toward the institution."[153]

Medoff and Freeman made pioneering estimates of union costs and benefits that were tough to do at the time. Their research and other work that followed found that unions raised wages and benefits during this period by about 15 percent. Others found higher premiums.[154] Freeman and Medoff found, and subsequent research confirmed, that unions made the biggest difference for younger, less educated, blue collar, construction, and Southern workers. Data show little difference by gender or ethnicity.[155]

The competitive impact of the union wage premium varies considerably. In some industries, a labor contract that pays 15 percent above market may have little impact if labor is a small part of the company's product costs, as in some steel or chemical plants. In this case, raising pay may not materially raise total production costs or significantly affect a company's profitability or the price of its shares.[156]

Freeman and Medoff undertook their pioneering work in the 1980s before historical data for individuals or establishments was available. Moreover, union wage premiums are complex. They change by industry and over time. Researchers need to adjust for the impact of workforce skill, age, turnover, education, regional differences, and other factors.[157] With better data, analysts have made these adjustments, which, despite the noise and bias they introduce, generally conclude that union premiums have declined by about half since the 1980s.

Most analysts believe that these premiums needed to decline. In 1990, researchers compared the cost of unions to US employers vs. those in other advanced countries. They determined that unions in the United States obtained significantly larger wage premiums than did unions in other advanced nations. They concluded that substantial wage premiums contributed to the faster decline in American union density than occurred in other OECD countries, in part because in many OECD countries, unions set wages at the industry level, not one enterprise at a time.[158]

Unions appear to help increase productivity in some cases – usually by helping reduce turnover and using a more experienced workforce to grow measurable output. They may produce benefits that are hard to measure or otherwise not captured by research. For example, workers often value the fairness implied in a formal process for resolving grievances. Fairness and legitimacy at work are hard to measure, but most managers think they help preserve trust.

Unfortunately, enterprise unions carry hidden costs that are ignored by nearly all economic research. Unionized companies spend a lot of money that does not benefit workers directly, for example on Industrial Relations staff, specialized attorneys, arbitrators, and in earlier times, on strikes. Moreover, unions impose metabolic costs on employers that economists rarely capture. Enterprise unions slow companies down (and frequently, these companies were not exactly sprinting before they were unionized). Union contracts can discourage talented workers by setting salary ceilings as well as floors. Often seniority, not merit, determines work schedules and promotions so professional advancement can take much longer. Work rules and job classifications can become rigid. These provisions not only slow an organization down, but they can also lead to litigious disputes that can cost more to resolve than is at stake.

Second, enterprise unions often erode trust, which is like oxygen or cash for many businesses. Running out of trust is lethal. Companies in banking, parts of health care, technology, and professional services can't operate without a trust-based relationship with clients and teams of service providers who trust each other. Trust is the lubricant that enables both teams and entire companies to adjust rapidly to changes in client needs or to competition. Trust erodes not only because unionized workers often don't trust their managers. It erodes because they have bargained detailed procedures for adjudicating matters that are resolved quickly in less formalized workplaces. To be sure, employers agreed to every one of these procedures—often in the naïve hope that doing so would preserve trust.

Freeman and Medoff argue that giving union members a voice at work can lead to higher productivity that helps to offset the cost of unions. A great deal of subsequent research has challenged the conclusion that enterprise unions contribute to productivity. Findings vary by industry and even by management, as might be expected, but the overall impact of these worker "voice" effects on productivity appears to be small.[159]

The Needless Misery of Union Organizing

When federal law charged the NLRB with enforcing the Reading Formula on most private sector workplaces, it was attempting to replace spontaneous strikes for union recognition with federally supervised elections. It turned out to be a minor improvement. Today, an employee who wishes to organize a union must wage and win a war at work.

By law, unions fire the first shot. Under rules overseen by the NLRB, one or more unions must petition for a representation election. Once petitioned, the Board determines an appropriate bargaining unit based on its view of which workers share common interests.[160]

When a manager learns that workers are gathering signatures to petition the NLRB for a representation election, she rushes to the phone. Her first call will be to a union prevention consulting firm, now termed "persuaders" by the Labor Department. Persuaders are a specialized $200 million industry that collects about $2,500 for every worker who votes in a representation election.

Persuaders follow a predictable plan. First, they identify suspected union organizers. Second, they fire them, in flagrant violation of federal law. Historically, very few employers crossed this line. One researcher found that in the 1950s, unions accused companies of firing about one union sympathizer for every 200 workers they petitioned to represent. As competitive conditions became more severe, the number rose to nearly one in twenty.[161]

In 1981, Ronald Reagan decided to break the striking air traffic controllers union. The only US president ever to have served as a labor union president, Reagan signaled employers that the federal government would not penalize aggressive anti-union tactics. Many employers had already discovered that the consequence of violating the NLRA was trivial. The maximum penalty for firing a pro-union worker after years of litigation is back pay, less any money the fired worker earned in the meantime. When scholars studied the question in 1990, they found that the average penalty to a company for firing an organizer was $2,733. A number ten or one hundred times this amount would still be much less than the expected cost of a union under most circumstances.[162]

Once they have fired the instigators, persuaders meet individually with remaining employees, who are now paying rapt attention. Following a series of mandatory group meetings, there is another round of sackings if the unionization fire is still smoldering. In desperate cases, the persuaders replace the managers that triggered the campaign. (Disrespectful managers cause more workers to organize unions than greedy ones do.) By Election Day, union support has invariably diminished. Persuaders are quite persuasive.

Union organizers have adapted to these tactics. They now select small bargaining units, carefully prepare workers for combat, and impose strict need-to-know information controls. They build an organizing committee of workplace thought leaders who ideally possess bravery worthy of French Resistance fighters. In the end, however, only the most desperate or politically motivated workers succeed in organizing a union.

Organizing campaigns in the private sector are traumatizing for both a company and its employees. Trust, which was often low going into the drive, is shot by Election Day and takes years to rebuild. That workers and companies must endure this sort of grim industrial combat for workers to exercise a right to bargain income is an unspoken policy travesty and a direct consequence of making the Reading Formula the law of the land.

Employers have forced unions to organize ever-smaller bargaining units. Between 2008 and 2013, unions petitioned for certification elections for fewer than one hundred US workplaces that employed more than five hundred people.[163] They know that big campaigns under NLRB rules heavily favor employers. Workers have narrowly voted against unions in recent large campaigns at RJ Reynolds in Winston-Salem, at Boeing in Charleston, and at Nissan in Canton, Mississippi. In these campaigns, which featured billboards and local TV and radio commercials criticizing the union, persuaders were, once again, very persuasive. Even worse for traditional NLRB organizing, however, was the 2014 UAW organizing drive at Volkswagen in Chattanooga, Tennessee. Under pressure from its German unions, Volkswagen gave UAW organizers access to the plant and agreed not to oppose the union campaign. The UAW lost 712 to 626, thanks in part to the campaign waged by Tennessee Senator Bob Corker promising that VW would expand jobs at the plant if workers rejected the union.[164]

By organizing smaller groups of workers, unions increased their election success rate from about 50 percent to almost two-thirds. Focusing on smaller units, however, means that unions organize fewer workers overall. Although unions petitioned to represent more than 100,000 workers as recently as 2000, by 2012, they sought to represent fewer than 40,000. In recent years, only SEIU and the Teamsters have attempted to organize more than 10,000 private sector workers annually.[165] As unions have petitioned to represent fewer workers, the median bargaining unit has shrunk to twenty-five to thirty employees—a far cry from the 47,000 workers who stirred the nation with a sit-down strike at the GM Flint, Michigan, plant in 1937.[166]

Organizing campaigns progress through three stages. First, workers petition the NLRB for a secret ballot representation election. Unions withdraw about a third of their petitions before the NLRB conducts an election, typically because persuaders have persuaded them that they will lose.

A campaign ensues. Unions win about two-thirds of all representation elections. If the union wins, contract bargaining follows. Unions that win representation elections succeed in bargaining a first contract about 60 percent of the time.[167]

In other words, a union must petition the NLRB for almost four workers to yield one new member. To maintain their current market share, unions need to organize about 400,000 new workers each year. Therefore, under current NLRA rules, they would need to petition to represent about 1.4 million workers each year just to stand still. Recently, unions have petitioned for about 85,000 workers on average—although the numbers are trending down.[168] Using this average, unions might organize 21,000 new members each year—about 6 percent of what they need not to shrink.[169]

For at least four decades, unions have blamed their dismal organizing results on management opposition. There is no question that corporate persuaders make large-scale organizing challenging. Unfortunately, the problem runs much deeper. Imagine that unions could certify workers based on petition ("card-check") instead of election. Imagine further that employers agreed to universal neutrality and to negotiate a first contract every time.

At current organizing rates, unions would add 85,000 new members a year. But with the return on their organizing investment skyrocketing, unions might increase their organizing activities fivefold. Complex organizations led by elected leaders take many years to increase any activity fivefold but imagine it could happen immediately. In short, indulge America's current labor unions their best-case, fantasy scenario.

Unions would grow twenty times faster than today. They would add 425,000 new members each year—a screaming success—until unions looked up and noticed that the US economy has more than 100 million private sector workers. Under perfect conditions, at this extraordinary rate of growth, unions would barely reach the AFL-CIO's survival threshold. They would add less than one-half of one percent of all private sector workers to their ranks each year. After accounting for standard membership attrition due to companies that shrink, die, or move overseas, private sector unions would stop losing density. Even under their dream reforms, American labor unions can't grow to relevance under NLRB rules that require them to wage company-by-company wars for exclusive representation.

Unions have good reasons for condemning illegal, immoral, and dishonest management opposition to organizing campaigns. However, the major irritant isn't always the fundamental source of the problem. The structure of exclusive enterprise representation, not managers, is the main obstacle to labor's resurrection. Progressives and Democratic Party politicians who imagine that stricter enforcement of current labor laws will allow unions to play a role in restarting income growth need to consult a calculator. For good and logical reason, diverse observers ranging from conservative governors to AFL-CIO presidents have called for the repeal of the NLRA and the abolition of the NLRB.

The demise of American private sector unions was the result of a design failure. Congress created a legal framework for unions in a context and an economy vastly different than today. The progressive reformers who wrote American labor laws failed to foresee an era of much more vigorous economic competition. They also designed unions that would face little pressure to adapt as conditions changed. The first way they did this was by awarding unions exclusive bargaining rights.

5. The Hidden Cost of Exclusive Bargaining

When Congress permitted unions to earn the exclusive right to bargain income, they imposed on unions a corresponding obligation. Unions were required to fairly represent all employees in the bargaining unit, a requirement known as labor's "duty of fair representation". It is the logical consequence of an exclusive bargaining right. Most states that copied federal law gave public sector unions a "duty of fair representation" either legislatively or judicially. A duty of fair representation is effectively part of an exclusive bargaining right.

A duty of fair representation created two unintended consequences. It created a collective action problem: forced to represent every worker in a bargaining unit, unions reasonably argued that every worker should contribute to representation costs. Unions argued that every worker should either join the union and pay dues or pay fees in lieu of membership, whether they personally support the union or not. With the passage of the Taft-Hartley Act over Truman's veto in 1947, states gained the right to ban compulsory union membership. Taft-Hartley led directly to fights over Right to Work laws in most US states, and to the recent Supreme Court decision that removed the ability of public sector unions to compel workers to pay union fees.

Second, the fair representation doctrine promoted a legalistic, highly procedural "jailhouse lawyer" approach to representing workers. Union contracts became lengthy. Grievance procedures became judicial and often slow. Focused on contract enforcement, unions took little notice of new products, markets, competition, worker demographics, or technology that steadily transformed the work itself. Perversely, unions benefitted from undermining workplace trust, in part because it reinforced their *raison d'être* under a system of adversarial, enterprise bargaining and in part because employers paid for the cost of a low trust relationship.

The Symbolic Fight Over Right-to-Work Laws

From their earliest days, unions bargained "security provisions". Unions wanted to discourage free riders, so they required every worker to either join the union and pay dues or pay fees to support the cost of union representation.[170] Some workers and many employers objected to union security provisions as unjust coercion. They pointed out that US law generally reserves for the government the power to compel payment for services. They argued that even if they enjoy the benefits, no citizen can be forced to pay a church that cleans up a park, a Rotary Club that supports a public charity, or a public radio station that broadcasts news. They are free to enjoy those benefits without paying for them.

When the Taft-Hartley Act allowed states to ban union security provisions, several states immediately enacted Right to Work laws. Employers, scholars, politicians, and union leaders commonly reason that if union security provisions make unions stronger, Right to Work laws weaken unions. They are right: nobody sympathetic to organized labor ever proposes Right to Work laws.

Interestingly, however, the data suggest that Right to Work laws may weaken unions economically, but they may strengthen them politically and as bargaining agents. In Right to Work states, 82 percent of workers who are covered by a union agreement join their union voluntarily. In states where unions can compel membership, the share is 92 percent—suggesting that union security provisions are hardly decisive for a union's revenue.

Surprisingly, workers join unions more often in some Right to Work states. More than 90 percent of workers who are covered by a union agreement join their union in Alabama, Indiana, Tennessee, West Virginia, and Wisconsin—a higher rate than in nine so-called "Fair Pay" states that allow union security provisions.[171]

If Right-to-Work Laws cause unions to decline, as both liberals and conservatives often assert, then Right-to-Work states should lose union members more rapidly than Fair Pay states. But they don't. Between 1983 and 2015, private sector unions lost more than 35 percent of their members in both Fair Pay and Right-to-Work states. In both types of states, unions failed to make up the loss of manufacturing jobs. Likewise, public employee union membership grew about 30 percent in both types of states as government services grew and unions organized new city, county, and state public agencies. Only construction trades shrank faster in Right-to-Work states. However, this was not because members refused to join a union. It was because nonunion contractors refused to sign labor agreements.[172]

The most significant difference in Right-to-Work states is not that workers refuse to join unions—it is that they are less likely to organize a union in the first place. Union agreements cover only 6.8 percent of employees in Right-to-Work states compared with 16.5 percent in Fair Pay states. Since Right-to-Work laws don't affect a worker's organizing rights, however, these regional differences are more likely to be the cause of Right-to-Work laws than the result.[173]

In short, when enemies of unions in their current form enact Right-to-Work laws, it imposes only a modest membership penalty on unions. They don't threaten the existence of unions—they just exploit the fact that coerced payment of dues is something that many Americans and some courts oppose on principle.

Interestingly, the world's most influential labor unions rarely bother to compel membership. Few unions outside the US and Canada require workers to join or pay fees. The result is a difference between the share of workers covered by union contracts and the share that join a union. The gap can be enormous, as the table below illustrates.[174]

	Union Coverage	Union Membership
France	98%	8%
Belgium	96%	50%
Austria	95%	28%
Portugal	92%	19%
Finland	91%	74%
Sweden	88%	70%
Netherlands	81%	20%
Denmark	80%	67%
Italy	80%	35%
Norway	70%	52%
Spain	70%	19%
Greece	65%	25%
Germany	62%	18%
Switzerland	51%	21%
Ireland	44%	31%
United Kingdom	29%	26%
United States	11.7%	10.5%

Source: European Trade Union Institute, Current Population Survey

These data conceal substantial variations within industries and within companies. As a general rule, workers are more likely to join unions in sectors with large employers. Together with the modest impact of Right-to-Work laws, these differences in worldwide union coverage and membership should cause unions to ask whether it is wise to force workers to pay fees when the strongest unions in the modern world don't coerce their members to do so.

Exclusive Unions Become Legalistic

Unions can operate as service organizations, social/political organizations, or legal advocates. Enterprise bargaining and its duty of fair representation create a powerful incentive for unions to prefer the latter. Attorneys are omnipresent in New Deal unions. They oversee the negotiation of legally detailed labor agreements and support the diligent surfacing and prosecution of grievances. Over time, union contracts inevitably grow lengthy—sometimes hundreds of pages long. Grievance procedures become slow and judicial. The life of a union comes to revolve around contract enforcement—not the organization of work or the consequences of new products, markets, competition, worker demographics, or technology. Exclusive representation guarantees that for many workers, a union is merely an insurance policy against oppressive managers.

A union absorbed in contract enforcement pays little attention to changes in how the work itself is changing. As technology changes, processes evolve, new business models and practices come to dominate, and the demographics of workplaces change, union inattention is cumulative. The result can be union officials who have spent decades out of the workplace and speak the language of a bygone era. Like emigrants returning home after a fifty-year absence, their language and mindset have frozen in time. The workplace and much of the workforce has moved on without them.

To an extent little appreciated by labor scholars, unions emerge and thrive in forms consistent with the demands of the work that its members do. Effective unions are organic; they reflect the social and cultural habits of their members. These habits both help screen for certain types of workers and shape the work itself.

In *Trampling Out the Vintage*, a sweeping history of Cesar Chavez and the United Farm Workers Union, Frank Bardacke grounds his analysis of the rise of the UFW in the nature of agricultural work. Bardacke dropped out of Harvard not to write software, but to spend several seasons working in the fields. He describes how the stages of food production, the crops, and the various regions of California influenced the ability and willingness of farmworkers to organize. He explains why farmworker organizing was often sustained by the tightly knit, highly skilled *lechugeuros*, the celery cutters, not the more isolated garlic or asparagus workers or those in ladder crops.[175] Waitresses, housekeepers, nurses' aides, fast-food workers, janitors, bartenders, machinists, baggage handlers, mechanics, cannery workers, and assembly workers all reveal similar differences in how their work shapes their propensity to organize.

The nature of the work shapes not only a worker's inclination to organize but also the character of the workplace organizations that emerge. The fights between the skilled white craftsmen of the AFL and the semi-skilled African-American and immigrant factory workers of the CIO were legendary. Their differences were rooted not only in race, class, and immigrant or ethnic communities but in the work that each group did. It would have been extremely difficult for privileged mechanics to link arms with Sicilian assembly line workers, who spoke broken English and shared a workingman's disdain for the tradesmen who thought himself a cut above.

In most industries today, technology is reshaping processes, skills, and business models.[176] Workers often need slightly different skills this year from last. The level of required coordination and information sharing may change. When the changes are continuous, workers may not realize that after several years, they have a new job and have learned to work differently. James Bessen has shown how, over time, the same position may begin to reward or penalize different skills and personality types.[177] Unions engaged in legalistic enforcement of contracts based on exclusive representation are almost always oblivious to these changes.

If they are to defend worker interests, unions need to be fully engaged in a wide range of workplace changes. For example, low-cost sensors and analytic software have made most work more measurable. Nurses, lawyers, accountants, fast-food workers, retail workers, and airline pilots today have their work measured in dozens of ways that were impossible a decade ago. These measurements exert a strong influence on the work itself.

Measurements can be helpful or they can be pernicious. Managers know that "what gets measured gets done." They understand that measurements of output, quality, or customer satisfaction strongly shape their priorities. Metrics often enable managers to automate routine tasks, however, so "what gets measured gets automated."[178] Industrial unions rarely engage in constructive discussion about the use of these metrics unless they affect contract provisions or staffing levels.

Ignoring fundamental changes in the workplace is a recipe for union irrelevance. Exclusive unions failed to respond in a timely way to changes in the workforce, the structure of work, and the nature of competition. This failure led to a peculiar explanation of why unions died. Analysts asserted that organized labor declined because employment "grew more slowly in unionized industries". This invites the question of why workers in emerging industries were not attracted to unions. Other than union neglect, what exactly makes accounting firms or commercial banks a "nonunion sector"?

Data reveal the idea of "nonunion sectors" to be bogus. Unions lost density even *within* their most active sectors. Nonunion employment grew as quickly within construction and manufacturing as in other industries because, in many cases, employment declines were concentrated in companies that unions had unwittingly penalized. Explaining union decline by noting that the economy grew more in new industries overlooks the relatively low price unions paid for failing to adapt or innovate to incorporate new industries—until they paid a massive price.

Requiring a single union for all members of a bargaining unit restricted the ability of workers in the same workplace to join different unions. Thus did Congress, and the unions they created, confuse solidarity with homogeneity. Then, in one of history's great ironies, unions restricted worker choice even further by forming a federation that banned unions from competing with each other. In doing so, organized labor inadvertently contributed to its downfall.

6. The AFL-CIO: Solidarity or Sedative?

Dues-based organizations learn how to count members. If membership is growing, these organizations, including labor unions, feel healthy. But if the overall workforce is growing faster, counting members is a dangerous way to measure progress. A more accurate gauge of union health is density—the portion of all workers who belong to a union. A business that happily grows revenue as its market share declines is making precisely the same mistake.

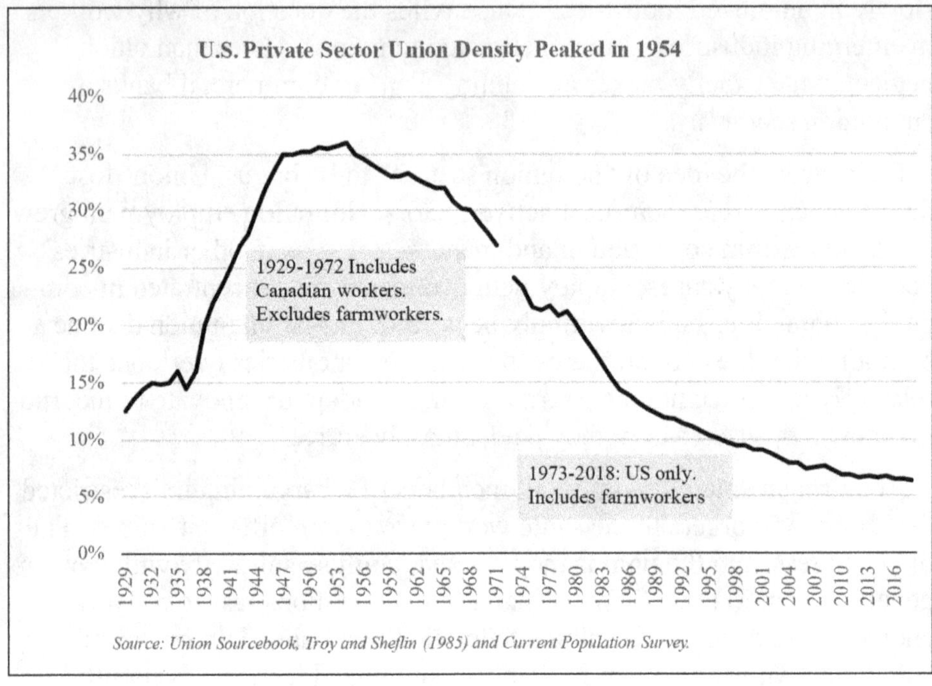

It is useful to divide the growth of private sector unions in the United States into three periods. The time plot shows that union density increased from 1935 to 1955. Unions grew both their membership and their "market share." Private sector union density peaked in 1955 at 35 percent. From 1956 to 1975, many unions thought themselves healthy because their membership continued to grow. But it grew more slowly than the workforce, so density declined. Unions were getting bigger but also weaker.[179] Since 1975, both membership and density have dropped every year as private sector unions have entered a phase of terminal decline. Today, unions represent a lower share of all private sector workers than they did when Congress passed the Wagner Act in 1935.[180]

Why did union density suddenly reverse starting in 1956 after growing steadily for two decades? Analysts frequently overlook an obvious factor: in December 1955, organized labor decided to ban competition between unions by merging the nation's two major labor federations. By design, the merger severely restricted worker choice.

How the AFL-CIO Suppressed Union Competition

The suppression of competition between unions was the declared purpose of the AFL-CIO merger. Once they formed a legal cartel, unions with exclusive representation rights felt little pressure to evolve as new industries emerged, technology transformed work, and demographic shifts changed the workforce.

The AFL and the CIO hail from entirely different industrial and labor traditions and were never natural allies. The American Federation of Labor emerged from the federations of craft guilds that appeared in the founding days of the American republic. It represented the more skilled, privileged, conservative, and often European craft workers who sought to control access to their occupation, as guilds have done since the Middle Ages.

The AFL fought the Knights of Labor, predecessors to the CIO. The Knights organized by territory rather than by trade. Like the CIO, the Knights rallied workers around the ideals of class solidarity. The CIO emerged from the large mass production industries in the early decades of the 20th century. CIO unions represented large numbers of unskilled or semiskilled workers who had migrated to American cities from farms or from poorer parts of Europe. Industrial unions were more inclusive and less elitist than their craft union brethren. The Mineworkers, for example, admitted black members from its earliest days. Socialist and other collectivist ideologies flourished in their ranks.

When the AFL rejected "wall-to-wall" organizing, mineworker John L. Lewis led the formation of the Committee on Industrial Organization. When FDR signed the Wagner Act in 1935, they changed their name to the Congress of Industrial Organizations and split from the AFL.

During the next twenty years, CIO unions fought each other and AFL unions hammer and claw. Labor's battles were fierce, epic, and colorful. Skilled workers battled the unskilled for the right to represent workers. Socialist leaders fought conservative ones. Entire towns became involved, as did local or national politicians. Fierce competition propelled record union growth in part because it led unions to reach out to new communities, including women and African Americans, who joined unions for the first time amidst these battles. In 1936, one percent of black workers were union members. By 1954, 40 percent of black men working in the private sector belonged to unions.[181]

Militant CIO unions like the United Automobile Workers (UAW) or United Electrical Workers (UE) drove many companies to recognize more company-friendly AFL unions. For example, Westinghouse, General Electric, Boeing, and Lockheed all recognized the white, southern, segregated, AFL-based International Association of Machinists (IAM) to avoid bargaining with the socialist and racially integrated UAW.[182]

The intensity of these fights is hard to overstate. Having prevailed over the UAW through physical violence at the Battle of the Overpass in 1937, Henry Ford established his notorious Service Department, a group of more than 3,000 thugs hired to maintain an antiunion reign of terror in Ford factories. Henry Ford was sincere in his view that "Labor union organizations are the worst thing that ever struck the earth."

Undeterred, the UAW petitioned for a vote at Ford's massive River Rouge plant. The final vote was split between the UAW and AFL unions that made a late entrance. Ford was stunned that only 2.6 percent of Rouge workers voted for no union. The resulting contract made Ford workers the highest paid in the industry and led directly to the disbanding of the hated Service Department.[183]

In the face of the obvious success of CIO union campaigns, many formerly craft unions began to adapt. The Teamsters stopped representing only truck drivers. The West Coast longshoremen quit the AFL and formed the International Longshoremen's Association with a CIO charter. The IAM successfully organized airlines, aircraft manufacturers, and industrial plants, notwithstanding its affiliation with the AFL.

Did these intense conflicts compromise labor's political solidarity or lessen its organizing? Hardly—it was the time of the most rapid private sector union growth in US history. From a low point of 2.7 million members in 1932, union membership grew to 10 million by 1941.

Competition Complements Solidarity

Accustomed to steady growth, union leaders came to view fights between unions as zero-sum and fratricidal. Competition between unions violated deeply held feelings of class solidarity. Many leaders concluded that the members they managed to win came at the expense of another union and decided that fights between unions were destructive to the labor movement overall.

This conclusion is both understandable and profoundly mistaken. Labor leaders were fooled by the availability heuristic: they could see and calculate the financial cost of competition. They felt it more useful to focus on organizing workers in nonunion companies than on zero-sum fights with other unions. As with trade and technology today, the benefits of competition were hard to see and impossible to count. These benefits included stronger local and national leaders, more adaptive local unions, greater local initiative, more determined and creative tactics, and a more engaged membership.

Why is competition so valuable, especially when companies and unions alike try so hard to avoid it? Competition forces specialization. Specialization enables organizations to differentiate, prevent head-to-head competition, and increase their odds of survival.

It isn't easy for union leaders to see this. Like Saudi oil sheiks, union leaders imagined that a cartel would make them stronger. Like the sheiks, they were wrong. Even enterprise unions grew so long as they competed with each other (and as long as employers could pass union costs to customers without penalty). The moment they stopped competing, unions had little incentive to adapt by specializing. The moment the American labor movement restricted what union a worker could join by preventing unions from competing with each other for workers, it stopped growing.

Scholars have argued that that the separation of the CIO from the AFL in 1935 enabled new forms of unionism and the emergence of dynamic new leaders and tactics. They rarely consider how the reunification of the two federations achieved precisely the opposite.

The AFL and the CIO merged for many reasons. They had worked together in 1949 to fight international communism by organizing the International Confederation of Free Trade Unions. They had collaborated the following year to form the United Labor Policy Committee to develop public policy responses during the Korean War. New leaders, especially the CIO's Walter Reuther and the AFL's George Meany, trusted each other more than prior leaders had. It helped the merger that the AFL had purged corrupt unions and the CIO exiled communist ones. Both federations faced a shared adversary in that both distrusted the coming Eisenhower Administration. Both Reuther and Meany thought that the growth of one labor federation often came at the expense of the other—something that organized labor could ill afford. The deep-seated belief in labor solidarity shared by every union leader made this conclusion instinctive.

In December of 1955, the federations merged to form the AFL-CIO. The merger was controversial at the time.[184] As head of the smaller federation, CIO leader Reuther emerged subordinate to George Meany and came to regret the merger almost immediately. He fought with Meany constantly and ultimately withdrew the UAW from the AFL-CIO in 1968. The UAW did not reaffiliate until 1981.

The entire purpose of the merger was to end competition between the two federations. The new AFL-CIO constitution contained a clause that every union leader soon learned to recite as Article Twenty. It decrees that "No affiliate shall organize or attempt to represent employees as to whom an established collective bargaining relationship exists with any other affiliate." Article Twenty prohibits unions from organizing workers in new jurisdictions. "Each affiliate shall respect the established work relationship of every other affiliate." Initially, Article Twenty was controversial. Today, it means that restaurant workers may not seek representation by the Service Employees (SEIU), nor auto mechanics with the UAW.

A labor cartel is legal because the authors of the Wagner Act let stand an obscure provision of the Clayton Antitrust Act of 1914 that exempts labor unions from antitrust prosecution. The exemption is understandable. It makes no sense to prosecute unions for fixing the price of labor since that is the entire point of collective bargaining. Because lawmakers drafted the exemption broadly, however, the same law permits unions to agree to not compete with each other. Unlike companies, unions are free to form cartels. The antitrust exemption makes Article Twenty legal, even though a similar arrangement among companies wouldn't be. It is why baseball team owners can use collective bargaining to cap player salaries, but technology companies in Silicon Valley pay hundreds of millions of dollars in fines when they are caught colluding to cap the salaries of highly paid software engineers.

Article Twenty remains a cornerstone of American union design. It is no longer controversial. It would be hard to tell exactly how much damage Article Twenty has done, except that two big unions were not affected by it. The National Education Association (NEA) never joined the AFL-CIO, and the AFL-CIO expelled the International Brotherhood of Teamsters for pervasive corruption in 1957. Because they were free to compete with AFL-CIO affiliates and vice versa, these unions provide a useful natural experiment.

During the thirty years that the Teamsters lost Article Twenty protection, the union was free to organize workers to switch unions. The Teamsters became the wolves of the union ecosystem, preying on the weak and infirm—and every AFL-CIO union returned the favor. When the Teamsters raided the IAM, for example, the resulting battles were hard-fought, occasionally with tire irons. When the dust settled, each union won a few elections and lost a few. Both unions worked furiously to strengthen their local organizations. Machinists became more responsive, negotiated more aggressively, conducted more training, and handled concerns more promptly. Both the Machinists and the Teamsters improved their game—a positive sum outcome for workers and affected unions—even as leaders of both organizations decried the wastefulness of zero-sum "raids" on each other's members.

Two unions fought especially vigorously for the right to represent schoolteachers. The National Education Association began as a conservative professional association representing small-town school administrators. Initially, it disdained collective bargaining. During the 1970s, however, the union shifted to representing teachers as a full-fledged labor union. During this time, the AFL-CIO had affiliated a teacher's union, the American Federation of Teachers (AFT), led by the estimable Al Shanker.

The NEA and the AFT fought frequently and hard. The fights were often expensive. As a result, however, teachers became America's most heavily unionized occupation and the NEA America's largest labor union.

Both unions were forced to replace ineffective local leaders, lest their members become vulnerable to the entreaties of the opposing union. Both learned to absorb weak local organizations into stronger ones. Both developed impressive grassroots political organizations and a reputation for highly engaged members. Both grew strong in Right-to-Work states. Whether teachers' unions have strengthened American schools is a subject for the next chapter, but there is little doubt that decades of competition helped to produce two of America's strongest unions.

Shanker died in 1997. In 1998, the two teachers' unions reached a tentative merger agreement, but NEA members rejected it. Nonetheless, five NEA state affiliates merged with their AFT counterparts. A decade ago, the AFL-CIO announced that standalone NEA locals could join state and local labor federations. An imperfect cease-fire took hold.

What happened? The NEA, having grown to 3.2 million members in 2007, immediately began to shrink. Observers estimate that its membership has dropped about 1.5 percent annually for each of the past six years; the union today appears to represent fewer than three million members.[185]

Competition and choice animate both markets and democracies; nothing else does. Perhaps there is another factor that explains the rapid membership growth when unions competed and the immediate end of growth when the AFL-CIO made competition illegal. Maybe another factor explains why unions got stronger once members had a choice of the Machinists or Teamsters. Perhaps the fierce competition for teachers had nothing to do with the creation of powerful teachers' unions. The evidence isn't decisive, but it is strong enough that the burden must shift to those who wish to defend restrictions on worker choice or exclusive union monopolies.

The evidence suggests that competition is a compliment to solidarity, not a rival. Solidarity without competition is a sedative that dulls innovation and reduces the consequence of poor performance. By sharply restricting member choice, imagining solidarity to be more valuable than innovation, and dramatically decreasing pressure on unions to create new forms of representation, organized labor effectively stood united on its own air hose.

As with most unintended consequences, those who designed American labor unions saw none of this coming. Accustomed to oligopolistic industries, Congress could not imagine that markets would become competitive enough that enterprise unions would punish companies. Steeped in poorly developed notions of workplace democracy, Congress could not foresee exclusive representation descending into industrial combat, the unproductive battle over Right-to-Work, or the growth of hyper-legalistic union representation.

Perhaps most perversely of all, Congress failed to foresee that exclusive representation designed for oligopoly industries would end up thriving in the one part of the economy where competition is minimal and political pressure replaces market pressure. They never anticipated the rise of labor unions in the public sector.

7. The Challenge of Public Employee Unions

Public services help to compress real incomes by providing more services to those paid the least. Some services, like health care and housing assistance, represent measurable cash transfers to low-income families. Most services, however, are hard to value. What are police services worth if they reduce crime or preserve social trust? How can analysts value a library that not only loans books, but strengthens small towns with preschool and ESL classes, tutoring, espresso bars, and space for local startups?[186] The cost of these services reveals little about their value.

The quality of every public service depends on the skill and commitment of the professionals who deliver it. No school ever outperforms its teachers. No police department is better than its officers. No public hospital rises higher than its clinical staff. Funding and leadership are critical, but high-quality public services depend heavily on skilled, committed professionals.

American public service professionals are often represented by a labor union designed for the private sector. Public employee unions now represent teachers, nurses, police officers, firefighters, clerks, janitors, parking inspectors, and hundreds of other public occupations. Nobody expected this. Indeed, unions of public employees were once considered unthinkable, even by labor leaders. They raise issues today for those concerned with restoring middle-class incomes.

Liberal and conservative public officials alike voice three concerns about the impact of unions on public services. They claim that union political donations inhibit accountability and create a needlessly partisan civil service. They accuse unions of raising costs. Most seriously, they assert that by protecting incompetent members, unions obstruct reforms essential to strengthening prison, police, education, and other public services. Before evaluating these concerns, it is worth reviewing the unlikely rise of labor unions in the public sector.

The Surprising Success of Public Sector Unions

The explosive growth of public sector labor unions in the 1960s and 70s surprised almost everyone. The architects of the Wagner Act had opposed unions for public employees. Franklin Roosevelt thought unions for government workers a hopeless idea. Most union leaders agreed, noting that companies and governments differ fundamentally. Government workers don't generate profits—so a union would be forced to negotiate against taxpayers, who had already elected representatives to reflect their spending priorities.

A year after he helped found the AFL-CIO, George Meany asserted that "It is impossible to bargain collectively with the government."[187] His view reflected the mainstream belief that voters, not bargaining representatives, should have the final say on public policy and public spending. Through the 1940s and 50s, even leaders of public employee unions thought that advocating for civil service reforms made more sense than collective bargaining.

This preference for civil service protection over collective bargaining emerged directly from the collapse of appointments based on political patronage, which still ruled most American states and cities at the turn of the 20th century. Patronage-based hiring treated government jobs as the proper spoils of political victory. Teachers, police officers, and firefighters typically held their positions for only a few years before a new mayor or state commissioner replaced them with his political supporters. Professional public services were difficult because competence and commitment were always less important than political loyalty to the mayor, governor, or President making the appointments. Labor unions were politically impossible because they would have directly challenged the patronage system.

After World War I, state and local governments began to replace patronage appointments with civil service systems throughout the US.[188] This transition was complete by the end of the Second World War. Civil service reforms created a cadre of public service professionals that could govern continuously between different city, state, or federal administrations. It created a stable workforce with high levels of job security that was organized into large agencies containing thousands or even tens of thousands of workers.

By 1960, the civil service had unwittingly created ideal conditions for the rise of public sector labor unions.[189] The postwar baby boom caused demand for public services, especially schools, to explode. America's intense social activism during the civil rights and antiwar movements added political fuel and trained organizers to the nascent movement for public sector unionism.

During the 1960s, pressure grew for the federal government to set bargaining rules for federal employees. States also had to legislate how state, county, and city employees would organize unions. Legislators mostly copied the Wagner Act rather than risk a completely new approach. Most state laws provided for workers to vote for an exclusive bargaining representative within agency-level bargaining units.

By duplicating the Wagner Act in the public sector, state legislators handed public employees rights and bargaining structures that had been expressly designed for stable, monopoly industries. Since no industry is more stable or monopolistic than government, the design of the Wagner Act turned out to be a strong and lasting fit for government workers.[190] Exclusive representation at the agency level fit so well and the nature of government services changes so little that public sector unions have proven resilient. In contrast to the private sector, public union density has held constant at about 35 percent or a bit higher for the past three decades.[191]

By 1980, AFSCME (state, county, and municipal employees) had reached almost a million members. The AFT (the smaller of the two teachers' unions) had grown to half a million. That year, public worker unions achieved the same 35 percent density that private sector unions had achieved in 1955.

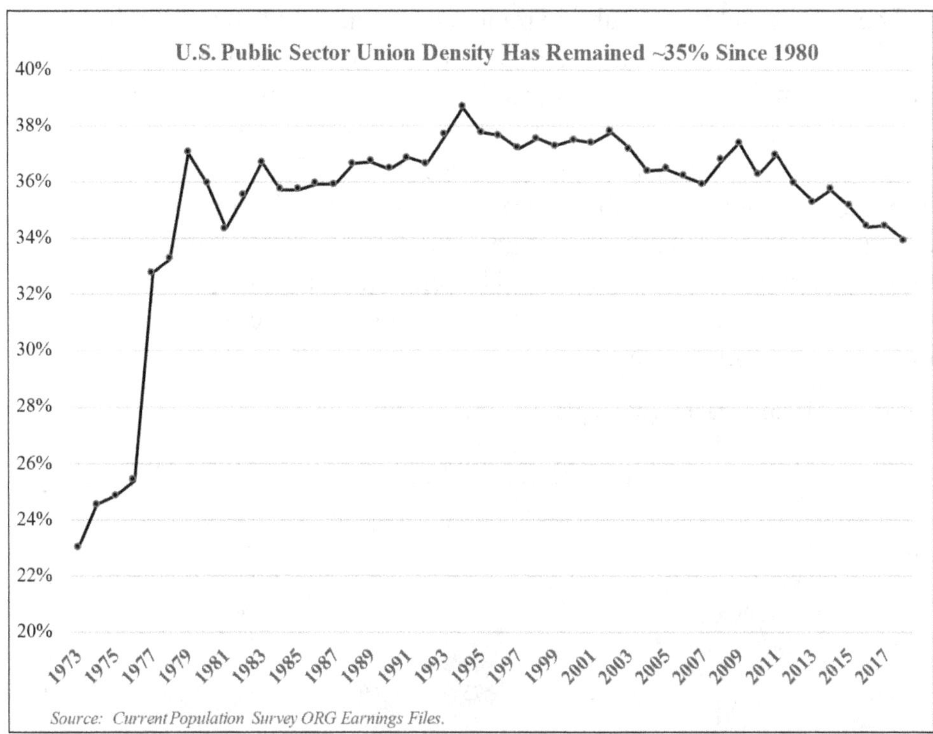

Source: Current Population Survey ORG Earnings Files.

The authors of the Wagner Act would be shocked to learn that the public sector today employs 15 percent of all workers but accounts for nearly half of all union members.[192] Public employees are five times more likely to be covered by a union agreement than employees in the private sector. As in the private sector, public employee union density varies enormously by occupation and region. Unlike the private sector, variations in state laws compound these differences.

Some form of public employee unionism ended up becoming legal in almost every state.[193] Even states that banned collective bargaining often permitted "meet and confer" sessions, which were similar enough to bargaining that they enabled unions to represent public employees effectively. Alabama, for example, bans public sector collective bargaining, but allows "meetings to discuss matters of mutual concern." It is a Right-to-Work state, but 85 percent of teachers in Alabama are union members. Public employees learned long ago that any union that represents a sufficiently high share of a workforce need not worry much about its formal bargaining rights.[194]

The demographics of public employees changed substantially during the past six decades. Today, most public employees are over age 45, and most are female.[195] Fifty-four percent of public employees have a four-year college degree compared to under 30 percent in the private sector. Twenty-eight percent have done graduate work.[196] This demographic is more politically and socially liberal than average and is made more so by the strong social convictions and genuine desire to serve the public that motivate many public employees. The tendency of growing public sector unions to mask the collapse of unions in the private sector is even stronger in Canada than in the US.[197]

State and local government employee demographics, 1960-2010

	1960	1970	1980	1990	2000	2010
Real annual earnings	$35,843	$43,194	$39,105	$45,010	$47,982	$51,552
Years of education	12.2	13.1	13.7	14	14.2	14.3
Bachelor's degree only	11%	15%	15%	21%	24%	26%
Graduate education	11%	20%	24%	21%	21%	28%
College graduates plus	22%	34%	39%	42%	45%	54%
Age	41	42	40	42	43	46
Female	26%	42%	46%	49%	53%	57%
Married	77%	75%	69%	69%	67%	67%
Teacher	11%	21%	20%	20%	20%	25%
Observations	72,278	128,967	422,135	484,578	582,663	144,125

Source: US Census and ACS Survey

Many private sector workers look with envy on public sector health care benefits, pensions, annual pay raises, and bosses who rarely measure performance, fire anyone, or lay workers off. To those who have seen their incomes stagnate, their health plans cut, and their pensions removed altogether, public employment looks like paradise. At the same time, many educated workers with attractive alternatives see government work as stultifying. As these tensions have come to a head, public employee unions face serious accusations. Critics charge them with subverting democracy, raising the cost of government, and inhibiting vital reforms by protecting incompetent workers.

Do Public Employees Elect Their Own Bosses?

The rise of public sector unions rekindled an age-old problem. Since Napoleon formalized the French civil service, public service professionals have been offered exceptional job security in exchange for political nonpartisanship. The US developed civil service regulations to end patronage hiring and firing. Although these regulations prevent politicians from firing public sector workers who are not sympathetic to their views, they don't prevent public employees from mobilizing to elect politicians sympathetic to theirs.

This isn't a new problem, nor one confined to the United States. Napoleon grappled with these issues in France and the man to whom he sold the Louisiana territories, Thomas Jefferson, struggled with the challenge of how to create a nonpartisan bureaucracy as well. Jefferson declared that while it is the

> "right of any officer (federal employee) to give his vote at elections as a qualified citizen… it is expected that he will not attempt to influence the votes of others nor take any part in the business of electioneering, that being deemed inconsistent with the spirit of the Constitution…."[198]

No country has lived up to Jefferson's ideal. Today, public sector labor unions actively use the Democratic Party to shape state, county, and city governments.[199] The Center for Responsive Politics calculates that four public employee unions (two teachers' unions, SEIU, and AFSCME) are among America's top ten all-time campaign contributors. They contribute almost exclusively to Democratic candidates, even though public employee union members register as Democrats only slightly more often than their nonunion counterparts.[200] OpenSecrets.org has documented $5.4 billion in contributions between 1990 and 2018 from the most active one hundred companies, PACs, unions, and law firms. About half of all dollars came from labor unions, which steered 95 percent of their contributions to Democrats.[201] This fundraising prowess makes public employee unions a protected species in blue states and a perpetual target in red ones.[202]

As public unions grew during the 1960s and 70s, they built formidable political operations. Jerry Wurf reformed AFSCME from a union that lobbied for civil service reform to an activist union willing to strike, undertake large-scale political mobilization, and oppose the complacency of the AFL-CIO. Al Shanker did something similar with the AFT. As their power grew, many public employee union leaders spoke openly about electing public officials who were sympathetic to their bargaining demands. The beloved AFSCME leader Victor Gotbaum famously bragged in 1975, "We have the ability, in a sense, to elect our own boss." This statement was widely quoted—a viral tweet long before Twitter.

Private sector workers cannot elect their own boss. Private sector unions do raise money to pursue partisan political objectives. But if a private sector union leader were to donate money to an employer in expectation of a better labor agreement, she would expose herself and the employer to criminal charges of commercial bribery. In the public sector, however, raising money to influence the boss you bargain with is business as usual.

Union support for Democrats appears to have little impact on political outcomes. Although unions contributed alongside many individual and PAC donors to the 2018 "blue wave" mid-term elections that produced the largest Democratic margins in history, when the dust settled, Republicans still controlled not only the White House and the US Senate, but thirty-three of fifty governorships, and sixty-two out of ninety-nine state legislative chambers.[203] In twenty-three states representing 40 percent of the population, Republicans controlled the governorship and both houses of the state legislature. Democrats achieved one-party rule in fourteen states, representing a third of the population. Only sixteen states have multiparty government. Union campaign spending, especially by public employees, may be unseemly, but it has hardly run amok over the preferences of American voters.

State campaign contributions appear to offer public employee unions the worst of all worlds. Union political donations distract leadership focus from organizing and membership services. They foster at least the appearance of self-dealing. Yet in most states, public employees don't successfully elect their own boss. For one, money influences election outcomes less than unions imagine. A substantial body of research suggests that American activists, donors, and pundits are especially likely to overestimate the impact of campaign contributions on state and federal election outcomes.[204] (At the same time, Americans tend to underestimate the role of gerrymandering and campaign contributions in funding lobbyists to shape legislative outcomes.)

Campaign contributions can make a much bigger difference in local elections. Local elections are ostensibly nonpartisan, so contributions are harder to raise and small contributions often have a disproportionate impact. For example, the powerful California correctional officers' union cultivates and finances candidates for District Attorney in counties throughout the state. The California Correctional Peace Officers Association (CCPOA) backs candidates who promise to incarcerate the guilty so that plenty of Californians end up in prison.[205]

The union is an unabashed champion of imprisonment. Many California politicians and their advisors describe the CCPOA as California's most powerful, feared, and destructive labor union.[206] The union raises $22 million each year from its 31,000 members and uses it to grow the prison business. They won a statewide "three strikes" laws to force judges to hand down harsher sentences. They defeated a measure to decriminalize certain nonviolent offenses.

The CCPOA has led the drive to change the face of California prisons. Since 1852, California had embraced rehabilitation. By 1984, the state had built only a dozen prisons. Since then, however, California has built twenty-one large prisons, forty remote camps, twelve correctional facilities, six youth facilities, and five facilities for mothers. Spending on prisons jumped from two to seven percent of California's general fund. Prisoners grew three times faster than the state population. The California Department of Corrections and Rehabilitation became the state's largest government agency, with 62,000 employees.[207] Today, the CCPOA is a massive and embarrassing obstacle to reforming the California prison system and is indirectly responsible for defunding the University of California, whose budget has shrunk to finance state prisons. New York has a similar problem, featuring Riker's Island and an equally brazen, if less politically adept, guards' union.[208]

Governments have attempted to limit the political influence of public employee unions in two ways: by reforming campaign finance generally and by directly limiting public employee political activity. Voters in many states have sought new ways to finance political campaigns. In 2016, Seattle and South Dakota passed forms of voucher-based public financing. These laws are under appeal, but most provide for every citizen to receive a coupon worth $100 of public funds that each registered voter can donate to a political cause or candidate. Candidates and causes would agree to accept contribution limits and to forgo out-of-state money.[209] This reform would take public sector unions out of the campaign business and allow public workers to contribute individually, just like everyone else.

A less obvious but more comprehensive approach would be to render all campaign contributions anonymous. This is counterintuitive; Americans instinctively favor transparency as the cure for almost everything related to money. This isn't always smart. Transparency strengthens markets, but the goal of campaign finance reform is to prevent the buying and selling of politicians, not to make it more efficient.

An analogy illustrates the point. Before 1892, voting was transparent. Because nobody in the US voted by secret ballot, politicians could openly purchase votes. But in 1856, the Australian state of Tasmania pioneered secret ballots. The US decided to test "Australian ballots" during the election of Grover Cleveland. Many people who met President Cleveland doubtless assured him, "I voted for you." Like every politician since, he learned to take these affirmations with a smile and a grain of salt.

It turns out that transparency was a problem, not a solution. Secret ballots destroyed the market for votes. Politics became more democratic—meaning that election outcomes reflected voter sentiment, not market power. Today it is unimaginable to ask citizens to elect leaders in open meetings (although the tradition persists in many state caucuses, including the crucial quadrennial party Presidential caucuses in Iowa).

Secret ballots made it difficult for politicians to buy voters but did nothing to prevent interest groups from buying politicians. Displeased at the appearance and occasionally solid evidence of corruption, campaign finance reformers have demanded transparency, even though the public interest may be better served by treating contributions like votes and keeping them secret.

Two legal scholars at Yale outlined how this might work. A candidate would receive funds from a blind trust managed by the federal or state government, depending on the election. The trust ensures that a campaign donation can no more be traced to the individual behind it than a vote can. Under their scheme, each citizen would receive a campaign voucher, which they could donate to causes or candidates.[210] (After the US Supreme Court decision in *Citizens United*, it is probably necessary to enable PACs to contribute as well.) The blind trust would sterilize and anonymize all contributions. Candidates would be no more certain about who donated how much money than they would know with certainty who voted for them. Now in addition to hearing, "I voted for you", every politician would hear, "I donated to your campaign." Donors and non-donors alike would receive the same warm but skeptical smile.

This provision would powerfully change a donor's expected return on investment. Investing in hope of a specific favor or increased access would be difficult because a politician can only repay a favor that she can verify. Because candidates could not verify an individual donor's generosity, donors would invest in leaders who share his or her general political orientation. Having diminished the market for votes with secret ballots, America would degrade the market for politicians with anonymized donations. (As with secret ballots, this is a directionally useful reform, not a foolproof one.) Public employees could not create a *quid pro quo* with politicians they help elect.

The second approach is to legislate restrictions on the partisan political activities of public employees and their unions. American state and federal governments have tried this with mixed success. During the New Deal, local politicians expected workers to show their appreciation for receiving federally financed WPA jobs by making regular "campaign contributions." To prevent this, Congress passed the Hatch Act. It restricts the partisan activities of federal employees, employees of the District of Columbia government, and employees of state and local governments funded by federal money. Affected workers may not run for partisan public office. They can't campaign for or against a candidate or slate of candidates in partisan elections. They may not make campaign speeches, raise money, distribute partisan campaign material, organize partisan rallies or meetings, lead political clubs or parties, circulate petitions, register voters for one party only, or wear political buttons at work.

Hatch Act limits apply to unions as well, and the Supreme Court has repeatedly upheld these restrictions.[211] Thanks to the Hatch Act, soldiers are barred from wearing red Donald Trump MAGA hats. FBI vehicles never sported bumper stickers for Bush or Obama. TSA screeners may pat travelers down, but not request that they sign petitions to give them a raise. The Hatch Act is strict: violations end careers. Most states have enacted "Little Hatch Act" legislation concerning the partisan conduct of state, city, or county employees. According to one legal analysis, four states are more restrictive than the federal Hatch Act and thirty-one are less restrictive.[212]

Hatch Act–style reforms try to reconcile two ideas that will always conflict. On the one hand, citizens prefer and expect a nonpartisan civil service. On the other, civil servants are citizens with rights, not just public servants with duties. Some limits on financial contributions to officials who oversee income bargaining are desirable, which is why campaign finance reform may serve as a less comprehensive but also less invasive method of improving the nonpartisanship of public employees. These reforms wouldn't rule out Hatch Act–style restrictions in the future.

Do Public Employee Unions Increase Government Costs?

Economist Barry Bluestone is the son of UAW leader Irving Bluestone. As a college kid, Barry pressed his father's best friend, UAW President Walter Reuther, to publicly oppose the Vietnam War. As a pro-labor economist, Bluestone has warned that if public sector wage growth consistently exceeds the growth of private sector wages, a political backlash becomes likely. He demonstrated that between 2000 and 2008 the cost of state and local public services increased by 41 percent nationally, compared with 27 percent for comparable private services. He questioned whether these increases were advisable or sustainable.[213]

Similarly, Harvard's Richard Freeman, who co-authored *What Do Unions Do?*, has become organized labor's most steadfast Ivy League ally. Freeman has warned that public employee unions not only raise the price of labor but often add more of it to state and local government. He cautioned that "public sector unions can be viewed as using their political power to raise demand for public services, as well as using their bargaining power to fight for higher wages."[214]

Former Clinton Assistant Secretary of Labor for Policy Jack Donahue has warned of unions contributing to a "talent death spiral." Likewise, many progressive mayors and governors now worry about the economic impact of public unions as growing federal entitlements that consume discretionary tax dollars. These are warnings not from free-market conservatives, but from scholars who have devoted their professional lives to understanding how traditional New Deal unions can be more successful in the future.

Academic research finds that the impact of unions on public sector pay is mixed and often varies by occupation.[215] However, abundant evidence indicates that unions have helped compress public sector incomes.[216] Janitors and clerks earn more working for the government than they would in the private sector. Attorneys, physicians, economists, and senior managers usually earn less.[217] By compressing pay across job categories, public sector unions confirm the tendency of collective bargaining to compress income.

Public sector benefits are nearly always more generous than those in the private sector. Health and retirement benefit costs substantially increase the premium that government pays for unskilled workers and help to reduce the compensation disparity between highly paid workers and private sector pay.[218]

Defined benefit pension plans represent the most substantial difference. These are the old-fashioned pension plans that provide retirees a lifetime annuity based on their highest income earned. The private sector all but eliminated defined benefit plans in the 1980s and 90s, but they have survived in the public sector. Many are severely underfunded and, in some states and cities, they represent substantial public liabilities. The Pew Foundation has calculated that unfunded state pension and health care obligations exceed 1.4 trillion dollars.[219] Even fast-growing, prosperous cities like Dallas face bankruptcy due to unfunded public employee pension obligations.[220]

It is common for pundits to blame unions for these pension costs, but state legislatures control the structure, scope, and funding of public employee pensions. Unions defend these plans and may bargain to have certain workers included, but the crucial work of defining benefits, authorizing investment assumptions, and funding pension obligations is the work of state legislatures. Legislators often participate in these plans and in any case, don't account to labor unions for their investment assumptions or funding decisions.

State legislators face powerful pressure to minimize current pension funding obligations by making optimistic assumptions about future investment returns. For these reasons, public employee pension benefits differ little between states with high levels of unionization and those with low levels.[221] Union members benefit from these plans and unions defend them, but legislators, not unions, determine how generous state pensions are and how well to fund them.

Public sector unions bargain not only pay and benefits—they regularly seek to increase staffing. Teachers bargain to limit class size, classroom hours, and transfers to other schools. Police insist on a minimum number of officers at large construction sites. Bus drivers fight transportation reforms that reduce the number of routes. Nurses argue that "every patient needs a nurse" to increase staffing, often in the name of better patient care. Some of these efforts succeed. Presumably, some should.

When unions bargain staffing increases, however, they often confront public sector managers who can't say no. Bargaining over staffing, however, is discretionary in every state. Government managers need to discuss staffing with unions only if they wish to do so. Unions can propose anything. They may and sometimes do suggest new public services. They can and often do demand lower management salaries. They are free to suggest that the state paint its bathroom walls in union colors. Managers can negotiate these things if they wish. They are much wiser to say, "If you have thoughts on those topics, drop me an email. They are outside the scope of our agreement." It is disingenuous to blame unions for bargaining generous staffing provisions when managers are entitled by law to decline to discuss the matter.

Union protection can impose a cost on federal, state, and municipal governments that is large but hard to measure: they discourage talented people from joining or remaining in public service. Public-policy scholar Jack Donahue has researched public sector talent. His book *The Warping of Government Work* documents the influence of lifetime employment in the public sector.[222] He shows convincingly that by restricting the ability of managers to remove misfits and poor performers, public-employee unions reduce government efficiency and responsiveness. Over time, government work repels the talented and performance-oriented who find more attractive prospects in the private sector.

Vibrant workplaces regularly lose high-quality people to organizations that offer them better jobs. They also transition their lowest-performing workers out of the organization. For this reason, persistent low turnover rates are often a sign not of a committed workforce, but of a stagnant one.

Private sector workers quit three times more often than public sector workers. The Bureau of Labor Statistics reports that during the first half of 2016, between 2.2 percent and 2.3 percent of all private sector workers voluntarily quit their job each month. These are employee-initiated, voluntary separations and exclude retirements, which the BLS reports separately. It is a reasonable indicator of the share of people finding a better job (although some people quit for medical reasons, to care for a parent, raise a child, or to relocate). Public sector quit rates were between 0.7 percent and 0.8 percent each month—one-third of those in the private sector.[223] State, city, and county employees were 50 percent more likely to quit their jobs than federal employees, who are less likely to quit than workers in any other sector.

This is a substantial difference. In some cases, low turnover is the unavoidable result of government monopsony. Firefighters rarely leave government employment because nobody else hires firefighters. However, low turnover also reflects the higher total compensation of many government jobs. Pensions that take ten years to vest and grow in value after that hold people in place. It may indicate an aversion by government workers to risk changing jobs and potentially a reluctance of private employers to hire government workers if they see them as slow or excessively cautious.

Do Public Employee Unions Reduce Professionalism?

The third and most serious charge against public sector unions is that by protecting their least competent and committed members, they degrade service quality and inhibit critical reforms. To understand the damage this causes, one need look no further than to American police or teachers' unions. Police unions were once "benevolent associations" and most still go by that name. They were charities and standard bearers of professionals who proudly served their communities. Today's police are more professional than ever, but police unions now protect the most dishonest and corrupt officers in their ranks.

The Washington Post investigated thirty-seven of the nation's largest municipal and county police forces. Together, these departments had fired 1,881 officers in the previous decade but union contracts enabled nearly a quarter of the terminated officers to win back their jobs. The *Post* report details a San Antonio police officer filmed on a dash cam challenging a handcuffed man to a fight for the chance to be released. They document a Washington, D.C., officer convicted of sexually abusing a young woman in his patrol car. A Boston officer openly lied while drunk and removed a suspected gunman from the scene of a nightclub killing.[224] Eight officers were fired and reinstated more than once. At least thirty-three of the reinstated officers had been charged with crimes.

Campaign Zero documented the protections afforded police by labor agreements or state "police bill of rights" laws. They reviewed police union contracts in eighty-one of America's one hundred largest cities and in all fourteen states with police bill of rights laws. They found that time limits inhibit police accountability following a shooting. Four states and twenty-five cities disqualify misconduct complaints submitted too many days after a shooting occurs. Others dismiss investigations that take too long to complete.[225] Fifty cities and thirteen states limit the length of time that investigators can interrogate an officer suspected of wrongdoing. They restrict who can conduct an interrogation. Contracts restrict the types of questions that interrogators may ask officers and even the time of day when an interrogation can occur.[226]

Forty-one cities and nine states give an officer under investigation access to information that a civilian suspect in their custody would never receive. Sixteen cities allow an officer to review all evidence against him or her before being interrogated. These restrictions reinforce each other and damage independent fact-finding. They allow officers to review ballistics reports, to confer with colleagues to get their stories straight and prevent the separate, intense, and immediate interrogation that is a staple of any officer's daily investigative work.

Other union restrictions help accused officers as well. Sixty-four cities and seven states limit disciplinary consequences for officers, for example, by preventing an officer's past misconduct from being considered in future cases. Others limit the capacity of civilian oversight structures or the media to hold police accountable.

Forty cities and three states require cities to pay costs related to police misconduct. These costs include paying officers while under investigation, paying legal fees, and/or paying the cost of settlements. Finally, forty-three cities and three states erase records of misconduct, sometimes after two years or fewer.[227] The group concluded that police union contracts in seventy-two of the eighty-one cities they reviewed, and thirteen of the fourteen statewide police bill of rights, impose at least one substantial barrier to police accountability.

Perverse incentives abound. In Oakland, California, police convicted by internal procedures are routinely given back their gun, badge, and lost pay because they can appeal any decision to secret arbitration. These proceedings never disclose the name of the presiding judge or prosecutor, nor do they produce a public transcript. As a result, an officer found to have shot his victim in the back multiple times and a group of officers convicted of having sex with underage girls on the job have all been returned to the city police force. When an outraged federal judge demanded a review, he noted that out of fifteen police arbitration cases, the city had prevailed against the union in only three.

Without transparency, city attorneys have little incentive to prosecute these cases aggressively. They rely heavily on police cooperation to convict criminals. They cannot afford to lose police support, so they face strong incentives to present weak appeals cases. For this reason, arbitrators are much more likely to return a violent officer to work than they are to reinstate a terminated private sector employee.

Union protective provisions today demean professional law enforcement officers whose work requires them to regularly confront troubled and hostile individuals. Washington, D.C., police chief Charles H. Ramsey knows the problem first-hand. As the chief in Philadelphia, he was required to rehire eighty fired officers—three of them twice. As he told *Post* investigators,

> "It's demoralizing, but not just to the chief—it's demoralizing to the rank and file who really don't want to have those kinds of people in their ranks. It causes a tremendous amount of anxiety in the public. Our credibility is shot whenever these things happen."[228]

In many cities, schoolteachers put police unions to shame. Teachers make up one-quarter of all US public employees. Parents and concerned voters watch their work closely because they understand that teachers influence the economic prospects of the children in their classrooms.[229] No profession in America is more closely scrutinized than schoolteachers—and none to so little effect.

"Rubber rooms" have become the enduring symbol of incompetent teachers protected by union agreements. The United Federation of Teachers in New York City insists that teachers who repeatedly failed in classrooms remain on the payroll, including teachers who were chronically abusive or drunk. Unable to fire these teachers, school districts in New York, Los Angeles, Chicago, and other major cities confined them for years to isolated rooms.[230] Even pro-labor Democrats sympathetic to teachers and willing to support attractive public employee benefits express little tolerance for foolishness of this sort.

With schoolteachers, there is little honest debate about the value of raising professional standards. High-quality teachers profoundly affect the future earnings of students. They represent a hugely profitable public investment.[231] Eric Hanushek and many other researchers confirm what every parent and every student already know: good teachers make an enormous difference. Hanushek documented the stakes:

> "A teacher one standard deviation above the mean effectiveness annually generates marginal gains of over $400,000 in present value of student future earnings with a class size of 20 and proportionately higher with larger class sizes. Alternatively, replacing the bottom 5-8 percent of teachers with average teachers could move the US near the top of international math and science rankings with a present value of $100 trillion."[232]

Hanushek's colleague Caroline Hoxby has summarized the broad research findings on teacher quality. She defines quality as value added: the ability and propensity of a teacher to raise student achievement. She notes that a teacher who is in the top 10 percent of the current distribution of value-added increases student achievement by several times what a teacher in the bottom 10 percent does. It is no accident that affluent families choose school districts able to hire the highest quality teachers.

Hanushek demonstrates that teacher quality translates directly to future student earnings. If all US teachers added as much value as the current top 10 percent of teachers do, the average American student would achieve at the level of students whose parents have incomes in the top 10 percent of the family income distribution, the equivalent to the level the average student in Singapore achieves.[233]

In an extensive and famously careful study, Raj Chetty and a team of five researchers took data from a Tennessee study of 11,571 students and concluded that more experienced kindergarten teachers increase the income of students two decades later.[234]

Defining and measuring a teacher's value-added is methodologically fraught. It can be especially challenging to control for powerful selection effects.[235] That does not render assessment impossible. Most research finds that some widely used indicators do not predict measurable teacher effectiveness. Teacher evaluation tests such as the Praxis, Master's degrees, especially in education, and credentials generally don't predict a teacher's value-added. There is some evidence that teachers improve their value added when exposed to outstanding teachers and when they are paid based on their value added.[236]

It isn't yet possible to predict a teacher's value-added without a year of teaching. After a year, however, experienced teachers can reliably determine a new teacher's ability to add value to students. A second year improves the accuracy of judgment slightly, but subsequent years do not.

Great teachers are both valuable and scarce. Researchers estimate that even with imperfect information, most schools would only invite one current teacher in four to teach a second year.[237] Those who can teach effectively, however, could command attractive salaries. (In 2015, the salary of the average American teacher was $56,383.[238] The average dentist earned $172,350 and contributed much less to the long-term wealth of his or her patients.)[239] A union or professional association that aspires to have teachers earn salaries commensurate with the value they add would not only welcome more stringent professional standards—they would demand it.

Tenure, meaning a grant of lifetime employment, makes this challenging. Reversing tenure for teachers, faculty, and other public employees would not only eliminate the expectation of lifetime employment, but also commit to replacing the lowest-performing 3-4 percent of teachers each year. In exchange for serious public responsibilities, a high level of pay and attractive benefits including pensions, the weakest performers in every occupation would leave public service with severance pay.

The deepest professional desire of talented people is to find and work with other talented people. As a result, public agencies that set steadily higher standards would soon discover that government work had become a badge of honor instead of a talent repellent. A forced attrition rate would transform most public services within five years. Within a decade, many of the original employees would marvel at the makeover. Many would quietly wonder whether they would make the grade in the new environment.

This is especially true for teachers, where the tradition of tenure has outlived what little purpose it may have once had. Those who wish to elevate teaching faculty to self-governing professionals able to command the status, respect, and salaries commensurate with the enormous value they can create must abandon tenure. Eliminating tenure and continually replacing the weakest teachers will allow the teaching profession to begin to attract top-quartile graduates of top-quartile colleges (many of whom will not survive the first year teaching evaluation). Steadily replacing weaker performers with stronger ones will increase the prestige of teaching dramatically. Along with soldiers in uniform, airlines might allow teachers to board first, to the hushed gratitude of other passengers. Former Chrysler CEO, the late Lee Iacocca, put it well, "In a completely rational society, the best of us would be teachers and the rest of us would have to settle for something less, because passing civilization along from one generation to the next ought to be the highest honor and the highest responsibility anyone could have."

In universities, tenure has created an embarrassing hierarchy of privilege. Undergraduate teaching has long been peripheral to the mission of top research universities, so many colleges outsource undergraduate education to adjuncts not eligible for tenure. As a result, fewer than 30 percent of college and university faculty today are eligible for tenure. Even full-time adjuncts make up fewer than 20 percent of all instructors. The majority are either graduate student Instructors or part-time adjuncts.[240] These academic day laborers may be inspiring and effective teachers, but with pay averaging $3,000 per course and no chance of job security, they quickly grow to resent the system of feudal privilege at the heart of modern research universities.[241]

Some argue that tenure protects a scholar's right to publish controversial or unorthodox research. It has never done this. University faculty gain access to prestigious publications, professional stature, and tenure itself by earning strong reviews from their peers. Peer review, with or without tenure, ensures conformity and rewards hyper-specialization. It penalizes the controversial or unorthodox. As long as academia relies on peer review, tenure can't protect academics from the adverse effects of controversial views nor from pressure to specialize and conform.

In 1988, universities in the UK decided to replace faculty tenure with a system of academic self-governance based on employment contracts that can be revoked due to redundancy, conduct, or performance.[242] What happened? Not much, except that it became possible to replace faculty who badly needed replacing.

Tenure persists because if a single university ended the practice, it would suffer competitively. Collective action problems of this sort are one of the problems that governments are meant to solve. The Internal Revenue Service could easily refuse tax-exempt status to nonprofit schools that accumulate multibillion-dollar endowments but refuse to grow admissions, set up campuses in underserved regions, or admit more talented students from low-income families.

Alternatively, the Department of Education can recognize that tenure contributes needlessly to costs that the government helps to finance and could refuse to authorize the release of federal student loan funds to any school with employment agreements longer than three years. Schools would be free to grant tenure and forgo public subsidies—but few would. Given the strong Democratic Party leanings of both teachers' unions, it will be surprising if the current, highly politicized US Department of Education does not contemplate an attack on tenure. If the federal government did the job, tenure at all levels would soon disappear. The experience of the UK suggests that few would notice or mourn its passing.

K-12 tenure is fading rapidly without government help. More than two dozen US states have either eliminated, restricted, or modified teacher tenure laws or are considering doing so. Florida, North Carolina, Kansas, and Idaho have eliminated K-12 tenure outright (although voters later reversed the Idaho initiative). South Dakota has eliminated tenure for new hires. Other states have added performance ratings to tenure decisions or returned teachers to probationary status if teacher performance is unsatisfactory. Some require that performance, instead of tenure or seniority, be the primary basis for any staff reductions. The courts have reviewed and curtailed tenure policies in many states, including California and New

York. To track the constant changes, the Education Commission of the States now maintains a database showing current developments in each state.[243]

Improving the performance of schools or other government operations is a complex undertaking, even without unions. It requires educational leaders who are willing to embrace school choice, as Arne Duncan in Chicago, Cami Anderson in Newark, and Michelle Rhee and Kaya Henderson in Washington, D.C. These leaders raise standards by focusing on a few key educational outcomes and insisting on the scrupulous measurement of results. They demand honest benchmarks and investment in strengthening teacher effectiveness. Without strong educational leadership, nothing unions do matters.

Nonetheless, public sector unions that advocate for a profession instead of focusing on defending their weakest practitioners can play a valuable role. By embracing a modified form of "at-will" employment, as the private sector reforms proposed elsewhere in the book would do, states would be able to renew employment agreements or pay severance unless termination is for cause. The amount of the severance would be bargained and would often vary depending on the age and years of service of the affected individual. The American Federation of Teachers has taken valuable steps in this direction, advocating for and achieving peer review agreements in Rochester, NY, Montgomery County, MD, and Newark, NJ. In Newark, the AFT agreed to performance bonuses.

Reversing tenure and creating an expectation of regular, performance-based attrition would require states to void contrary provisions in statutes or private contracts, including civil service law, police bill of rights protections, and labor agreements, which is politically and legally more achievable in some states than in others. As always, states that reform first and produce impressive results will be closely watched and quickly followed by others.

Will today's public employee unions embrace limits to their political contributions and the steady replacement of their weakest members?

As with political reform generally, public employee unions will evolve into professional associations only if they conclude that it benefits their members or if the cost of not evolving becomes too high. Without continued economic and political pressure, corrections officers will fight campaign finance reform, to say nothing of Hatch Act–like restrictions. Cops are not going to take lightly to employment at will, community oversight, and the loss of special "bill of rights" privileges. Public employee unions may feel like the fabled frog in the water that is slowly getting hotter. Fortunately, once the water is warm enough, the frog reliably jumps. Tales of amphibians quietly boiling to death are urban legends.[244]

Tragically, Congress designed labor unions for its day, not ours. The laws that resulted were unsuited to a competitive and dynamic private sector and too well-suited to the work of monopolistic government agencies.

How would modern income bargaining work? How would 21st-century unions overcome the weakness of unions created for a bygone industrial era? Counterintuitively, perhaps, the answer begins not with how workers organize, but how employers do.

PART THREE

Getting Even: A Modern Income Bargaining System

"At many stages in the advance of humanity, this conflict between the men who possess more than they have earned and the men who have earned more than they possess is the central condition of progress.... At every stage, and under all circumstances, the essence of the struggle is to equalize opportunity, destroy privilege, and give to the life and citizenship of every individual the highest possible value both to himself and to the commonwealth."

Theodore Roosevelt,
Speech outlining the New Nationalism
Osawatomie, Kansas
August 31, 1910

8. Bosses of the World, Unite!

Most people who advocate for income bargaining to address median wage stagnation are concerned with building stronger labor unions, not stronger employer associations. They are focused on the plight of workers like Adriana Alvarez, a McDonald's worker in Cicero, Illinois. Fast-food chains are no longer places for teenagers to pick up part-time work. The average age of a fast-food employee is 29 and, like Alvarez, a third have spent some time in college.

Indeed, Alvarez joined the Fight for $15, whose organizers have helped win wage increases for some 22 million workers in America by fighting for higher minimum wages. Alvarez still earns $11 per hour, however, not because she isn't in an organization to fight for her interests, but because McDonald's isn't.[245]

In the real world, worker and employer organizations are two sides of the same coin. This chapter asserts that not only do strong unions require strong employer associations, but that wage bargains that do not punish individual companies require them as well.

Chapter Nine argues that employer organizations are essential to solving several festering problems facing US labor markets: the rise of non-compete and non-solicitation agreements, the growth of restrictive occupational licensure, and the critical need for large-scale career and educational training. Chapter Ten considers how modern unions and proportional bargaining might work and how Americans might adopt something like German works councils. Chapter Eleven puts forward some of the rules, rights, and information needed to support proportional bargaining.

When McDonald's opened for business in Denmark, it expected to pay workers the way it pays Adriana Alvarez: the lowest wage that an adequate worker would accept. It did not expect to provide hourly employees with health care, a defined benefit pension, or five weeks of paid vacation. These provisions, however, were standard under the agreement between 3F, the leading Danish fast-food workers' union, and the fast-food employer association.[246] Together with robust public health care, housing, and transportation services, this income agreement gives fast-food workers in Denmark something approaching a middle-class life.

McDonald's resisted, leading to what *The New York Times* called "nearly a year of raucous, union-led protests". Eventually, McDonald's yielded to local customs.[247] The decision was easier because when it joined in the industry-wide pay agreement, the company suffered no competitive penalty—nor would it sustain a competitive advantage by paying less.

This was no free lunch. McDonald's may have been forced to charge more for burgers to pay for higher staffing costs. They may have hired fewer people on each shift. They either attracted more productive workers, raised prices, cut spending, or made less money. The decision to adhere to the industry agreement was not costless, although McDonald's appears to have managed the pain. Denmark has 5.7 million people, about the same size as greater Atlanta or Detroit. But McDonald's operates about 40 percent more restaurants in Denmark than in these comparably sized cities.[248]

McDonald's may have experienced efficiency wage effects. The company reports lower staff turnover in Denmark than the US, where employees quit after an average of only eight months. McDonald's breaks out its operating margins and pretax profits for Denmark, which appear comparable to those it reports in the US. Evidently, McDonald's has found ways to compete other than by paying their employees as little as the market will allow.[249]

Unlike in America, McDonald's encountered not only organized workers but also organized employers able to bargain for an entire industry. It seems fair to presume that employers quietly put as much pressure on McDonald's to embrace the industry agreement as labor and regulatory organizations did.

Labor market policies designed to compress income and reduce wage polarization need to make it attractive for employers to compete like McDonald's in Denmark: with innovative services and products, better distribution or branding, by being faster, more efficient, or better informed—not by lowering wages or benefits for their least powerful employees. Doing this requires that employers be able to construct industry platforms that standardize wages and create a much more vibrant market for skill. It involves a system of income bargaining which, absent

Danish traditions of social solidarity, provides employers with substantial economic incentives to not compete by reducing wages.

Fixed, Variable, and Social Costs

McDonald's succeeds in Denmark by distinguishing between fixed, variable, and social costs. Fixed costs represent medium-term contractual obligations for building or equipment leases, loans, or service agreements. Every company worries about these costs before committing to them. Once agreed to, however, "fixed" costs are sunk (although no cost is truly "fixed", contractual commitments and market friction mean that some costs are much more expensive to reduce than others).

Managers worry most about variable costs, including labor costs. They are large, more controllable in the short term, and directly affect margins and pricing. Variable costs matter, even to companies forced to compete based on the commitment, expertise, speed, and agility of their employees.

There is a third type of cost that most operating managers ignore, although business leaders and lobbyists do not. These are social costs, which include taxes, Social Security payments, and the cost of regulatory compliance. Every American employer has other uses for the cash they pay into Social Security or payroll taxes. Because all competitors pay equally, however, most managers treat social costs as a "cost of doing business". They focus on controlling variable costs. Employers are never indifferent to costs of any sort, but most think differently about costs like Social Security that the law requires all employers to pay.

McDonald's discovered that industry wage agreements turn once variable labor costs into social costs. Thanks to their contracts with 3F, the fast-food workers' union, McDonald's must compete with faster or better food, cleaner facilities, and more helpful staff. Paying workers less money is not an option.

Private agreements that standardize wages in each region and reduce them as a factor in competition are essential to grow the incomes of low-paid workers and rebuild their confidence in America's economic and political systems. At present, American labor market organizations are designed to amplify wage competition. Neither markets nor enterprise unions can turn variable wages into a social cost. Only agreements that include all competitors in a sector can remove wages as a significant competitive factor.[250]

Interestingly, when a single industry dominates a region and a single union dominates an industry, the result is something like industry bargaining that socializes labor costs. Wendy Almada learned the difference when her Arizona employer fired her after she became pregnant. She moved to Las Vegas and took a job cleaning rooms for a large hotel. She discovered that the Culinary Workers Union represents employees at every major hotel in Las Vegas. She joined 57,000 cooks, bartenders, waitresses, porters, housekeepers, and bellhops in Local 226, where she now earns $17.65 an hour plus health and pharmacy insurance, a pension, and freedom from the sort of arbitrary management decisions that caused her to lose her previous job. It is a certainty that her employer would prefer to pay her the going nonunion rate, about $10 an hour—but it is also clear that so long as every large hotel in town plays by the same rules, they are not substantially disadvantaged.[251]

What about companies with overseas competitors that enjoy lower labor costs? McDonald's competes locally, as do Las Vegas hotels. Would exporters or importers be penalized by wage agreements bargained in the US? The answer is that pay in tradable goods industries are not America's main problem. It is only a slight exaggeration to claim that the entire challenge of polarized US incomes is a problem of the non-tradable sector. Brutal overseas competition has already forced tradable goods companies to become more productive than non-tradable ones—and for the most part, the pay in these sectors is already well above the median.

Economist Michael Spence has documented the enormous value added by companies in tradable sectors. He describes how, under the pressure of global competition, tradable goods companies have become more productive. They use technology to shift low- and mid-skilled work to other countries.[252] The employees who remain are higher-skilled, well-paid workers whose salaries have grown rapidly. These companies look nothing like those in lower productivity, non-tradable sectors like health care, retail, construction, hospitality, education, government services, transportation, or distribution.

As a result, most export companies are much less sensitive to labor costs. They have shifted production overseas and automated much of the work that remains. A ton of US-produced steel, for example, now contains many more dollars of information than dollars of labor. Like most exporters, steel companies worry more about the quality of their talent than the cost of labor per se.

McDonald's discovered that unions that bargain for an entire sector are much less punitive than those that bargain for a single enterprise. That a large, dominant industrial union would be much easier to accommodate than a small enterprise union is a shocking discovery to most American managers. Unions increase employment costs (that is, after all, their purpose). Unless they improve productivity by attracting more skilled or committed people, this will lead to reduced staffing, increased prices, or greater automation. Less staffing can mean harder work or fewer services. But like Social Security payments, higher wages need not impose an absolute competitive penalty, so long as the same agreement covers all competitors.

The experience of income bargaining everywhere suggests that it strengthens middle-class incomes. By increasing the wages of lower-paid workers, bargaining moderates the growth of above-median incomes. It guards against an exploding college wage premium, in part by defining more skill categories that pay well without college degrees. Industry-based income bargaining helps to preserve a middle class by requiring winners to live up to their social obligation to share the gains with those who are otherwise punished by trade and technology. A requirement, or at least a strong incentive, for employers to bargain income for below-median earners ensures that the winners of technology and global competition do not cheerfully run off with the surplus.

Wage Subsidies for Employers Who Bargain Income

American law prohibits employers from collaborating to set wages, even as the law permits unions to form cartels. This is backward. If companies are to agree on a wage schedule that pays above-market wages to their least-skilled employees, a monopoly industry association matters far more than monopoly labor unions. To avoid competitive penalties caused by different income agreements, businesses need monopoly industry associations that can bargain wages, benefits, procedures, and skill standards across their entire sector.

Any scheme that enables employers to collaborate in wage-setting faces at least three risks. The first is that employers are naturally inclined to conspire to drive wages lower. The second risk is the one faced by any cartel—that individual employers will defect from the group and reduce wages on their own. Finally, if the first two problems are somehow solved, organizing employers is complex. A "region" or even an "industry" may be too ill-defined to form the basis of a coherent organization.

Adam Smith understood the first problem exceptionally well. The Scottish father of modern economics warned that:

> "We rarely hear... of the combinations of masters, though frequently of those of workmen. But whoever imagines, upon this account, that masters rarely combine, is as ignorant of the world as of the subject. Masters are always and everywhere in a sort of tacit, but constant and uniform combination, not to raise the wages of labour above their actual rate…
>
> "We seldom, indeed, hear of this combination, because it is the usual, and one may say, the natural state of things, which nobody ever hears of."[253]

Adam Smith was doubtless right in 1776 and is undoubtedly right today. In the modern day, leading corporations including Apple, Pixar, Google, and the Detroit Medical Center have paid multimillion-dollar settlements for conspiring to restrict pay. *De facto* employer collusion remains the rule, not the exception. The ban on direct employer wage and salary collusion has long fueled a large market for consultants, websites, and innocent-looking salary surveys that help employers efficiently collude to set pay within an industry and region. Machine learning based on diffuse large data sets makes this problem difficult to regulate. If wage or salary decisions result from black-box algorithms that neither reveal nor explain their reasoning, then companies cannot always tell if they are conspiring, engaged in predatory pricing of products or wages, redlining, or discriminating.

Income bargaining solves a vexing problem precisely because Adam Smith is right about the chronic tendency for employers to collude. Far better that employers conspire in the presence of worker organizations designed to check their natural impulse to reduce wages. Redesigned unions will be as committed to seeing wages rise as employers are to controlling or reducing them. Better that collusion is open and collaborative—or open and adverse—than it takes place in secret with no protection for those who will otherwise find themselves victims of "the usual, and one may say, the natural state of things, which nobody ever hears of."

An industry association is a social enterprise devoted to a sector. As many do today, they would serve employers in the same industry, often with regional subsidiaries. An association would provide business services as well as a forum for income bargaining. The next chapter explores how industry associations can improve the functioning of labor markets by sharpening skill standards and defining vocational education and certification programs to promote more accurate job matching and better hiring. They can promote occupational certification over licensure, and, thanks to pressure from labor organizations, they can orchestrate the end of non-compete agreements.

Industry associations are natural vehicles for secondments. A British invention rarely used in the US, secondments are temporary assignments to external organizations. Rather than hire a full-time employee, an industry association might invite a local professor, manager, or labor leader to spend a year working with the association on a particular project. These individuals may bring expertise and a professional network that improves the quality and reach of the organization. After a year, secondees return to their former employer stronger, thanks to newly sharpened skills and relationships.

Over time, many of the best industry associations would function as platforms. The value of a platform comes from increasing the number of connections in a network, not from building or controlling assets. Networks depend on the trust they build with both buyers and sellers. The focus of an industry association would be on the industry, building services and agreements to promote skill matching, smarter hiring, consistent regulation, smarter workplace audits, benefits administration, best practice dissemination, reputation management systems, and much else. Associations would be run not by managers experienced at operating efficient supply chains but by social entrepreneurs comfortable maximizing the value of networks—a skill that requires very different instincts.

America has no corporate tradition of "social solidarity," so most companies will instinctively find collaboration uninteresting. Some companies will hope to sustain a lower pay structure than their industry peers. Others will prefer to avoid the bother or risk of coordinating with competitors. Nor is it practical to legally compel companies to bargain, as current labor law demonstrates. Ordering parties to "bargain in good faith" is like ordering an indifferent couple to date in good faith. Instead of mandates, companies need a powerful economic incentive to engage in income bargaining.

One approach would be to rely on a wage subsidy delivered to employers as a tax credit for each full-time equivalent worker they employed who earned below the regional median. Suppose the regional median income is $45,000 and a company employs the equivalent of one hundred full-time workers who earn this amount or less. If Congress set the bargained wage subsidy at $2.00 per hour (or $4,160 per full-time worker), a participating company would receive a tax credit of $416,000 if they signed the agreement negotiated between their industry association and participating labor organizations. How the tax credit would translate into wages would be subject to bargaining.

The cost of the program would depend on the size of the bargaining subsidy and on the share of employers that elect to sign the income agreement negotiated by their industry association. If employers representing 70 percent of all below-median workers were to participate (a level that would see twice the share of workers represented by labor organizations as occurred at the height of New Deal–style collective bargaining), the program would cost about $233 billion. Tax receipts and a reduction in the cost of the Earned Income Tax Credit (EITC) would reduce this cost by perhaps $60 billion, as workers paid taxes on the income and would not be eligible to claim the EITC to avoid a double subsidy.[254] (The EITC is America's current approach to subsidizing low-income wages and is much loved by both political parties. By paying the tax credit to employers, however, eligible workers would see larger paychecks instead of waiting until tax time to receive larger refunds.) At $172 billion, a bargaining subsidy of this magnitude would constitute about five percent of the federal budget.

Businesses like hospitality or custodial services with a higher share of workers earning low wages would receive larger subsidies, giving them a greater incentive to participate. It would disproportionately promote job creation in regions hurt by shocks from global trade with China. Companies would receive tax credits only on their workers earning below-median pay, so Facebook or Google, where pay averages more than $100,000 per year, would derive significantly less benefit.

All subsidies create moral hazards. If employers can earn money on below-median workers, they should rationally cut below-median pay even further to shift payroll costs to taxpayers. Bargaining and minimum wage statutes would inhibit but not completely prevent this. Therefore, to qualify for the tax credit, a company would need to demonstrate that its corporate Gini coefficient had not increased. The Gini is a simple measure of income dispersion that is the most widely used measure of income inequality. To allow for bargaining and management flexibility and to prevent companies from either reducing pay to scam the wage subsidy or diverting it to highly paid workers, a company would not receive a subsidy unless it had compressed its internal distribution of income.

So long as moral hazards are contained, wage subsidies have widely recognized advantages. They reinforce the value of work. A wage subsidy might grow labor participation if companies could induce workers to come to work for perhaps $15 per hour even if the job is worth only $12 to an employer. They are a very efficient way for those who emerge better off from the global flow of goods and money to compensate those who end up worse off. Wage subsidies are a far more effective use of tax credits than funding federal retraining programs. They are easier to allocate than Trade Adjustment Assistance, which needs to cover the butcher and the baker when the candlestick maker's job moves to China. Even conservatives opposed to subsidies in principle are more likely to support a payment that subsidizes work, not unemployment.

A wage subsidy has practical benefits as well. By subsidizing the lowest wages and enlarging the pool of income that can be bargained, a tax credit makes initial income agreements much easier to settle. A tax credit helps newly reformed unions secure initial agreements, when employers may be better organized than employees. For these reasons and others, wage subsidies are staples among both liberal and conservative policy geeks. The liberal Urban Institute proposed one in 1974. Nobel economist Edmund Phelps proposed one in 1997. In 2017, Senator Marco Rubio introduced a law to subsidize wages in hurricane-ravaged Puerto Rico.[255]

Tying a wage subsidy to income bargaining provides a powerful incentive for employers to bargain income, especially in low-wage sectors. It would help preserve a strong middle-class by raising lower incomes faster than higher ones. Substantially reducing corporate taxes using tax credits to subsidize wages for companies that bargain income is politically appealing as well. It marries an idea embraced by conservatives with one favored by progressives—and both companies and workers benefit economically.

How would the US pay the cost of a wage subsidy? Ideally, by a mix of taxes on carbon, extraordinary wealth, and consumption. Conservative economist John Cochrane has proposed a creative and straightforward approach: use anonymized electronic value-added tax (VAT) payments at the point of purchase to adjust a VAT according to income.[256]

Encouraging Employers to Organize

In many sectors, industry boundaries are straightforward. Employers know who they compete with for talent. These employers would join together in industry associations built around a small number of principles. Employer associations would be mutually exclusive—one per industry. To prevent employer associations from competing to bid wages lower, they need to be chartered, regulated monopolies. Employers would define industry boundaries and determine their preference for regional associations, subject to regulatory oversight. Employers would be free to form new associations or to merge or divide associations as competitive conditions evolve and new industries emerge. Regulators would approve splits and mergers so long as they do not overlap and are not designed solely to frustrate or subvert bargaining.

As a practical matter, many of the 200,000 or so companies in the US with more than one hundred employees would ask an existing industry association to obtain a federal charter to bargain income. To the extent that companies found themselves aggregated in ways that worked poorly, they would separate or merge associations. For example, airlines would surely elect to bargain income and set skill standards separately from the rest of the travel industry. Would regional airlines define themselves clearly enough to separate from national and global carriers? Acute care hospital employers would likely wish to separate from the rest of health care and from skilled nursing facilities. Research hospitals might form organizations that are separate from acute care hospitals.

Employers would decide whether to emphasize national or regional organizations. Some, like airlines, might prefer to bargain a national agreement with regional wage schedules that adjust for differences in living costs. Grocery store chains or construction firms that compete based on regional density more than national reach may prefer to organize stronger regional associations. Compelling research contrasting Germany, where workers in the lower-productivity east earn less than those in the west, with Italy, which requires national wage standards even in the lower-productivity south, confirm the importance of regional wage-setting.[257]

Very large employers with vastly different kinds of businesses might participate in more than one association. Much of Amazon looks like any other software development business. They hire a large number of engineers, data analysts, user interface experts, marketers, and product managers. But with more than 575,000 employees worldwide, Amazon operates a fast-growing grocery business and more than two hundred fulfillment centers in the US.[258] Amazon might decide to join three (hypothetical) associations, starting with the Software Development Association with Facebook, Google, and Apple. It might join the Grocery Group with Safeway, Kroger, and Publix. It could also join the Logistics and Fulfillment League with UPS, DHL, and FedEx. Employers would enjoy flexibility in defining the boundaries of their industry and geography so long as every company (or section of business in the case of large or complex companies) is covered under one and only one agreement. That's where regulators come in.

For this bargaining system to work, employers need the ability to redefine and reshape their associations. Industries evolve continually, and the lines between them are not always crisp. The governing principle is that employers who compete for the same customers and employees belong in the same association. In most industries, this grouping is logical and obvious.

The purpose of chartering associations is to allow flexible monopsony (sole buyer) organizations that avoid overlapping jurisdictions or gaps in coverage across industries. Federal regulators (potentially assisted by private workplace auditors, described later) would ensure that industry associations are mutually exclusive. They would also make sure that a majority of employers within an association ratify income agreements. Some might offer online services to enable employees to ratify or reject contracts through their labor organizations, much as some unions do today.

This model of employer organization is not the state-led model that is widespread in Europe. Many researchers suspect that the inability of European industry associations to evolve with changing circumstances has reduced their utility. The problem is especially acute in industries with complex supply chains that force small, specialized suppliers to bargain alongside their large customers, whose needs and motives are entirely different.[259] Some European countries have reintroduced enterprise bargaining—sometimes with the proviso that enterprise-based labor agreements must provide at least the same level of wages and benefits as agreements for the related industry do but can include provisions tailored to specific, large enterprises.

Income bargaining backed by wage subsidies gives employers more choices with respect to employment costs. Should wages reflect an individual's contribution or should they reflect a group's output? Should health care benefits be handled at the company level or via the industry association? (Put another way, can associations help turn health care insurance into a social cost?) When can companies earn higher returns on their training investments by providing internal training and when are they better off funding training through the industry association and socializing the cost of losing a trained employee to a competitor?

Industry associations are a proven source of research, political advocacy, and labor market planning. It would be useful for industries to develop a view of how skill and staffing needs are likely to evolve by region. They should have a view of foreseeable economic growth and technology adoption in their sector to educators make smarter investments in vocational training. They could then create vocational or professional training programs based on demonstrated market need rather than faculty interest. In some industries, these associations could build robust talent pipelines to address chronic skill shortages. Above all, revitalized employer associations could create wage and skill standards that deepen the market for talent and skill.

9. Organizing Employers to Strengthen Labor Markets

The central job of employer associations would be to bargain income with the revitalized labor organizations described in the next chapter. But in many cases, their most valuable work would be to strengthen both regional and national labor markets. Where employers can improve their selection of job candidates and hire more accurately, they improve productivity. When workers have more options, changing jobs is easier and pay typically improves. Strong labor markets help everyone.

A strong labor market requires skill standards, occupational pathways, and work-based career and technical education (CTE). It also requires an end to America's chaotic and wasteful approach to occupational licensing.

Organized Employers Can Better Support Fluid Labor Markets

As Adam Smith warned, individual employers who seek to restrict worker opportunity can badly distort labor markets. Smith would immediately recognize today's routine use of no-poach, non-compete, and non-solicitation agreements for what they are—instruments to limit worker bargaining power. He would likewise recognize the weed-like growth of occupational licensure as an understandable but dysfunctional response by workers seeking to recover bargaining power by restricting access to their occupations.

The first line of defense against these practices is employee and professional organizations strong enough to check the power of organized, monopsonistic employers. The second is laws that support the creation of robust, fluid labor markets.

Non-compete and non-solicitation agreements are designed to restrict employment opportunities. A non-compete agreement prohibits an employee from taking a job at a competing firm. Non-solicitation agreements prohibit an employee enticing their former co-workers to leave by offering them new jobs. No-poach agreements are illegal agreements between employers not to compete for each other's workers. Nonetheless, Alan

Krueger and Eric Posner found that "over half of major franchises forbid their franchisees from competing for one another's workers, up from 36 percent in 1996".[260]

The use of non-compete and non-solicitation agreements has snowballed in recent years. A recent survey of 11,505 employees concluded that one in every five workers are subject to non-compete agreements—about 30 million employees nationwide. Those affected by non-compete and non-solicitation agreements are now litigating these contracts at record rates.[261]

Employers justify non-compete and non-solicitation agreements by asserting that they allow them to share trade secrets with employees or to invest in training. Neither argument holds up. AnnaLee Saxenian documented the different rates of innovation between Route 128 in Massachusetts and Silicon Valley. She concluded that California (which declared non-compete agreements void under state law) benefits enormously from the ability of talented people to move between competing companies and to start new ones.[262]

Trade secrets are a weak rationale for non-compete and non-solicitation agreements. Most companies never recognize, much less codify, their proprietary business insights. When they do, they discover that the half-life of product and process secrets is shrinking and that few "trade secrets" create an enduring competitive advantage. Worse, employers require as many workers without access to so-called trade secrets to sign a non-compete agreement as those whom they claim have such access. Fourteen percent of workers earning less than $40,000 are required to sign non-competes even though they are only half as likely to possess trade secrets as their higher-earning colleagues.

Most companies that use non-compete agreements rely on them as a form of social control or to improve their negotiating leverage with workers. An employer who can contractually bar a worker from changing jobs obviously acquires a great deal of bargaining power. Indeed, the mere threat of litigation from a non-compete appears to reduce wages. A 2016 report by the US Treasury Department notes, for example, that California employers are more likely to require an employee to sign a non-compete, even though California courts ignore them. Fifteen percent of workers without a four-year college degree (including all US-based

Amazon warehouse workers) are subject to non-compete agreements.[263] The Treasury report found that workers earn more over time in states that do not enforce non-compete agreements than in states that vigorously enforce them, suggesting that these agreements restrict wage growth more than they encourage training.

There is a strong case for banning non-compete and non-solicitation agreements entirely. A non-compete agreement asserts that an employer owns a worker's most valuable assets—his or her professional skills, reputation, and relationships.[264] When litigated to the letter, an employer can persuade a court to bar a worker from taking a new job or force a new employer to fire him or her, even if the former employer had laid off or dismissed the affected worker. Worse, employers impose 37 percent of these agreements *after* an employee starts a new job, meaning that the affected worker could not factor in these restrictions into his or her decision to accept the job offer.[265]

Organized employers are, perhaps paradoxically, less likely to favor non-compete agreements for the simple reason that the universal use of these agreements would severely restrict their access to critical talent. They are likely to find that a deal to ban the use of these agreements more acceptable than the risk that their use become even more widespread.

Likewise, workers able to bargain skill and income standards directly with employers would have less need to resort to state occupational licensing boards. Today, these boards license occupations ranging from cosmetologists and dentists to electricians and dog walkers. They are now the country's most potent labor market institutions and directly undermine the creation of robust, fluid labor markets.

Certify More. License Less.

Without strong labor organizations, workers find other ways to use skill standards to increase their pay. Increasingly, they have turned to state occupational licensure. They form licensing boards that make it illegal to practice their chosen occupation without a license that the board issues. These groups almost always seek to raise pay by limiting entry to their chosen occupation.

Without robust employer and labor organizations to set skill standards, licensing boards have become the untamed weeds of the US labor market. More than 30 percent of American workers find their jobs controlled by one of America's 1,790 occupational licensing boards. These boards block access to hundreds of occupations by millions of workers. They raise prices and create an artificial scarcity that costs consumers an estimated $116 billion annually.[266] In almost every case, they are controlled not by government administrators committed to bureaucratic impartiality, but by the people they license.

Excessive licensure has real consequences. Sonia Ufot from Brooklyn learned to braid hair in the shop of a family friend at age 15 in Warri, Nigeria, where she was born. Demand for skilled hair braiding is high, so Ufot can work 12- to 15-hour days and charge from $100 to $250 for braiding, depending on intricacy. New York has distinguished braiding from cosmetology, but in some states, even those with prior knowledge of braiding must pay tens of thousands of dollars to attend 2,000 hours cosmetology training that has little to do with styling black women's hair. Many cosmetology schools don't even offer braiding instruction.[267]

A paper on licensure by Northwestern's Beth Redbird begins:

> Over the past few decades, occupational closure, and particularly licensure, quietly became the norm for a broad swath of US occupations. Where only a small set of "traditional" professions once determined entry through regulation, today the practice governs a much wider range of occupations, from doctors to engineers, carpet layers to massage therapists, agricultural inspectors to wilderness guides, and fortune tellers to legal document assistants. The most substantial growth has been in blue-collar occupations, and particularly the production and transportation sector, which more than doubled its licensed workforce over the past 30 years.[268]

In the 1950s, only five percent of all US occupations required a license. Redbird calculates that nearly one-third of all jobs require one today. The increase is due not to job growth in licensed professions but to the rise in the number of occupations that demand licenses.[269] Jobs that now require a license in some states include hairdressers, auctioneers, makeup artists, tree trimmers, upholsterers, packagers, scrap metal recyclers and, in New York City, dog walkers.[270]

Licensing blocks access to certain occupations and prevents adjacent occupations from pursuing opportunities and income. Doctors frequently prevent nurses from performing routine medical procedures. For this reason, physicians have spent millions of dollars lobbying against nurse practitioners or physician assistants. Dentists in most states block hygienists from opening teeth-cleaning or whitening clinics. Insurance brokers in Utah try to ban free equivalents of their service. Funeral directors frequently seek a state-sanctioned monopoly on the right to sell caskets.[271] Researchers find that men suffer more than women from excessive licensure and that whites suffer more than blacks. In short, licenses are a surprisingly large but hidden tax on workers and consumers.[272]

Occupational licenses restrict worker mobility because states rarely honor each other's licenses. An Iowa manicurist license requires nine days of training but is not valid in Alabama, where the same license requires 163 days of training or practice. Inconsistent standards mean that workers cannot move across state lines to increase their income. A New York cosmetology license is not valid in Iowa, where obtaining one takes sixteen months. Most states do not license interior decorators, but those that do often require more education and training than emergency medical technicians. Occupational licenses place a special burden on military families that move frequently. In an era of reduced geographic mobility by low-income workers, these barriers are not helpful.[273]

The consumer benefit of licensing is also debatable. At a time when Yelp, Angie's List, and sector-specific rating systems enable consumers or companies to easily determine the public reputation of a plumber, painter, or manicurist, it is the rare consumer that cares about licensure in professions not directly related to public health or safety.

Finally, occupational licenses are frequently used to exclude workers who have been incarcerated, reducing opportunities in many semi-skilled fields.[274] Worse, licensing appears to be contagious. As it grows, it creates pressure on legislators to license even more occupations.[275]

The positive impact of licensure found by some researchers appears to be the result of training programs, not of licensure per se. Redbird suggests that the training required by licensing regimes can provide trainees valuable professional networks and occupational onramps. She notes that in states without licenses, legal assistants tend to be middle-class individuals with friends who are attorneys. California trains and licenses paralegals and systematically exposes students to attorneys during their training. Redbird finds that this enables graduates to find employment more quickly than in states without licenses.[276] However, these benefits are arguably the result of training programs tied to licensure, not to licensure itself.

Until recently, excessive licensing has proven a difficult problem to address. Federal authorities have cannot regulate or standardize state licensure practices. Although state Sunset Commissions and the Institute for Justice have made modest progress reducing licensing in a few states, progress was piecemeal until a landmark court decision in 2018. In *North Carolina State Board of Dental Examiners v. FTC,* the U.S. Supreme Court held that a dental board controlled by "active market participants" (practicing dentists) enjoyed no immunity from antitrust prosecution. Research indicates that almost every occupational licensing board is controlled by "active market participants". As a result, a door has suddenly opened for State Attorneys General or adversely affected citizens to sue occupational licensing boards on antitrust grounds and for state legislatures to ban practitioners from serving on licensing boards.[277]

Occupational certification is an alternative to licensure, but the distinction between the two is not clear to many employers. Licenses are state-mandated—it is illegal to practice an occupation or to hire a practitioner without a license. Certificates document demonstrated skills. Sometimes called micro-certificates or badges, occupational certificates are an effective alternative to licensure. Badges help employers classify and verify specific skills, which can be especially valuable for those without four-year college degrees. A badge documents experiences, achievements, or completed courses. Some certificates take advantage of transparent badges that certify specific and sometimes narrow occupational skills, experiences, or achievements: a tested level of software proficiency, the completion of an online course, the attainment of a clearly defined technical certification. Certificates improve earnings because they help employers make smarter hiring decisions in a noisy marketplace.

Professional and vocational certificates are now the fastest-growing credential in higher education. The US Census Bureau reports that 19 million US adults have earned a certificate, including 6.4 million whose formal education ended at high school. Whether due to signaling, skills, or selection effects, these certificates are associated with incomes that are 10 percent higher overall and 17 percent higher for those who never graduated from college.[278]

The explosion of occupational licensure, no-poach, non-compete, and non-solicitation agreements are symptoms of weak and fragmented labor markets. They are the natural result of a failed system of income bargaining that has left behind inadequate employee, employer, and training organizations. Absent organized employers to bargain with, craft unions and professional associations persuade state legislators to raise their incomes by restricting access to their profession or craft. Without organized workers to restrain them, employers seek to control even workers they no longer employ, restricting opportunity and suppressing wage growth. The cost of lost income and opportunities to millions of working Americans is much higher than those who benefit ever gain.

Standards Strengthen Labor Markets

Strong industry associations would allow employers and organized workers to continually define and strengthen skill standards. Appropriate standards make hiring less risky for employers and they make it far simpler for workers to move between jobs. They make chronically sticky labor markets more liquid. These standards are broad and in many industries so fluid that they are the opposite of the narrow job descriptions of yore.

Skill standards matter. Consider an employer with two full-time job openings, one for a maintenance electrician and the other for a graphic designer. Electricians arrive credentialed by an apprenticeship or vocational program and either certified or licensed by a state board. Unless the job is highly specialized, employers are likely to pick between applicants with well-documented skills.

Selecting a graphic designer is riskier. Skill standards are less clearly defined, and designers are less likely to be certified, except potentially for software proficiency. Even committed designers must hope that a portfolio designed for a different company and context will resonate with a new employer. Because it is riskier to hire someone based on a portfolio, however, wages suffer.

For many economists, a skill shortage is impossible because the whole point of markets is to fulfill unmet demand. A labor shortage must be a signal to raise wages. While this is true at some margin, it is comically untrue in industries that change quickly or grow suddenly. For example, increasing wages may be necessary to produce the estimated 209,000 cybersecurity specialists that American employers would hire if they could find them. Wage increases alone will not suddenly enable thousands of new workers to diminish a company's attack surfaces, harden firewalls, lock routers down, and protect websites against a variety of attacks.[279]

To take a more common example, the Conference Board reports chronic national shortages of therapy aides/assistants in health care.[280] These are positions that require on average one year of education beyond high school, attract few immigrants, and are unlikely to be automated. Likewise restaurants in many large cities cannot find pastry chefs. Demand has soared, but even if restaurants pay more (as they inevitably must), employers need to be able to guide interested workers to the requisite training or certification.[281] If a worker aspires to work as a therapy assistant, pastry chef, or cybersecurity specialist, they need to be able to quickly discover what experience, training, or skill certification employers want. Organized employers can make skill requirements explicit, and they can help forecast talent requirements for regions and industries so that fewer shortages arise.

Employers not only need skills that schools do not teach, they often look for skills that they cannot specify precisely. Some are "soft skills" like the ability to listen, present, write, and collaborate. Employers value these capabilities, but schools rarely teach or measure them. Without the ability to specify the real skills they need, hiring becomes riskier. Employers are forced to hire people based on what they hope are relevant signals, add unnecessary requirements to the job, take a risk, and pray that the new worker can acquire relevant skills on the job. Often, the uncertainty leads employers to require a college degree for any job that requires soft skills. The result can be a "Credentials Gap", as when 16 percent of production supervisors actually have a college degree, but 73 percent of recent job postings for production supervisors demand one.[282] Staffing surveys often report that more than a third of employers have trouble filling jobs, a market failure that often can be more easily solved by groups of employers in a sector than by individual ones.

Skill standards help workers as well. An employee with a skill valued by only one employer does not really have a market for his or her skill. Skill only translates into higher income when it is sought by multiple employers and workers are free to change jobs. Without standards, the market for any particular skill can become thin and illiquid, especially if the skill is an emerging one. James Bessen shows that highly skilled 19th-century textile weavers were critical to mill productivity but remained poorly paid as long as their abilities remained tacit and non-transferable. He shows that for nearly seventy years after the introduction of the power loom, wages for skilled weavers did not increase and mill owners reaped outsize profits. Once work became standardized enough that workers could move between mills, however (and as competing forms of work outside of mills advanced), factory owners were forced to pay more. As long as a weaver faced a market of one employer for his or her skills, his or her increased productivity did not lead to wage increases. Bessen demonstrates that weavers could not transfer their skills to new employers and earn higher pay until manufacturers standardized production processes and skill categories.[283]

Skill standards alone do not help an aspiring pastry chef or therapy aide. These potential workers need pathways. Just as labor markets become stronger when employers specify relevant skills (often by working closely with occupational educators), markets are also strengthened when vocations have clear pathways from either high school or college to a credential that employers deem relevant. These standards need to be explicit, but ideally not European in their rigidity. (In France, a pastry chef serves a ten-year apprenticeship. A bookstore clerk serves a five-year apprenticeship in Germany.)

Some analysts worry that career pathways lock young people into a career at an early age, but young people choose different paths, including college, in most countries with strong training systems. Nor is it today's problem: in the 21st century, as the US has steadily grown four-year college completion rates, the completion of two-year associate's degrees has leveled off. Expanding occupational pathways would create onramps and signposts to help high school graduates negotiate an otherwise bewildering occupational world.

The US military understands the value of onramps and skill standards. Recruiters do an outstanding job of providing access to military careers for high school graduates, and they can be extremely precise about which skills recruits can train for. Organized employers would serve their interests and those of young people by learning from military recruiters.

Worker and employer identities sometimes pose a subtle challenge to occupational pathways. Workers often have trouble imagining themselves doing jobs for which they have many of the requisite skills. Employers may have the same blind spot. For example, research suggests that many of the skills possessed by workers in declining jobs are applicable to growing jobs. Operators of coal mining equipment may be able to rapidly retrain as CNC machinists, for example, but neither miners nor employers recognize this.

To avoid identity mismatch, it helps for employers to be specific about the competencies they need.[284] Innovative training and placement programs, including Opportunity@Work and Markle's Skillful initiative, challenge workers to think more broadly about how to apply their skills and aptitudes to new occupations. They challenge employers to cast a broader recruiting net as well.[285]

In developing occupational pathways, employer associations are beginning to use data from online talent platforms. LinkedIn, Facebook, Monster.com, Glassdoor, and Google capture massive amounts of data on jobs posted, filled, and unfilled in every region and industry. They know which skills and degrees prevail in major occupation groups. They can document the most frequently trodden career paths from education and entry-level positions to more fulfilling work. Which architecture school within two hundred miles produces the most partners in design firms with more than three hundred employees? They know.

Google has used machine-learning algorithms to refine a mountain of data. They distilled more than 17 million online job postings and 200 million resumes to create about four million unique job titles. Perhaps 15 percent of these are in everyday use. As Career Builder or Dice use this technology to show job seekers more relevant openings, companies are starting to adopt a more standard occupational vocabulary.[286] An active employer association that saw itself as a platform for developing talent markets in their sector could dramatically accelerate this process.

These data can help managers, labor organizations, and educators see the demand for skills and occupations evolve in real time. Traditional labor statistics cannot do this. By sharing this information with educators and labor organizations, industry associations could create new visibility into which educational institutions and programs produce higher incomes.

Working with talent platforms, industry associations can help make public the skill and earnings outcomes of particular schools and degree programs.[287]

In short, skill standards shape labor markets. Employers and workers who bargain with them can and should develop these standards and help them evolve. With standards in place, they can then ask what mix of formal training and on-the-job experience is needed for workers to acquire relevant skills.

Career and Technical Education Requires Organized Employers

The single most widely shared belief in all of labor economics may be that American vocational training serves students, employers, and educators very poorly. Students lack pathways or even the means to evaluate the meager occupational offerings of the local community college. Employers find job applicants' hard skills to be highly inconsistent. Educators confront locally controlled school boards and frequently complain that high school graduates are academically and emotionally unprepared for serious study. Without reliable and comparable outcomes information, even programs that produce successful results are not able to scale up.

Employers participate in what is now termed career and technical education (CTE) in one of three ways, depending on how big they are. A gigantic company like Amazon can backward integrate into the community college business. Amazon effectively runs its own community colleges to train workers for advanced skills that the local market needs, even if Amazon itself does not. At many fulfillment centers, Amazon offers training for occupations with high local demand, preparing workers to become, for example, aircraft mechanics, computer-aided designers, machine tool technologists, medical lab techs, and nurses.

Amazon's goal is to train warehouse workers for better jobs outside of the company. They pay 95 percent of annual tuition costs under $12,000. They host the classes behind glass doors in their fulfillment centers, which ensures that the classes will be both convenient and widely observed. Sixteen thousand employees in thirteen countries have taken advantage of the program. They have committed to offering communication, resume writing, and basic computer skills to more than 50,000 hourly workers. This is an excellent model for companies with a half million semi-skilled workers concentrated in a handful of locations. Auto manufacturers should take heed.

Much more common, however, is the situation of European energy giant Siemens. They employ 1,600 people at an energy hub in Charlotte, North Carolina, and were not attracting as many high-quality skilled people as they needed. Inspired by the dual system in Germany, where qualified students work part-time for Siemens and receive specialized training part-time, the company launched an apprenticeship program in the Charlotte area. Because Siemens pays all tuition and books, students graduate with an AA degree, a journeyman certificate, no debt, and a job paying more than $50,000. The program recently welcomed "its largest-ever class of incoming apprentices" and is widely heralded as a model in books and articles about CTE in America. Although Siemens has plans to grow the program in Sacramento, Atlanta, and Fort Payne, Alabama, this "largest class ever" consisted of eight fortunate students.[288] It is a terrific program, but even large employers are not able to scale up single-employer programs to meet America's crying need for CTE.

Lockheed Martin did something similar but opened its program to companies in other sectors. Facing a skills shortage in San Antonio, Texas, Lockheed worked with the local community college to create the Aerospace Academy in 2001. The community college provides instruction for high school juniors and seniors, who receive paid summer internships at Lockheed. These interns now account for about 20 percent of the company's newly hired full-time workers. Individual manufacturing, health care, and IT companies have been inspired to follow the same approach: courses for both high school and college credit combined with summer internships.[289]

Individual employers sponsor student projects, competitions, and internships. Unfortunately, however, these employers tend to limit their support for the program to their own needs. As a result, individual companies can rarely furnish training that is extensive enough or involving enough occupations to make a fundamental difference to young people. Over time, these programs are often captured by a single dominant employer or by the community college partner. Without a committed group of employers, these programs invariably stagnate.

Toyota chose a third way. They built a solid training organization, enrolled suppliers and competitors, then spun the program off as a nonprofit run by a consortium of companies. Starting in Kentucky in 2005, Toyota collaborated with a local community college to create an advanced manufacturing technician certificate. They created a multiemployer group called the Federation for Advanced Manufacturing Education (FAME). Toyota controlled FAME at first but soon gave up control to the consortium. FAME has grown to twenty-two AMT programs in nine states, involving more than three hundred companies.[290] Students receive internships, which are effectively tryouts for full-time jobs. Students graduate debt-free, and 95 percent receive offers of full-time jobs with their sponsors. Employers fund the program, direct it, and shape it to meet their needs.

As is often the case, some of the critical factors that caused these programs to succeed are subtle or hidden. CTE programs often recruit committed managers to critique student presentations or to judge contests for innovative products, business plans, services, or initiatives. They invite the most effective managers to guest-teach a class and perhaps to co-teach a course. Managers find themselves mentoring students and hosting events to help students build their professional networks. Many managers discover that this work improves their hiring accuracy since projects and internships allow them to observe students more fully. Invariably, a few managers become full-time faculty. Experienced practitioners who can teach are the secret sauce of the most successful CTE programs.

A defining feature of successful training programs is that employers, not students or schools, are the main customer. Employers bear much of the cost. They hire students who are still in school and devote time to training them on the job. They retain graduates afterward. Unless employers can define training programs to meet their needs, there is no reason for them to bother with it.

Organized employers are essential to large, successful CTE. A hospital may need medical records technicians who are familiar with constantly evolving federal billing codes. They are likely reluctant to invest in training workers who may quit and go to work elsewhere—but willing to increase their contribution to an industry association that builds strong CTE. They know that they will benefit since about as many workers will come to them as leave. By allowing individual employers to socialize the cost and risk of training and turnover, industry associations can expand high-quality CTE programs.

Public funding is vital for successful CTE—but without the collective engagement of employers, public funding is not enough.[291] Without engaged employers, federal training funds end up in the hands of political supporters. A 2011 audit by the US Government Accountability Office found that the federal government ran forty-seven overlapping training programs costing $18 billion. Few had ever been evaluated for effectiveness. Those that had been evaluated had failed to deliver meaningful results. A 2016 review of a large Labor Department training effort found that it was unable to increase either earnings or employment.[292]

Labor unions have a long history of collaborating in CTE. Apprenticeships are a large part of the craft tradition of the AFL and a small part of the industrial tradition of the CIO. Labor organizations are well-situated to recruit young people into programs and to participate in both the design and delivery of curriculum. Today, fifteen Building Trades unions operate more than 1,900 training centers across the US and Canada that train two-thirds of all formally registered apprentices.[293] If this system were a college, it would be the largest degree-granting institution and the third-largest public university system in the US. The Machinists, Autoworkers, Culinary Workers, and Steelworkers also operate substantial training and apprenticeship programs.[294]

Unionized apprenticeship programs have two problems. First, they evolve slowly, in part because they inevitably become wedded to craft jurisdictions. On a strict union job, a pipefitter does not do plumbing, nor does a finisher touch up the paint. The best apprenticeships evolve with their craft; the worst cement jurisdictions in place.

The second problem is "agency risk", the chance that a union representative will represent their own interests, not the workers'. Agency risk occurs any time one person represents another's interest. A Congresswoman who represents citizens, a manager who represents an owner, and a lawyer who represents a client all face agency risk. In the past, unions have failed as agents when they have misused apprenticeship program funds or restricted access to training programs. For these reasons and others, apprenticeship programs often work best if a group of employers in the same industry play a central operating role, and unions play a monitoring and marketing role. Industry-based employer associations enable employers and unions to do exactly this.

Marty Walsh knows the power of labor unions in marketing innovative apprenticeships. Walsh came up through the Laborer's Union and the Boston Metropolitan Building Trades before he was elected mayor of Boston in 2013. Concerned about formerly incarcerated men who lacked marketable skills, he helped start Operation Exit in 2014.

Nate Awan, who grew up near Walsh in Dorchester, was kicked out of four schools and sent to prison at age eighteen for trying to shoot a rival gang member. A former prosecutor helped Awan into Operation Exit, where he sampled carpentry, sheet-metal work, and other trades. He chose pipe-fitting and as a second-year apprentice made $30 an hour—enough to support his small family.[295]

If the main requirement of successful CTE is multi-employer leadership, Operation Exit shows that the second is strong outreach and career counseling. Counselors are crucial in high school. They are even more valuable in vocational or professional schools, where students wish to begin work in their newly chosen field upon graduation, if not sooner. Counselors help students create or discover internships, balance the demands of work and study, and execute an effective campaign to secure a position as graduation approaches if the internship is not going to convert to a full-time job. A high-quality counseling operation that helps smooth the transition to work adds enormous value for students, especially for those facing difficult personal challenges.

Employer associations that are regulated monopsonies with powerful economic incentives to bargain income are essential to improving job matching, increasing job churn, raising productivity, and compressing income. But it takes two to bargain: how exactly are workers to organize?

Labor unions do not need to be complicated. Workers, high paid or low, salaried or wage-earning, young or old, should be able to form or join any organization they wish. Labor or professional organizations would operate as freestanding social enterprises. The result would be a market for worker representation that, when combined with employer incentives to bargain income, would produce organizations strong enough to ensure that income grows inclusively and dynamic enough to evolve as economic conditions change.

10. A Market for Worker Representation

Competition forces organizations to focus and innovate; nothing else seems to. To remain strong enough to bargain income effectively, labor organizations must specialize and adapt. As a result, America needs something that Robert Wagner never contemplated in drafting his bill: a carefully designed market for worker representation. America needs not a few traditional unions, but an ecosystem of labor organizations devoted to equitable income growth. These social enterprises include labor and professional organizations, a system of low-cost compliance with public and private rules, and advisory workplace councils designed to increase trust and voice in local workplaces. These labor market organizations would stand in sharp contrast to today's unions, professional associations, licensing boards, and regulators that are shielded from competition and innovate slowly, when they innovate at all.

Labor organizations can be voluntary membership organizations, as easy to join or quit as membership in a local gym, church, or public radio station. Voluntary membership organizations can grow quite large; the AARP has twice as many dues-paying members as all American labor unions combined.

From Exclusive to Proportional Representation

History and logic suggest that left to their own devices, workers in every field will organize by industry, occupation, region, and shared concerns. Industry organizations with local subsidiaries are best suited to bargain with employer associations. Here they are called labor co-ops to distinguish them from industrial unions with exclusive bargaining rights and an enterprise focus.[296]

Co-ops would offer membership, representation, services, and bargaining to all workers in a sector like health care or hospitality. Similar in some respects to "open source unionism" envisioned by two labor scholars before the Great Recession, labor co-ops would likely offer tiered membership.[297] Associate members might register and get a free newsletter and the right to vote on income agreements. Supporting and sustaining members might be eligible for specialized services. Co-ops would bargain with regulated, industry-based employer associations described earlier. They would negotiate with individual companies only by rare and regulated exception and would be governed by the minimum provisions of related industry agreements.

Income bargaining would be proportional, not exclusive. If petrochemical workers formed three different industry co-ops, they would compete for members but over time would face a substantial incentive to either merge or differentiate and cooperate effectively in bargaining, lest they serve their members poorly. Ultimately, the pressure on overlapping labor co-ops to specialize or combine would inevitably influence and be influenced by the boundaries and regional structure of employer associations.

As they have from the beginning of time, workers would also organize by shared occupation, profession, or craft. The resulting professional associations or craft unions would emphasize training, certification, and networking for specific occupations. In the case of professions or trades like nurses, carpenters, or credit analysts that concentrate heavily within an industry, occupational organizations would be a crucial part of the labor coalition that would bargain income with federally chartered employer associations. Nurses frequently do this today.

Craft unions or professional associations for occupations that span many industries, like graphic designers, security guards, or project managers would end up participating in bargaining coalitions with multiple industry co-ops. Setting wages by industry may seem awkward for occupations that span multiple sectors. IT managers, copywriters, and public relations staff turn up in every industry. But employers would be inclined to copy each other in setting salaries for these workers, just as they do now. Industries that hire a lot of IT managers will find them well represented in bargaining. They will set minimum skill and pay levels. Other industry associations will tend to copy these standards or risk losing talent.

As work specializes, professional associations and craft unions will unavoidably reflect both the trunk and the branches of occupations or crafts. Today, an association may represent physicians. It may have branches that represent pediatricians, subbranches for pediatric oncologists, and even associations of pediatric oncology surgeons. Likewise, a craft union for plumbers may have a separate chapter for pipefitters, who may have chapters of specialized steamfitters certified to work on pipes carrying toxic chemicals under pressure. Whether members join the main organization, a specialized branch, or both is likely to vary by personal preference and identity as it does today.

Few union leaders realize it, but workers with advanced degrees are much more likely to organize unions or professional associations that bargain income than are workers without high school diplomas. In 2003, 6.6 percent of workers who had not graduated from high school were union members, compared to 15.4 percent of workers with an advanced degree. Nonetheless, more union members have only a high school education or less (6.1 million in 2003) than have a bachelor's degree or higher (5.1 million in 2003).[298]

Professional associations and craft-based unions naturally seek to shape skill certification programs. For example, the Project Management Institute maintains standards and a registry of those who have earned any of eight different certificates related to project management. The organization has 450,000 members in over 280 local chapters around the world with annual revenues approaching $200 million. PMI has proven adept at bringing students into companies around a specific set of tools and competencies. Its members mentor students and set up internships within their businesses, which encompass a large number of different industries. PMI, like other occupational associations, has developed valuable data that could enable co-ops in a variety of industries to bargain income for project managers at different skill and certification levels.

Of course, employers would soon discover that they classify the same work and workers differently. A product manager does a different job at two different companies and may be called a program manager at a third. There will emerge a continuous tension between occupational categories in every industry. Employers will agree on standards and certification only if it minimizes hiring risk and increases candidate pools. In most sectors, occupational certifications will serve to signal worker motivation, skill, and commitment but not serve as a prerequisite to advancing to a new position.

Craft unions and professional associations must be able to evolve with changes in the structure of employment. As physicians become employees of large hospital or provider networks, for example, medical associations are frequently starting to bargain income.[299] Under this scheme, they would participate in bargaining alongside labor co-ops.

Advocacy organizations would represent a third type of worker organization. Employees who share workplace concerns across multiple sectors and occupations, such as women, immigrants, veterans, or parents, might organize to bring a subset of issues of intense interest to their members to the bargaining table.

The legacy of the Automobile Labor Board notwithstanding, proportional bargaining sounds chaotic to those accustomed to collective bargaining under systems of exclusive representation. An analogy to proportional political representation might help. Consider a state with five Congressional Districts. For simplicity, each district consists of 40 percent Democrats, 30 percent Republicans, 20 percent Greens, and 10 percent Zombies. Say, Oregon. Assume that in the exclusive, winner-take-all model (known by horse-loving Brits as "first-past-the-post"), a single representative can be elected by plurality, so Oregon would send five Democrats to Washington. Sixty percent of the population would not have their views represented in Congress.

Instead, Oregon could merge the five districts and seat the winning candidate from each party. Under this proportional representation model, everybody would have a representative. Minority views would be heavily represented and representatives of larger parties would have much stronger mandates than others. Political scientists have debated the merits of exclusive vs. proportional representation for years and show no signs of stopping.

The great advantage of proportional representation schemes is that a robust variety of organizations produces a much wider range of individual choice than exclusive representation every can. An electrician who works on the staff of the local college may know enough about campus electrical systems that she is indispensable. She may command a wage or salary much higher than required by the income agreement that covers her work. What organization would she join? She might choose to join a labor co-op of college and university employees out of solidarity or to take advantage of benefits or services that a co-op can offer. She might join a craft union of electricians to meet those who share her professional interests or to benefit from advanced skill certification. She could join an organization that advocates for women at work. She may decide to form the Society of Academic Electricians to engage with people very much like herself. She could do all of these things. Or she may prefer to go home after work and attend a reading group, raise kids, or restore antique German motorcycles.

Organizing or joining a labor organization would be a simple First Amendment right. Any individual worker or retiree would be free to go online and join as many co-ops, craft unions, or labor advocacy groups as he or she wished. Organizations that engaged their members more deeply, offered better services, bargained or helped bargain better agreements, or mobilized workers for better causes would grow faster and replace those that did not.

To flourish, worker co-ops must be easy to form, grow, merge, and dissolve. Trial and error, improvisation, surprise, incremental changes, and pragmatism will grow stronger labor organizations than sheer determination ever will. Left to specialize and compete, labor organizations will be forced to experiment. In a robust market for workplace representation, a few organizations will become strong enough to advance the cause of income growth. As in all competitive markets, many attempts to innovate will fail and make way for stronger groups to take their place.

Raising Pay, Raising Money, and Raising Hell

Labor co-ops, craft unions, and advocacy groups would be membership organizations devoted to advancing the interest of a specific sector, occupation, or concerned group. Like all social enterprises, they would require revenue in the form of dues and service fees to be economically self-sustaining.

Labor organizations of any sort are high-fixed-cost operations that require a minimum number of members. Today's labor unions derive virtually all of their $8 billion in annual revenue from dues.[300] In contrast, the labor organizations described here are likely to obtain some of their income from dues and significant revenue from services that they offer to members. The search for diverse sources of revenue will force these organizations to adopt new models, surface new leaders, and test new approaches. These organizations will quickly evolve ways to advocate for their members, whether they are salaried professionals, hourly employees, freelancers, consultants, temps, or retirees. Those unable to recruit enough members would specialize, concentrate geographically, merge with larger organizations, or cease operations.

Unions are today prohibited from taking revenue from any employer—even ones they don't bargain with. The law is designed to prevent employer-dominated unions, which can be a severe problem if exclusive bargaining restricts workers from changing unions easily. Non-exclusive labor organizations do not have the same problem. If a worker or group of workers conclude that their organization should not take money from employers to provide health and safety training or workplace audits, they are free to quit and form or join another organization. Labor organizations that bargain proportionately require transparency (financial disclosure, fair elections, and fair ratifications) but do not need nearly as many restrictions on revenue as do unions that bargain exclusively.

As social enterprises, every labor organization would have an incentive to test new revenue models and services. Many would seek to maximize revenue and would learn from other membership nonprofits like churches and public radio stations that offer basic as well as multiple levels of sustaining memberships. Any membership organization without the ability to mandate fees must trade off higher dues and the number of members willing to enroll. One study of seventy-one professional associations, which are almost always voluntary, reported average annual dues of $250 with the 80th percentile paying $350. In contrast, US union dues appear to average about $650 annually with substantial variation across unions.[301] There is little question that the ability to compel membership leads to higher dues.

Co-ops would be free to raise funds, build loyalty, and grow membership by offering valuable services. Professional associations do this today and, as a result, derive only about 30 percent of their revenue from dues.[302] The experience of today's professional associations and innovative labor unions suggests an outline of many of these services.

Professional Training and Conferences. Hundreds of professional associations and craft unions credential skills. Many host specialized conferences to educate members and strengthen professional networks that enhance fluidity, mobility, and earnings. Some of these services are moving online, but practitioners in many occupations are willing to pay for an annual trip to an attractive city, mix with thought leaders, network with peers, and confirm their status and professional identity within their chosen tribe. These events are a major source of revenue, an enjoyable getaway, and a catalyst for people who share interests and experiences.

Employment Services. Either industry associations or the labor organizations they bargain with can finance online talent platforms, and career support focused on their industry. These platforms enable employers to post job openings and workers to post resumes. If the service charges an employer a small fee only when they hire successfully, sector-specific employment platforms can generate meaningful revenue. If well integrated with standard platforms like LinkedIn and supportive of industry certifications and badges, they can provide talented applicants and temporary workers to firms, and information about jobs to tens of thousands of industry workers who are more qualified than applicants who use open platforms to apply for jobs indiscriminately.

The information embedded in talent platforms is extraordinary. Which program in Des Moines graduates the most certified welders? Graduates of which nursing, business, or data science program earn the highest incomes? How do people prepare to become solar repair technicians or PR professionals? Today this information is not easy to discover—and employers, as well as students, are worse off as a result.

MGI has concluded that by 2025, platforms like LinkedIn, Relationship Science, or Monster will add $2.7 trillion to global GDP. They will substantially improve the functioning of world labor markets.[303] As these platforms grow, they will naturally form vertical subgroups. Because they are sector-focused, labor, professional, and industry associations can leverage these platforms and make imaginative use of the data that they provide.

Career counseling is a related and undervalued employment service. Delivered via classes and online meetings, counseling can be exceptionally cost-effective. Skilled counselors with knowledge of local labor markets can make a big difference to workers who may value help writing a resume, generating employment options, or understanding the fine points of job searches.

Benefits Administration. The rise of gig work has caused many observers to note the need for benefits earned according to hours worked. These benefits need to be portable across multiple employers of temporary, part-time, freelance, and consulting workers. Health care, vacation, retirement savings, sick leave, and other benefits can be financed this way. For purposes of designing portable benefits, it is useful to distinguish three types of gig economy workers depending on whether their primary allegiance is to an industry, an occupation, or neither.

Many consultants and temps in media, software development, performing arts, specialized education, and other services commonly work within a single industry sector and sometimes for a single employer. Under the terms of industry agreements, employers would contribute either a percent of pay or a fixed amount per hour to fund benefits, which would manage Social Security payments, health and dental insurance, retirement savings, and vacation or sick day accounts. A worker with several employers could earn contributions from each based on total earnings or hours worked.

Other professionals work across multiple sectors within a single occupation, a challenge entirely familiar to American craft unions. Most building trade work ends when workers finish construction. A carpenter or an electrician might work a dozen jobs in a year in residential construction, commercial construction, remodeling, or repair. Portable benefits with contributions for each hour worked are part of every building trades agreement. These plans offer substantial and comprehensive benefits often comparable to those earned by regular employees of a large company. Even though there has always been a solid economic case for separating health care coverage from employment altogether, temporary or freelance work need not condemn a worker to forgo health insurance, vacations, or other social benefits.

The remarkable Sara Horowitz has built the 350,000-strong Freelancers Union to provide a wide range of retirement, life, and health insurance benefits, especially in New York. The Freelancers both originate insurance for networks like Guardian Dental and own and operate the Freelancers Insurance Company and a 401(k) plan, which provide benefits directly. The Union also runs the Freelancers Medical Center in downtown Brooklyn, which it operates in partnership with a local medical group.[304]

The Freelancers Insurance Company is set up as a "social purpose enterprise," but either private businesses or professional associations can offer these benefits. In Silicon Valley, where IT consultants are as thick as traffic jams, MBO Partners provides bookkeeping and billing services to independent consultants. It enables consultants to deduct pre-tax contributions for health, workers' compensation, disability, and 401(k) retirement benefits.

Creating employer-funded portable benefits for the third type of gig work is a substantial challenge. These are workers who work neither within a single industry nor a single occupation. They work temporary jobs across multiple skills and sectors. A person who waits tables part-time, edits social media posts, drives for Lyft, and works a day each week at a local retailer needs benefits that are portable across sectors and occupations. Several states, including Washington and New York, are considering portable benefit schemes that would reach across multiple occupations and industries. These experiments will be closely watched, because they provide benefits that are tied neither to a single occupation nor to an industry—and thus benefits enormously from local government innovation.

Pension Funds. Labor co-ops are likely to be better at designing and delivering portable benefit schemes than at managing them directly. Some employee advocates have long favored union co-management of health and welfare benefits. For example, many unions are tempted to help manage pension funds, which can accumulate a great deal of capital. Current law allows unions to co-manage pension funds, as multi-employer Taft-Hartley trusts ("multis").

Most multis are plagued by agency problems. They perform poorly, thanks to their small scale and political risks. The smaller size of most multis concentrates risk and increases overhead compared with larger, independently managed funds. Multis also face myriad of perverse incentives. Employers are always tempted to shift liabilities to competitors by failing to fund their pension or health care obligations. Unions are tempted to pressure multis to either support or boycott individual companies, sectors, or projects. Building trades pensions are often invited to invest in construction projects that agree to sign labor agreements. It is a short step from this to the sort of corruption that plagued the nation's largest multi—the notorious and now-bankrupt Teamsters Central States Pension Fund. According to the Center for Retirement Research at Boston College, America's 1,400 multis face $553 billion more in claims than in assets. Congress is debating a bail-out.[305]

Some labor reformers have proposed a so-called "Ghent system" approach to administering benefits. Under these programs, common in northern Europe, labor organizations manage unemployment funds directly. Named after the city in Belgium that first implemented (and since abandoned) worker-managed benefits, the Ghent model helps explain why union density is higher in Scandinavia than in France, where the state manages unemployment benefits. David Rolf has called for labor to experiment with a Ghent system in the United States to be administered by "worker advocacy organizations" based on the experience of unions in Denmark, Finland, Iceland, and Sweden.[306]

The appeal of worker-managed unemployment service is understandable. Because they pay generous unemployment benefits, these plans enable employers to reduce staff or use temps more easily. Moreover, it creates a strong incentive for workers to join a union to qualify for unemployment benefits. (In some countries, workers are required to join the plan, but not the union itself.)

It is critical to design smart incentives into these programs. Today, all Ghent model systems are under economic pressure due to a common problem with insurance markets. When conditions change, and rates rise, senior workers defect because they face the lowest risk of unemployment. The result is that the same risk is shared by fewer people, so rates rise. Unchecked, an underwriting "death spiral" results. Many analysts have associated the sharp rise in unemployment insurance premiums with the decline of union membership in Nordic countries.[307]

In short, contractual seniority protection from layoffs undermines Ghent programs. Thanks to seniority, experienced workers with little risk of unemployment withdraw from the insurance pool and drop their union membership. (The underwriting death spiral for unemployment insurance among workers protected by seniority is the opposite of the one for health insurance, where young, healthy workers have the strongest incentive to defect. Health insurance is nationalized in most Nordic countries, but a clever American union might bundle the two.)

Because governments can mandate participation, they are better able to socialize unemployment risk than private organizations. As with multiemployer benefit funds, labor co-ops are sometimes better positioned to design plans, sign up workers, and troubleshoot problems than they are to dispassionately invest funds or manage payouts.

Reputation Ranking. Most employers care a great deal more about their reputation than they do about legal or contractual compliance per se. Public scoring of employer compliance with a set of standards can therefore serve as a powerful motivator of employer behavior.[308]

Employee organizations can help develop and leverage a robust marketplace for corporate reputations. Most companies despise a below-average ranking, even when they understand that half of all companies will receive one. Labor organizations can choose their metrics: health and safety violations, pay fairness, the share of women in senior ranks, environmental sustainability, productive investments in training, management quality, or the number of employment-related lawsuits.

Ranking companies, workplaces, and managers creates incentives to bring bottom quartile companies closer to the average on any particular metric. Labor co-ops can have fun with this: urge workers to nominate companies for best and worst in each category and hold a black-tie Academy Awards-style ceremony on Labor Day.

Working America, an affiliate of the AFL-CIO, got a start on this by holding a My Bad Boss contest. My Bad Boss was inspired and led by Karen Nussbaum of 9to5 fame. Nussbaum has long been one of organized labor's (and the Clinton Labor Department's) most imaginative and committed leaders. Many of the contest entries were grotesque. If this were a revenue-generating service, co-ops might reward best as well as worst, charge money to attend the event, take ad revenue from the live stream, and sell the complete report and detailed scorecard. If it worked, they could hold separate events by industry and present the results at an industry conference.

Financial Services. Members of labor co-ops buy homes, save for college and retirement, and invest. These organizations can arrange insurance, loans, and banking services for delivery on favorable terms by competent and sympathetic financial institutions happy to support affiliates that originate business.

It is no longer necessary for every labor organization to charter a bank, as many unions did in the 1920s. The Machinists opened the Mount Vernon Savings Bank in 1920. In 1923, the ACTWU (textile workers) founded the Amalgamated Bank. The following year, the Boilermakers founded the Bank of Labor. The year after that, AFL President Samuel

Gompers founded the Union Labor Life Insurance Company to offer workers health and life insurance. Each of these financial institutions survives in some form to this day (and, ironically, each is worth more in financial terms than the union that started it). Labor banks are popular and successful in other countries as well, notably Japan.

Ownership and Entrepreneurship Services. In most companies, investors own the business and "rent" the labor they need. In a few companies, workers own the business and rent the capital they need. Because the employee-owners of these organizations participate in varying forms of governance, they need broader business and leadership skills than do workers in most companies. Co-ops can help provide this. With a bit of creativity, they can derive revenue from these services.

Historically, unions and worker associations have contributed to cooperatives. Spanish dictator Francisco Franco strictly outlawed labor unions, so socially conscious Jesuits in Northern Spain built a conglomerate of worker-owned cooperatives in the Basque region around Mondragon. Today, the Mondragon Cooperative is a $13 billion multinational corporation with 75,000 employees and is far more studied than emulated. The United Steelworkers became active in employee ownership as troubled steel companies restructured and has formed a formal alliance with Mondragon.[309]

A few enthusiasts promote worker ownership as a strategy, not a tactic. Followers of third-way economic philosophers like Yochai Benkler and others influenced by kibbutz traditions advocate for production, distribution, and consumption without the strict use of market mechanisms. These strategies depend on business and labor enterprises that promote informed social cooperation.[310]

Labor organizations can play a useful role in co-operative enterprises. They can contribute to their design and governance and can help train employees in the business skills needed to participate in intelligent business decision-making. Worker-owned businesses raise capital and must therefore manage the familiar tradeoff between increasing wages and increasing returns to capital providers. Some have even had strikes. Employee ownership does not resolve the tensions between labor and capital, so much as it reshapes the discussion about the inevitable trade-offs.

Employees own all or part of about 7,000 US businesses, mainly because these companies issue employees shares as part of an Employee Stock Ownership Plan. ESOPs are heavily tax subsidized. Companies that sell 30 percent of their stock to an ESOP can defer or even eliminate capital gains taxes. The cost of buying owners out when they retire is tax-deductible, and an ESOP that owns all of a company's shares is exempt from income tax. Options on common shares are another form of ownership, especially popular in Silicon Valley. Options are lottery tickets. Most expire worthless, but if the company takes off, they can pay off nicely —even spectacularly. They (or restricted shares, which are taking their place) are essential to persuading talented engineers and marketers to join a high-risk startup.[311]

Two types of businesses are especially likely to benefit from ESOPS. In professional service firms, employees are the only real asset that a business has. As a result, ESOPs are common in architecture, engineering, law, and consulting. Other companies need to attract and retain service staff but cannot pay them high hourly compensation. Chobani, a New York–based yogurt maker, issued shares to its 2,000 full-time employees. Those who stayed with the company the longest are now millionaires.[312] Grocery businesses like WinCo or Publix have likewise built successful ESOPs.[313]

Labor co-ops can play a valuable role in helping members acquire the skills, relationships, and capital needed to start their own companies, especially in auto repair, residential construction, and other industries where skilled workers often become small business owners. Labor organizations can also help employees better understand the choices around ESOP shares, restricted stock units, stock appreciation rights, phantom stock, profit-sharing, and stock options, where even well-educated employees need help to understand the tax consequences of distribution rules or the exercise of illiquid securities.

American labor unions have used employee ownership defensively. When the steel and airline industries hit hard times during the 1980s and 1990s, employees discovered that like it or not, they were effectively unsecured creditors to their tottering employer. In distress, the company sought to reduce its obligations to lenders and employees alike. A lender received equity in exchange for debt forgiveness, raising the question of what workers would receive in exchange for wage reductions. A few investment bankers at Lazard developed a niche practice helping unions with these complex restructurings. Few unions would have sought to make workers into owners during normal times, but many airline and steel companies are alive today—and many workers still working—because of these deals.

Political Mobilization and Advocacy. Business and labor organizations often rally their members to support their political preferences. They may focus on issues facing an industry or profession, or they may build support for political candidates, causes, or parties. Labor co-ops and industry associations would engage their members around policy problems or opportunities, raise money for their respective causes, and use shared social concerns to enlist the support of their members, much as happens today. This is fundamentally healthy.

Labor organizing has always been a social cause as much as an economic one. Forced to compete, labor organizations will develop unique approaches to educating, engaging, and mobilizing members. As always, some will pursue narrow interests, while others will advocate for those outside their immediate ranks. US history suggests that labor organizations earned widespread public support by promoting broad-based improvements to work, including the forty-hour work week, Social Security, and overtime rules, even when doing so diminished the value of collective bargaining.

Many co-ops are likely to make political mobilization an integrated part of their appeal to new members. The history of social change is a history of popular mobilization, whether for voting rights, civil rights, or labor rights. Unions today honor a pantheon of heroes who led the sit-down strike in Flint, the general strike in San Francisco, or the hunger strike in Delano. Lesser-known mobilizations by Atlanta washerwomen, Lowell mill women, Seattle fast-food workers, or Los Angeles janitors all built political support for communities of workers outside of the influence of the NLRB. Labor co-ops are likely to test unique and modern political identities to both attract members and contribute to the vibrancy of American democracy.

American Work Councils

Companies, not industries, employ workers and determine their working conditions. If labor co-ops bargain income with industry associations, how do workers achieve a meaningful voice on the job? Workplaces vary enormously, but most of any size would benefit from workplace councils. These local councils would advise management at the workplace level. They would not affiliate with a labor co-op, nor would they have revenue or employ staff. Workplace councils would be optional. The law would require that a workplace form one only at the request of employees.

A workplace council would consist of between three and ten non-supervisory employees, depending on workplace size. In order to be effective, council members must be respected by both employees and managers. Workers could serve on a council irrespective of their membership in a co-op or professional association. While only non-supervisory employees would be eligible to serve on a workplace council, anyone, including managers, would have the right to nominate, advocate for, and vote for workplace council members.

A workplace council has several jobs. They resolve violations of an industry agreement, discuss changes in the workplace, and address concerns raised by managers, workers, or other council members. A council would serve as a sounding board or "kitchen cabinet" to operating managers. The councils would enjoy information and consultation rights, especially in areas of core concern like staff planning, changes to work processes, the introduction of new technology, training, health and safety, and the particulars of pay, bonuses, working hours, and holidays. As small organizations accountable only to workers in a workplace, they would not bargain side agreements or modify the industry income agreement, whether or not their employer was a party to one.

Workplace councils play both offense and defense. The defensive mission is to enforce the income agreement if the company has signed one through its industry association. Nobody is closer to the workplace, understands the agreement better, knows employees better, has more management confidence, and is in a better position to resolve disagreements than workplace council members. They will be entitled to receive information about and review decisions about matters like contract provisions, staffing, hours, and vacations. Council members need to be committed to rapid, trust-based, high-quality decision-making, and conflict resolution. Workplace disagreements need to be resolved quickly or passed from council members to professionals in a local co-op for formal or informal resolution. In some workplaces, the workplace council might hear and quickly resolve grievances not resolved at a lower level.[314]

The offense mission of a workplace council is to enhance the quality of the workplace, employee trust, and the quality of the company's goods or services. A council would do this because most people want to do work they are proud of and because employees who produce more or better services can earn more than the wages called for in the income agreement. Improving quality results requires that workplace councils become more deeply involved in measuring trust and quality. It requires council members who can advocate for a workforce and not settle for defending its weakest practitioners. It requires workplace leaders who are trusted and who build trust.

Kaiser Permanente has experimented with something similar to workplace councils. Kaiser is a large, integrated, managed care consortium founded in 1945 by industrial pioneer Henry J. Kaiser. It is today the largest managed care organization in the United States. (Kaiser named the Permanente Medical Group after the creek that ran by his mountain cabin and today runs through Google's main campus.) Labor unions helped to grow Kaiser by demanding it for their members where it was available. The model took off and, as Kaiser himself long predicted, it is the only one of his many businesses that survive. Today, at least half of Kaiser's 220,000 employees are union members.[315]

Starting in 1997, Kaiser and its 28 unions began to give unionized workers a role in management decisions. Today, Kaiser has some 3,500 unit-based teams of managers, front-line workers, and physicians that discuss the quality, efficiency, and efficacy of health care services. They determine specific improvements in patient care. Kaiser invested substantially in trainers and consultants for these teams.[316] Today, they credit their efforts "not only with improving patient care and satisfaction, but in making Kaiser Permanente a better place to work by giving employees a voice on the job."[317]

A valuable function of workplace councils is to help evaluate management effectiveness. Importantly, it enables workers to identify abusive managers without fear of retaliation. Abusive managers are not confined to Hollywood producers, Silicon Valley moguls, Washington, D.C., politicians, or tenured academics. The restaurant industry chooses to rely on middle-aged men to supervise young women, so, perhaps not surprisingly, it generates more claims of sexual harassment than any other sector.[318]

Active workplace councils may also help improve hiring. In service organizations, service quality typically depends heavily on the professional skills and commitment of those who get hired and promoted. Moreover, participation in the hiring process is a powerful tool for socializing members of an organization, as professional service firms have repeatedly demonstrated.

Workplace councils are, of course, an Americanized version of German works councils. Despite superficial similarities, however, Germany has a fundamentally different version of industry bargaining and workplace councils from the one outlined here.

Germany is not the United States. It combines things rarely found in the same country at the same time: powerful unions and efficient companies; high unemployment benefits and low unemployment; high-cost workers and globally competitive manufacturers; massive productivity with fragmented industries of small and medium-sized companies. German labor force participation rates and wages have both outpaced the US since the early 1990s. Germany is both more automated and more unionized—in part because unions have been a source of wage restraint and have encouraged long-term capital investment.

There is no parallel to the Eurozone in the US. The single Eurozone subsidizes high-productivity countries, so Germans can post both record-low unemployment and record exports and trade surpluses. German deficits, debt, inflation, and interest rates are all too low to matter. They have solid education attainment thanks to excellent teachers, a culture of learning, and good vocational programs. Like the US, Germany has a low fertility rate and has remained relatively open to immigrants—although this has come under intense political pressure.[319]

The labor market reforms proposed here are fundamentally different from those operating in Germany or elsewhere in Europe today. Germany lacks any provision for creating new unions or employer associations. A handful of unions have run the show for over a half-century. The solutions outlined here reflect America's entrepreneurial preferences. Likewise, European industry associations have no simple way to merge or divide (although in Germany, membership in employer associations is optional, giving weaker firms a way to opt out of sectoral income agreements). In the US, industry associations need to be able to adapt by merging or dividing, so long as they do not overlap and compete. European labor unions tend to be exclusive and to not compete for members. Workers either join the union designated to represent them or none at all.

The reforms here would create a robust market for representation in keeping with American traditions and preferences for private markets. Europe has regional variation across countries but relatively little within them. America needs to accommodate a much greater variety of economic conditions and can do so using these reforms. Germany enforces a form of co-determination that requires union representation at the level of each company's board of directors. Income bargaining, as outlined here, leaves the question of board representation up to bargaining in each sector. German works councils can bargain contracts. To overcome a culture of mistrust pervasive in most American unions and to prevent the penalties associated with enterprise unions, workplace councils as described here are strictly advisory, albeit with information and other rights.

New ways for workers to organize and offer services will not, however, be sufficient to build effective income bargaining. Bargaining requires rules, norms, information, rights, and incentives for organizations to adjust as conditions change.

11. Rules, Rights, and Information

To function effectively, commercial markets depend on customs, laws, courts, and dozens of supporting institutions. Likewise, labor market institutions designed to reduce income polarization require the support of a legal and social infrastructure, including rules that allocate rights and incentives to those who bargain income.

Three rights matter most. Workplaces need audited health and safety and wage-hour standards that safeguard workers without degrading normal business operations. Employer and labor organizations need rights that strengthen their ability to serve as active agents of employers and workers. Above all, both employer and labor organizations need to overcome the massive information asymmetries built into modern labor markets.

Complementing Regulators with Chartered Workplace Auditors

Like much else, workplace regulations have not kept up with the times. Divisions of the U.S. Department of Labor enforce at least fourteen complex laws, each containing thousands of rules, in some 8 million American workplaces.[320] Problems with wage or overtime violations are enforced by the Wage and Hour Division. Health and safety rules are enforced by the Occupational Safety and Health Administration (OSHA). The exception is mine safety, which is covered by a surprisingly large, well-hidden part of the Labor Department called MSHA (the Mine Safety Health Administration). Farmworkers, self-employed people, home health workers, railroad or maritime workers, and public employees often have their own laws and agencies. A farmworker who calls the Labor Department with a health and safety concern will be stunned to learn that Congress assigned the Migrant and Seasonal Agricultural Worker Protection Act not to OSHA, but to the Wage and Hour Division.

Many federal workplace laws are enforced by state agencies or by federal agencies outside of the Labor Department. Congress charged the NLRB with protecting workers who organize unions. The Equal Employment Opportunity Commission enforces laws against discrimination or sexual harassment. Worker compensation issues and laws protecting public employees are handled by state regulators. Many states have health and safety or wage-hour regulations that supersede federal rules because they are more stringent.

When they were created (mostly in the 1930s, although Nixon signed OSHA in 1970 and Clinton signed the Family and Medical Leave Act in 1993), these workplace regulations represented a valuable step forward for workers. As with the National Labor Relations Act, however, most have not evolved with a changing world.[321] OSHA plus inspectors from 22 states with OSHA-approved state programs together hire about 2,400 inspectors to monitor 8 million workplaces. In 2017, they inspected about 75,000 workplaces, meaning that most workplaces will see a health and safety inspector once every century or so.[322] Likewise, the Wage and Hour Administration employs a thousand inspectors to enforce thousands of pages of workplace rules. In 2017, it concluded about 20,000 investigations. In short, the enforcement of federal workplace rules in the US is at high risk of becoming largely symbolic.[323]

This enforcement model is fundamentally flawed. No approach to workplace regulation in which enforcement depends on trained public inspectors can regulate American workplaces—even if Congress were willing to increase staffing. Modern enforcement requires institutions that can specialize, scale, and evolve as workplaces change. Even increasing federal inspectors by an order of magnitude would not achieve this. Today, inspectors need to understand incredibly specialized workplaces. Meatpacking plants, solar energy construction sites, and hospital X-ray rooms face entirely different challenges. As workplaces in these industries introduce new technologies and work processes, workers' needs evolve quickly.

Federally chartered private auditors could ensure fact-based reporting and highly focused enforcement. Companies above a certain size would retain auditors that operate under a federal charter, much as publicly traded companies hire chartered accounting firms to audit and report their financial health and compliance with public accounting standards. Auditors would report on a set of standard measures of workplace health, safety, and compliance with relevant workplace standards. Auditors would charge employers fees to document and certify compliance and disclose relevant performance metrics related to health and safety and employment rules. Auditors would quickly specialize and employer associations would soon develop information as to which workplace auditing firms best understood operations in their industry.

Publicly chartered private auditors can scale and specialize. They have the same incentive that accounting firms do to learn about the specific conditions, economics, technologies, and competitive concerns facing each workplace they audit. Some may offer related services, like online ratification services or deciding to help resolve disputes quickly to ensure that agreements are applied consistently across companies.

It is not difficult to imagine requiring companies with more than one hundred employees or those undertaking hazardous work to audit their workplace annually. They would report standard wage-hour and health and safety results. Federally-chartered auditors would work with managers and the workplace council to develop a plan to comply with federal or state health and safety requirements. Audits would focus on the unique issues of each workplace: chemical or radiation exposure in hospitals, safety in automated manufacturing environments, ergonomics and lighting in almost every office, and sexual harassment prevention most places. Employers would pay the cost but would be exempt from federal or state litigation or inspection, absent a specific emergency safety complaint. Likewise, auditors could undertake a wage-hour compliance review. (Incorporating wage-hour regulations into labor agreements might simplify this further.)

Auditors would collect and report data as specified by the Labor Department. For example, companies might be required to disclose pay disparities (the ratio of the top and bottom decile, or something similar). Without legislating maximum pay, norms would rapidly emerge; companies would be reluctant to raise the pay of their most valuable leaders without considering those who take home the least.[324]

Workplace councils would help develop an employer's plan and education program. The plan and results would be public, so that managers, community members, current workers, and potential employees were all aware of it. The effect would be for companies to focus their efforts on the needs and vulnerabilities of their particular employees and for data and education to drive compliance instead of inspections and penalties. The

DOL would charter workplace auditors and would revoke the credentials of those that proved ineffective. Chartered auditors would hire or train people with deep expertise to surface workplace concerns and make comparable data widely available. Standardized public data would extend the impact of regulators and enable them to focus sharply on the most egregiously irresponsible employers.

Auditors are one way to leverage the limited resources and skills of government regulators. Awards to spur innovation are another. The Commerce Department has done this with the Baldrige Award for manufacturing quality. The Department of Education uses Race to the Top grants to encourage school innovation. If the Department of Labor were to each year award an industry association and its employee organizations a prize of 2 million dollars for original agreements that emphasized speed, effective conflict resolution, or innovative forms of compensation, it would encourage a lot of creative effort. Industry associations or labor co-ops could try something similar by creating awards for innovative workplace councils. These awards work best when agencies make the application process educational and helpful and allow panels of private sector experts to judge applications so that awards are not overly politicized. The Baldrige Award, for example, is widely credited as having an application process rigorous enough that companies derive value from merely applying to be considered for the award.

Earned Bargaining Rights

Income bargaining entails agency risk, the familiar possibility that agents of workers or employers will place their own interest ahead of their principals.[325] Bargaining rights can help address this by strengthening principals—meaning workers, not co-ops and companies, not employer associations.

Proportional bargaining favors rights that are earned, not endowed. The final rules might vary, but until all co-ops in an industry represent perhaps 10–15 percent of all hourly workers, industry associations might submit their proposed income agreements directly to employees for ratification. A third-party service, potentially workplace auditors, would manage the online ratification process under contract with the industry association.

They would publish the proposed terms, answer questions, and conduct private, secure online balloting for both employers and affected workers. If ratified by a majority of affected employees, employers would enjoy their wage subsidy. In this situation, workers have no bargaining agent.

Bargaining does not repeal the laws of economic gravity so much as force them into the open. A co-op with very few members would have little influence with employers or with its peer labor organizations. No set of formal rights conferred by government can overcome this weakness. If workers are indifferent to pleas of solidarity or professionalism from various co-ops, they can easily signal this to employers, who will assuredly get the message. The reverse is also true: as the example of Alabama teachers shows, formal bargaining rights matter very little if workers overwhelmingly support an agent to speak on their behalf.

Proportional rights are non-exclusive and likely to evolve. Once all labor organizations in an industry (including co-ops, craft unions, professional associations, and interest groups) achieve the agreed-upon membership threshold, they would collectively be entitled to ratify any proposed agreement. In sectors where co-ops achieve a higher membership threshold, perhaps a third, they might earn the right to arbitrate an agreement or other bargaining rights. A structure of earned rights gives co-ops a continued incentive to grow—and often to consolidate.

Current labor law spells out mandatory and discretionary subjects of bargaining. One such subject is seniority, which has always suffered agency problems. Senior labor leaders have been members longer, attend meetings more often, hold higher offices, know the rules better, and are much more likely to vote. They can and do use the organization to advance their interests over those of more junior members. Today's labor unions care about seniority rights much more than companies do—so companies nearly always yield to union demands to respect seniority in promotions, transfers, and layoffs. Employers end up agreeing to reward endurance over performance, which is as degrading to high-performing workers as it is to business performance.

Rules to support income bargaining that strengthens principals need to address obvious agency problems. The income agreements that result are likely to be broader but shallower than collective bargaining agreements. They would bargain income, but work rules, seniority provisions, and litigious, multi-stage grievance procedures would be optional subjects of bargaining. Employer associations would be wise to avoid them altogether.

By statute, income agreements would neither ensure seniority rights nor prevent an employer from utilizing seniority in making decisions. Income agreements would support the full right of managers to hire, lay off, assign, transfer, or promote workers. Managers could elect to use seniority as either a strong or weak factor in making these decisions. Note that abandoning strict seniority provisions in labor agreements would permit unions to implement Ghent-style unemployment systems without the risk of adverse selection faced by Ghent plans in Nordic countries.

Severance would be a mandatory subject of bargaining and an essential part of any income agreement. An employer could terminate a worker for nondiscriminatory reasons by making an agreed-upon severance payment. There are three rights embedded in this rule: a manager's right to fire a worker, nondiscrimination, and a terminated worker's right to severance.

Income agreements would not restrict the management rights, but terminating a worker would not be costless. A manager would retain the right to organize and direct work, hire, promote, assign, reward, or terminate people, with severance. Most labor agreements do this today: after a lengthy grievance and arbitration process, the matter is concluded when the company writes a severance check to the terminated employee. It is far easier to negotiate generous no-fault severance terms in advance, as executive employment agreements do. Severance (or advance notice of termination in lieu of severance) makes termination decisions simple—but the cost of the decision is shared, not transferred to the affected worker. When termination decisions cost money, employers take them more seriously.

How generous would severance be? It will vary. Employers will wish to avoid severance so expensive that it creates perverse incentives. Bargaining coalitions will negotiate severance, realizing that increasing the cost of firing employees guarantees fewer full-time hires, more temps, and smaller raises for workers who remain. Ultimately, all firing costs are hiring costs.

Discrimination would remain illegal. Discriminatory hiring, firing, pay, and promotions based on age, race, gender, sexual identity, disability, national origin, pregnancy, or religion would operate under the same bans they do today. As today, federal law would protect whistleblowers and handle claims of sexual harassment—a nontrivial and under-reported issue for women working in low-wage jobs.

Elaborate and litigious grievance procedures are a second agency failure. These procedures plague New Deal collective bargaining. Ultimately, they corrode workplace trust and serve workers poorly, even if they burnish a union's credentials as stubborn litigators. In order to resolve disputes promptly and impartially, without lengthy or legalistic grievance procedures, it is helpful for industries and co-ops to agree on arbitrators, perhaps a service offered by auditing firms, who can hear disagreements and render prompt decisions. Arbitrators who deal with other companies in the same industry agreement can be especially helpful in ensuring consistent standards and interpretation.

To prevent employers and unions from overusing their right to appeal to rapid arbitration, a rule used by the National Football League to avoid excessive appeals to referees may be useful. The NFL allows coaches from either team to appeal a field referee's call on a matter of fact. The issue receives an immediate video review. Both sides have a limit on failed appeals, however. (Not every appeal needs to be a failure for one side.) Faced with a limited appeal path, aggressive time limits, and negotiated limits on the number of failed appeals at each company, both employers and employees will wish to minimize prolonged disputes.

Income agreements would cover full-time and part-time workers hired by the company. Inside contractors, who perform the same work as regular employees, would be covered. Inside contractors provide vacation relief or surge capacity during busy times. At the Nissan plant in Smyrna, Tennessee, however, assembly-line workers are inside contractors employed by Yates Services. They work alongside Nissan employees and do the identical job as Nissan employees.[326] Under an income agreement, inside contractors would have the same incomes, making it much less attractive for employers to use them to avoid paying benefits.

Contractors who are full-time employees of a specialist company, such as security guards, food service staff, or janitorial staff, would be covered by agreements bargained between their employer associations and co-ops in their respective industries.

What about "independent workers," as Seth Harris and Alan Krueger termed them?[327] These workers are contractors, like Uber drivers. They choose their hours, although many work full-time. Independent workers could organize labor co-ops and join bargaining coalitions while remaining contractors. The agreement might obligate employers to contribute to portable benefits, such as health care, retirement savings, or paid time off. It might provide extra payments to contractors who work full-time, or convert them to employees if that is preferable.[328] Giving contract drivers the ability to bargain shift minimums is much more likely to optimize the tradeoff between the number of drivers and passenger wait times than city councils setting arbitrary limits on the number of people who can drive for hire within a city.

Overcoming Information Asymmetry

Economists have long recognized that information asymmetries between employers and employees introduce friction and inefficiency. Employers must extend job offers to workers whose productivity and fit they cannot determine fully in advance. Employees must accept or reject these offers without having spent a single day in the new workplace and with little sense of its culture or standards.

However, every market requires visible prices to operate correctly. This is especially true for labor markets, where information about salaries and wages is often closely held. For employers and labor co-ops to bargain income effectively, they must share common information about pay at different companies within a region and sector. Industry associations need to know the pay schedules and job classification schemes of their affiliated companies. Co-ops need to know which positions currently command higher pay. They need to know when a new workers accepts a job offer in order to determine the interest of a new employee in joining a co-op, craft union, or professional association. Employees want to be able to join or not join labor organizations—even though they also want their privacy rights respected.

The purpose of a National Employment Database would be to support these multiple goals. The database would also assist the Bureau of Labor Statistics to validate research surveys and improve their accuracy.

The mechanics of the database are straightforward: payroll services or software would automatically send the BLS a copy of each worker's name, job title, Social Security number, employment status, pay, benefits, company name, location, labor organization affiliation if any, and email address. The Labor Department would produce public reports that would be sanitized to protect individual salary information.

To support bargaining that is more fact-based, both employee and employer organizations would be entitled to standardized reports from the Employment Database. These would summarize salary data for each company and region covered by the agreement. The report might disclose the total number of employees in each salary bracket of each position, consolidated to avoid disclosing individual salaries. Knowing that businesses will make public the pay bands by job title will also encourage employers to standardize redundant job categories and incomes within job categories.

A National Employment Database would permit labor organizations to send employees two emails each year to determine their interest in joining while protecting workers from privacy breaches. An employee could opt out of these emails, as is typical under CAN-SPAM Act rules governing email, or they could learn more by providing additional personal information to the soliciting organization. Labor organizations would quickly become adept at direct marketing tactics. They would offer free courtesy memberships (get the newsletter), basic low-cost membership (eligible for services), and higher-priced, sustaining memberships for loyalists. Recruiting members on the job would also be protected. The number of employees belonging to each labor or professional organization (but again, not individual identities) would be public information, as it is today.

A National Employment Database would loosen the currently stringent protection of salary data in the US. In Holland, the police punch up individual tax records to set the penalty for a speeding ticket as a fraction of income. In the US, personal and business income and taxes paid were public information, on an individual basis, from the end of the Civil War until 1894 and again during the 1930s. They have long been public in Scandinavian countries, although not always online, free, or comprehensive. Norway now discloses to taxpayers the name of any person who asks to look at their tax return, which seems to discourage the neighbors from prying.[329]

Public disclosure of personal and corporate incomes and tax payments appears to build support for tax compliance, simplicity, and fairness. It may strengthen an ethos of income compression, although this may be more a cause of disclosure than an effect.

Full disclosure is neither likely nor necessary in the United States. The US weighs privacy heavily and has incomes so disparate that the information is more sensitive than it might have been in 1960. (It is interesting to consider what impact a full income and tax disclosure policy begun in 1960 might have had on the shape of present-day American earnings.)

The reports of the National Employment Database would be available to the public for each employer. As a result, labor, policy, or academic organizations could calculate an employer pay equity index using Gini coefficients (more accurate, less intuitive) or the ratio of the average pay of top and bottom deciles. Would this lead companies to compress pay? Maybe. It would reveal which companies pay more in each industry. Since pay disparities are higher between companies than within them, disclosing pay differences might help close the gap between companies within an industry. Or it might confirm that the disparities serve a strategic purpose.

Comparing pay between large firms would be complex since income agreements would frequently index pay to local conditions. The US is a large country, so the ten wealthiest counties (all urban and coastal) pay an average full-time worker $50 per hour (not to be confused with median pay rates)—three times more than the poorest ten counties (all rural, mainly southern) that average $16 per hour.[330] A company operating across a wider geography than its competitor may wrongly appear to have a highly disparate pay structure. Analysts seeking to figure out income equality coefficients for several large companies would need to adjust wages for nontrivial variations in local pay.

Information Tactics in a Reputation-Sensitive Economy

Information is never neutral—and employers and employees alike would take advantage of information transparency. It is useful to consider how breaking down information asymmetries is likely to affect proportional income bargaining. Proportional bargaining consists of three simultaneous negotiations. One is among employers with overlapping but not perfectly aligned objectives. One is among labor organizations—many representing a subset of occupations or workers with specific concerns. On the main stage, two bargaining committees conduct the actual negotiation. This is a substantial effort, so income agreements typically run from three to five years.

Employer associations may face pressure from some employers to raise wages and from others to lower them. Superstar firms might use bargaining to raise wages and punish smaller, less productive, or less monopolistic competitors. Most industry associations will face pressure to prevent large companies from dominating small ones, since association contracts are ratified via one company, one vote. Large companies with more workers may have more influence—but they do not have more votes.

Industry associations will exert a great deal of influence on the character of labor coops. Some of this is simple economics. Low-productivity industries that rely heavily on low-cost labor like hospitality, retail, or janitorial services will be highly tempted to use their bargaining power to force labor costs down. This will, of course, motivate the rise of determined, confrontational labor co-ops. Employers will face a decision: use their bargaining strength to keep wages low and risk promoting the growth of stronger, more adversarial labor organizations or devise more effective bargaining strategies. For example, a smart association will consider the extent and timing of natural turnover in their business as well as regional variations and preferences in structuring pay.

An agreement would take effect once ratified by a majority of affected workers and by a majority of companies in an association. By default, only members of a co-op would vote to ratify an industry agreement, but this too could be made dependent on representational density. Private firms, perhaps auditors, would offer to host secure online meetings, discussions, and voting for both companies within an employer association and workers who belonged to a co-op.

Within the labor bargaining committee will be one or more co-ops representing workers in every occupation as well as craft unions or professional associations representing major occupations. The largest co-op would typically convene bargaining and determine the scope for occupational or interest groups. These internal negotiations between unions and companies on a bargaining committee are part of the income bargaining process, which is broad (it covers many people) but not deep (it covers almost exclusively pay, benefits, and severance, not seniority or work rules). In nearly every sector, the advantages of scale would lead the largest co-ops to merge. The benefit of size will tend to limit employer interest in forming small associations unless the logic for doing so is compelling.

As today, workers whose skills, reputations, or relationships are so distinctive and valuable that they can bargain terms for themselves above those provided in the income agreement would be free to do so. When Silicon Valley companies bid the price of new AI engineering graduates to $500,000 annually, the professional associations for software engineers will applaud and take notes.[331]

Bargaining would therefore vary in extent and intensity across industries. As noted earlier, some sectors might see employers ratifying income agreements directly with workers and claiming their wage subsidy, as might occur if technology or financial services workers chose not to form or join co-ops. Many growing sectors concentrate regionally and attract skilled workers who can change jobs quickly if they are unhappy. Partly as a result, libertarianism thrives, and collective action is often repugnant to workers in these industries. These sectors attract managers who are both motivated to prevent turnover and strong enough to do so. Workers may find no real need to bargain, and employers can agree on wage standards, seek direct ratification from an industry or region's workers, and move on. Where "exit" is more attractive than "voice," workers may choose to bargain individually.[332] Once growth slows or workers decide employers are holding back, however, they will be able to form co-ops quickly.

Proportional bargaining is designed to reflect the changing sources of employer and worker influence. Craft unions have historically relied on skill as their primary source of leverage in bargaining with employers. They limited the supply of skilled labor by controlling access to apprenticeship programs and requiring employers to hire via a union-controlled hiring hall. These closed shops restricted worker opportunity and gave employers a powerful incentive to circumvent the arrangement, which was outlawed by the Taft-Hartley Act.

Industrial unions relied on solidarity—specifically the ability to credibly threaten to strike. Strikes are also a dying tactic. Strikes (and lockouts, which are employer-initiated strikes) have declined in the United States much faster than unions themselves. In 2017, the BLS reported only seven strikes in large workplaces in the entire country. Some lasted a day or less. Since the end of the Great Recession, days lost to strikes or lockouts have dropped below one-half of one percent, at which point the BLS decided to stop counting.[333]

Strikes by workers and lockouts by employers are legal in every country that outlaws compulsory servitude. Strikes play a role in some negotiations, but just because a worker has the right to walk off his or her job individually or collectively and an employer has the right to pause their operations and send employees home does not make it smart to do either. Both strikes and lockouts would remain legal but unattractive for the same reasons they are unattractive today—both parties have available to them tactics that are less risky, less costly, and more likely to produce results.

Employer and worker tactics would reflect the changing nature of an economy where reputations are precious and perishable assets. Income bargaining would operate through the same mix of economic facts, preferences, and strength based on alternatives to a settlement that characterize every negotiation. Changes in technology, information, dispute resolution, and competition have enlarged the sources of both union and employer influence and changed the negotiating terrain. Since they would bargain with an association of employers, labor co-ops might aim fewer of their tactics at individual companies. Or they may focus attention on an influential company that they believe will carry the opinion of their industry association. Because most industries wish to appear responsible and responsive, co-ops will become adept at using this desire to their advantage.

Companies exist to make deals. Literally, without this skill, corporations would not be needed. They are very good at preserving sustainable costs while achieving high-priority goals, including a productive, trust-based relationship with their workers that emphasizes speed and informal problem-solving. Structured correctly, a company's negotiations with its employees can be similar—except that preserving trust is arguably even more critical to people coming to work every day than it is with suppliers of products or services.

Any negotiation can hit an impasse. The tools used to resolve disputes today including fact-finding, mediation, arbitration, and a growing toolkit of alternative dispute resolution methods that have long served public employee negotiations, where many states either restrict strikes by statute or ban them altogether.

Final offer arbitration can go a long way to ensuring good faith bargaining. FOA is interest arbitration in which the arbitrator chooses one of the parties' final proposals (typically overall, but sometimes on each disputed issue). Arbitrators do not give each party "half a loaf," so parties to the negotiation have a strong incentive to create a reasonable offer. Arbitrators would in all cases consider the membership strength of a group of co-ops in evaluating its proposals. A proposal from organizations representing 60 percent of the employees in an industry would and should have much more credibility than one from an organization representing 10 percent.

Arbitration can be overused. A simple rule to prevent this is to pre-ratify all arbitrator decisions to bind both parties. Negotiators could only use arbitrators by turning over to them full control of the outcome—something most negotiators are understandably reluctant to do.

To recap: preserving middle-class incomes requires some form of income bargaining. Bargaining requires employers who organize to strengthen labor markets, regulators who help audit workplaces, rules on what does and does not get bargained, and information to support bargaining and overcome the information asymmetries that plague modern labor markets.

Our journey that began with a red racing queen and failing labor markets has now toured the demise of 20th-century labor unions and glimpsed a possible design for labor market institutions to help reduce income polarization and enhance democracy. It has primarily been an economic expedition, focused on institutions that can moderate profound changes in technology, production, demographics, and global integration. However, economics alone cannot give birth to new labor market institutions. Ultimately, political economy depends on politics.

Conclusion: The Politics of Pay

At their best, capitalism and democracy strengthen each other. They treat people as free agents unchained by heredity or tyrants. They preserve individual choice in matters of consumption, investment, occupation, and voting. They favor the rule of law and steadily expanding suffrage, property ownership, and civil rights. Their partnership has, for better and for worse, driven both the dynamism and the turbulence of the modern era.

The results are impressive. Transportation, communication, media, food, and medicine have become safer and more accessible. Americans are more diverse, less violent, and more connected than ever before. We pollute less and use fewer resources as we get richer. Each generation has produced entrepreneurs who create riches from new technologies and organizers of social movements who secure new rights for disenfranchised groups.

Both capitalism and democracy are social constructs that help us make certain kinds of social choices. Neither are in any sense "natural", ordained by God, or inevitable. Markets enable social choice based on dollars, so those with more money exert greater influence on social choices. At best, this enables those who are better at creating economic value for others to do more of it.

Democracies enable social choices based on one person, one vote. Adults debate who counts as a "person", how political districts will be drawn and minority rights protected, but most children grasp the basic fairness of majority rule.

As a result of these dynamics, capitalism and democracy enjoy nothing like a marriage of equals. Democracies design markets, not vice versa. Thinkers as diverse as Thomas Paine, Thomas Jefferson, Friedrich Hayek, and John F. Kennedy have all cautioned that unless America renews its political design and the institutions that support it, markets will reinforce plutocracy. Democracy becomes vulnerable to despots.

Michael Spence has suggested that democracies design markets with three goals in mind. They must prevent or mitigate market failure, oversee social investments that private investors cannot profitably undertake, and correct distributional outcomes that are so skewed as to be widely viewed as unacceptable.[334] Each of these tasks is complex, but the first two are well-researched and theorized.

Market failures are well understood. They can be caused by private companies shifting costs on to the public -- so-called externalities like pollution or the adverse consequences of global trade on some regions. We have seen that information asymmetries lead to market failure in hiring and often in competition. Finally, monopolies are a form of market failure that every democratic government debates and guards against.

Likewise, the need for public investment is well-researched and theorized. We can demonstrate that adequate public infrastructure, including intangible assets like the social harmony that comes from effective police and court systems, the value of an educated population from public schools, and the fundamental knowledge that comes from research universities cannot always be accomplished privately if the social benefit of these investments exceeds their private returns. As a result, governments everywhere debate the appropriate level of public investment by attempting to understand the future benefits of today's investments. As always, some governments turn out to be better at this than others.

The third function of government, to counter unacceptable distributional outcomes, is the least well developed theoretically and the most contentious politically. After all, who decides what level of income inequality is unacceptable? An extreme view of income inequality impedes the functioning of markets, whereas neglect of the question threatens the public confidence needed to sustain any system of social choices.

One common sense test is that income inequality becomes unacceptable when citizens lose confidence in markets, or worse, in the ability of democratic institutions to act as a countervailing power against companies that grow large enough to threaten economic liberty. If modern capitalism leads invariably to large, politically powerful corporations, then modern democracy needs to embrace public, nonprofit, and labor organizations that can counter corporate power, which will otherwise choke off not only competition, but democracy as well. In a healthy economy, countervailing powers balance each other out.[335]

Instead of revitalizing institutions of countervailing power like unions, employer associations, or regulators, however, America chose to rely on its visible superiority over totalitarian systems in the postwar period

-- even as markets began to subvert democratic norms. As a result, Americans are now much less confident that capitalism and democracy can secure a broad prosperity than they were in the postwar period. Following the Great Recession, which penalized homeowners more than it did equally culpable financial intermediaries, a 2018 survey found that half of young Americans no longer support capitalism. Many claimed to prefer a government of experts instead of one consisting of elected leaders. Just 19 percent of US millennials agreed with the statement that "a military takeover is not legitimate in a democracy."[336]

Addressing a crisis of legitimacy requires an acknowledgment of failure and a commitment to build institutions that rebalance power. Labor market institutions that can bargain a more equitable distribution of income are an excellent foundation upon which to rebuild civil society and support for capitalism and democracy. *A Better Bargain* has proposed seven federal reforms to help create these institutions:

- **Allow employers to form non-overlapping industry associations under federal charter.** These associations can be national or regional. They can merge or divide. Their purpose is to bargain income with labor organizations, set skill standards, and support employer-based occupational training.
- **Encourage workers to form voluntary labor co-ops, professional associations, and interest groups.** Co-ops are open to all workers in an industry. These will map logically onto industry associations. Professional associations or craft unions are open to members of an occupation. Interest groups are open to those who share an identity (parents, Latinos, women) or workplace concerns (health and safety, sexual harassment) that cross industries and occupations.
- **Define the parameters of proportional income bargaining.** The scope of negotiation would cover temps and inside contractors who do substantially the same work as employees. Subjects of bargaining would include wages, severance, audits, and rapid dispute resolution. It would exclude seniority and litigious grievance procedures. It would ban non-compete and non-solicitation agreements. Industry associations would be exempt from antitrust. No-poach agreements would remain illegal.
- **Offer wage subsidies to companies that sign and adhere to their association's income agreement.** Companies would receive wage

subsidies as tax credits. Congress would determine what fraction of each company's payroll below the regional median these credits would pay and what simple tests might prevent companies from gaming the subsidy by cutting wages broadly. Subsidies would replace the EITC so that low-wage workers would receive larger paychecks instead of larger tax refunds.

- **Legalize workplace councils.** Any workplace with more than ten workers could have a workplace council if employees request one. A council would consist of between three and ten non-supervisory employees, depending on workplace size. A council would resolve violations of an industry agreement, discuss changes in the workplace, and address concerns raised by managers, workers, or other council members. It would enjoy information and consultation rights, especially in areas of core concern like staff planning, changes to work processes, the introduction of new technology, training, health and safety, and the particulars of pay, bonuses, working hours, and holidays. A workplace council also helps build workplace trust and engages workers broadly in improving the quality of the company's goods or services.
- **Create a National Employment Database.** Income bargaining requires increased income transparency. A national database would collect weekly payroll data and issue reports summarizing company, industry, and regional pay brackets in a manner that maintains the privacy of individual incomes. The National Employment Database would also provide labor organizations with the ability to solicit membership by email twice annually unless workers opted out of these emails.
- **Require annual workplace audits.** Workplaces with more than one hundred employees would conduct audits, similar to financial audits. Working with management and the workplace council, auditors would collect standard information specified by health and safety and wage-hour regulators. Audits would be public and downloadable to facilitate comparisons. Companies that complied would be exempt from federal inspection absent an emergency safety complaint.

Can the reforms outlined here attract the support of a political coalition committed to building business and labor institutions that can power more inclusive income growth? Faced with a President actively subverting government and civic institutions, the question of the hour is whether a political center exists that can build a coalition to protect middle-class incomes.[337] Can the policies outlined here attract the support of corporations? Of business-minded Democrats and Republicans? Of liberal Democrats? Of libertarians?

Companies would each develop a unique view of costs, benefits, and risks of organizing to set skill standards, outline career paths, and bargain income. Few would suffer economically if wages became less of a competitive factor. Many larger companies already pay above-median wages, so an industry agreement might solidify their advantage. Mid-size companies would benefit from more explicit skill standards and certifications to reduce hiring uncertainty. Most would welcome a shift of training costs from their company to an industry association. Smaller companies with lower pay would benefit disproportionately from the wage subsidy.

Many businesses would prefer chartered private auditors to state or federal inspectors. (Just as they would prefer a private accounting firm to a free federal accountant.) Auditors would develop deeper expertise and knowledge of the company's products, services, people, and processes while being fully accountable to public standards. Likewise, workplace councils would improve the operations of most human resources departments and the quality and legitimacy of management decisions.

The approach undoubtedly contains hidden costs, even if the social, political, and economic value of a vibrant middle class justifies the required investments. Speed, agility, and focus are underappreciated competitive assets, and some managers will worry that an income agreement would slow down a company or divert its attention. The fear is worse because these advantages are hard to measure and the cost of mistrust is borne almost entirely by the employer. A large wage subsidy would compensate companies for some of these unanticipated costs.

Companies that today recognize conventional unions would likely embrace these reforms. They would no longer be required to negotiate enterprise labor agreements. For nonunion companies, the threat of destructive, federally sanctioned union organizing campaigns would vanish. Many business leaders would celebrate the end of the NLRB and the end of exclusive union representation. Some would value the creation of right-to-work laws throughout the land (even if both companies and unions appear to overestimate the impact of these laws).

Would liberal Democrats embrace income bargaining as described here? Most would. Populist Democrats may be more concerned with how income has polarized than how it has stagnated and thus more focused on corralling the top one percent than restarting income growth for the bottom two-thirds. Also, college graduates are overrepresented among Democrats (one reason that forgiving student loans is more popular than forgiving bankruptcy-inducing medical bills). If below-median incomes are to rise faster, the income of those earning above-median incomes would likely rise more slowly. That is roughly the definition of inclusive income growth. The median college graduate would not benefit (although many earning less than median pay would).

Conventional labor unions are backbones of Democratic Party fund-raising and field operations. Would they support income bargaining as described here? Income bargaining as outlined here, might appeal to strong unions, but would quickly eliminate those that do not engage their members. Freed from the need to win representation elections in order to grow, however, unions with imaginative leadership, strong recruiting skills, and an ability to develop new leaders might grow into formidable organizations. They would have access to a workforce of 140 million Americans.[338] The cost of acquiring a new member would drop radically. A well-led co-op that operated effectively in a low-wage sector might attract 5 million members. Unions have never proposed a set of political reforms to enable a better bargain than that.

The challenges facing public sector unions have been detailed already. Those that professionalize and commit to steady improvements in public service quality would see a renewed opportunity for growth and influence. For Democrats who value effective, well-paid, and widely respected teachers, police, and senior administrators, these reforms should be an easy decision. Politically powerful incumbent unions are likely to make sure that it is not.

Libertarian thinking is widespread and influential in the US, especially in the white male precincts of Silicon Valley, but also in New Hampshire, Idaho, and some rural areas. Libertarians often articulate what they dislike more clearly than what they like and some, like Ayn Rand, reserve their deepest vitriol for economic liberals like Milton Friedman. Nonetheless, libertarian thinking contributes importantly to policy debates and should. Many conservatives have come to embrace "Libertarian Lite," "Bleeding heart libertarianism," or, God help us, "liberaltarianism."[339]

Could libertarian thinkers support income bargaining? Milton Friedman famously did, but most would not. There is, however, a compelling argument to test the case. Canada's top-ranked think tank is the Fraser Institute. Fraser devotes itself to maximizing personal freedom and market forces. It is proudly libertarian and relentlessly empirical, bragging that "if it matters, we measure it."

Since 1986, Fraser has graded 159 countries on 76 measures of human freedom. They measure freedom of religion, association, expression, assembly, civil organization, movement, and relationships. They index civil and property rights, access to sound money, freedom to trade internationally, and the efficient regulation of credit, labor, and business. The result is the Index of Economic Freedom. It is a scorecard of economic liberty put together by libertarian economists, not truth on a tablet, but Nobel Laureate Douglass North termed it "the best available…description of efficient markets."[340]

The Fraser Index is revealing. It concludes that in addition to the United States and some island states like Hong Kong, Singapore, and Mauritius, the twenty top countries in the world for economic freedom in 2015 include Switzerland, Ireland, the UK, Australia, Canada, Denmark, Finland, and the Netherlands. These are among the wealthiest countries in the top twenty, and all rely on some form of income bargaining for lower-paid workers to preserve a strong middle class. It appears that income bargaining can complement liberty.

To be sure, each country also has a robust, well-functioning legal system and secure property rights. Some are homogenous, and none are the size of the US. Nonetheless, a prestigious libertarian institute acknowledges that private income bargaining can be compatible with economic freedom. Nations can construct labor markets that leave companies free to pursue creative destruction and countervailing institutions, mainly unions and employer associations, capable of paying the bill for the inevitable human cost. Not every highly ranked country pursued this approach, but most rich ones outside of the US have.

The Index also reveals that a Copernican revolution is underway in rich, complex economies. Companies no longer orbit their shareholders. Market capitalization, or shareholder value, is no longer the sole measure of business performance. Shareholders are a central part of a more complex constellation that acknowledges the claims of employees, communities, and nations affected by a company's work. Fraser shows that this change need neither compromise property rights nor threaten economic liberty.

In the US, pre-Copernican ideals of shareholder value are common in boardrooms but less common outside of them. Day to day, most companies pay a great deal of attention to the impact of their actions on communities, employees, and the country at large. In the US, however, the claims of communities and employees are often cumbersome and costly to assert. Well-designed employer associations and labor organizations can make this process less formal, costly, and legalistic.

What about workers themselves? Would those whose incomes have not grown favor income bargaining? Would they form or join co-ops? Would income bargaining meet the needs of part-time and contingent workers? Of unskilled and immigrant workers? History and several surveys suggest that it would, but there are no guarantees.

There are, of course political, forces aplenty to oppose income bargaining in any form. Some believe that markets alone should determine wages. They oppose income bargaining as rent-seeking, a crucial, if vague and unmeasurable, term that roughly means "using political power to earn money that the market didn't give you." Others favor capital over labor or have concerns that wage increases will slow overall growth. Not all of these concerns are silly, even if many are.

It is possible to imagine the political coalition that endorses corporate, antitrust, and labor market reform but, like income bargaining itself, it is not possible to know outcomes fully in advance. The Great Compression teaches America that "who gets how much?" is not a math question, much less a call for markets to work their magic unassisted. It is instead an invitation to bargain how gains from work become income. There is no predetermined answer: income need not flow exclusively to those who contribute most, nor to those with the greatest need, nor those with the most power. In most systems of distributive justice, each of these factors matter—but none determine the outcome.

Parties to a consensual agreement, however, nearly always consider the arrangement more legitimate than a solution imposed by an employer with greater political or market power. Legitimacy matters because, without it, employers, employees, or capital providers either withdraw from productive activity or subvert it politically. As analyst Will Wilkinson reflected:

> "...whenever we produce a surplus there's always the question of how to divvy it up. If it's a question about how to divide it fairly—about who ought to get what, rather than about who has the power to snatch the most—then it's a question of "distributive justice. "
>
> "Questions of distributive justice are hard. Who did how much work? How well did they do it? How relatively valuable were the efforts of the various contributors to the common enterprise? Maybe everyone agreed to the division in advance. But was the distribution of bargaining power that led to the agreement itself fair?
>
> "Our answers to these questions matter. When the distribution of the burdens and benefits of cooperation aren't fair, we get fed up. And we want to keep positive-sum games going. We need to keep them going. But if we keep getting less than those doing less, we feel used. So we fight for our share. We develop enforcement mechanisms to punish free-riders. We impose sanctions. We negotiate. According to some thinkers, the adaptive function of some of our most basic emotions is to police compliance with norms of cooperation and bargain over who does and gets how much of what. A fit of pique, slow-burning resentment, an explosion of anger—all are common "moves" in everyday distributional negotiation. If we can't negotiate a fairer deal, we'll withdraw or minimize our efforts, one way or another. The surpluses will get smaller. Positive-sum enrichment might turn into negative-sum conflict. Lacking good exit options, mainly we press on and bargain the best we can with the leverage we've got."

Advances in neuroscience help explain that people bargain this way not because we are spiteful, but because we are human. Mounting evidence suggests that sapiens triumphed due to a unique ability to cooperate in getting work done. More than an opposable thumb, the ability to collaborate and to convince others of the benefits of collaboration has made us successful as a species and wealthy as individuals. Our idiosyncratic, easily hacked stack of human wetware appears to have evolved complex mechanisms to justify beliefs that let us work together.[341]

As a result, reciprocation appears to be a core belief of every human culture. We are not selfless. We are acutely aware that individuals can free-ride in the name of cooperation. We therefore not only cooperate, but we also establish norms as to who does what and who gets what. We monitor whether others reciprocate to ensure that we are not getting less than those doing less. We police compliance and impose sanctions on free-riders to avoid zero-sum fighting.

This monitoring gives humans something akin to a justice gene. Workers, no less than managers and investors, either negotiate a deal that seems fair or withdraw or minimize their efforts. When this happens, the surplus shrinks, and there is less to negotiate over. Positive-sum efforts that make everyone richer become negative-sum conflicts that leave everyone poorer.

This is why humans react poorly to those who take more than their share. It is why alarm bells go off when managers who preach the virtues of cooperation to create wealth prefer autocracy when they distribute it. Unlike US Marine Corps officers who always eat last, these managers reserve a generous cut for themselves before the meal begins and denounce as uncooperative any who dare to object. We need to revitalize the norms, covenants, and institutions that make our economy and democracy work based on pluralistic capitalism, fiscal prudence, and education targeted at non-college workers.

Thanks in part to a painfully acquired genetic instinct for fairness, economic justice is always a negotiation and always has been. When the negotiation works, it strengthens civic life, produces more equitable outcomes, and legitimizes the surrounding political and economic institutions. It also confers dignity on those who earn the least, which, in the present day, can be as important as income.

For these reasons, considering known costs and risks, it is worth testing a new system of income bargaining.

Acknowledgments

My first thanks are to those who influenced me most: my parents, family, friends, teachers, coaches, and colleagues. They shaped my thoughts, emotional priors, and love of work. If I fail to name you here it isn't because I appreciate you any less.

During my decade as a union leader, I had the benefit of excellent friends and mentors. Like many college students, I was inspired by Cesar Chavez and trained as a community organizer by Fred Ross Jr. at Hospital Workers Local 250 SEIU, Tim McCormick, shop steward Marilyn Benson at Salinas Valley Memorial, and the late Bob Gerstenlauer taught me the practical steps of building a local union of health care workers. At the International Association of Machinists, where I attempted with little success to organize workers at several of Silicon Valley's early technology companies, I learned a great deal about leadership from my co-workers at Westinghouse, from Justin Ostro and the late Frank Souza.

My teachers during my years with labor included some of the finest leaders I have encountered anywhere: Marshall Ganz of the UFW, Andy Stern at SEIU, Morty Bahr and Larry Cohen at CWA, Leo Gerard and Ron Bloom at the Steelworkers, Peter Cervantes-Gautschi at the Santa Clara County Central Labor Council as well as Kim Fellner, Randy Barber, and many activists who joined them to debate labor's future. I learned as well from militants, communists, and dissidents at the edges of the labor movement who repeatedly demonstrated their courage and principle. You know who you are.

At McKinsey, my greatest debt is to Ted Hall, who took a chance on a guy with a nonstandard resume and held me and everyone else to high professional standards. Michael Dalby, Bob Kaplan, Paul Hasse, Lenny Mendonca, Don Waters, and many others showed me in deeds as much as words that relentless, fact-based investigations could yield honest, pragmatic results. Michael Dalby gave me valuable feedback on early drafts of the book. Ted and Lenny started the McKinsey Global Institute and today James Manyika and Michael Chui in San Francisco and their worldwide colleagues at MGI continue to bring smart, disciplined analytics to a broad range of social questions around the world. I cite a tiny fraction of their prolific output.

I appreciate the support I have had from colleagues, investors, clients, and cofounders in a variety of workplaces, including Katherine Boshkoff, Rebecca Churchill, Mariah DeLeon, Brian Elliott, Art Gensler, Steve Hodges, Chris Holmes, John Ingram, Amal Johnson, Paul Klingenstein, Mukul Kumar, Larry Louie, Jim McLean, Gabe Mendoza, David Pockell, Georgios Papadopoulos, Bob Rebitzer, Michael Schaffer, Michael Solomon, Dimitris Spanos, Gordon Tibbitts, Bernard Tyson, Bob Waterman, and Richard Weatherford. In case I neglected to say it at the time—my deep thanks to each of you.

At the Clinton/Reich Labor Department, I appreciated the work and wisdom of my colleagues, including Olena Berg, the late Joe Dear, Jack Donahue, Maria Echaveste, Tom Glynn, Kitty Higgins, Larry Katz, Karen Nussbaum, and the late Tom Williamson.

A Better Bargain owes deep intellectual debts to several labor economists who had nothing to do with the book. Researchers like David Autor, Raj Chetty, Richard Freeman, the late Alan Krueger, Dani Rodrik, Bob Solow, and Mike Spence affect the lives of working Americans far more deeply than commonly recognized. Their work has influenced me a great deal—if in places surely not enough. As Google Chief Economist Hal Varian warns, "the only thing more dangerous than a professional economist is an amateur economist".

In researching the book, I learned as well from the writings and in some cases the advice of James Bessen, Jared Bernstein, Alan Blinder, Barry Bluestone, Erik Brynjolfsson, Peter Cappelli, David Card, Claudia Goldin, Tyler Cowen, Brad DeLong, Arindrajit Dube, Jason Furman, James Heckman, Larry Katz, Tom Kochan, Paul Krugman, Robert Kuttner, Andrew McAfee, Larry Mishel, Tim O'Reilly, Michael Piore, Michael Porter, James Rebitzer, Robert Reich, Chuck Sabel, Emmanuel Saez, Betsey Stevenson, Cass Sunstein, Larry Summers, Alex Tabarrok, Laura Tyson, Richard Thaler, Hal Varian, Steve Weber, David Weil, Justin Wolfers, and Gabriel Zucman. Cowen and Tabarrok's blog *Marginal Revolution*, Russ Roberts' podcast *Econ Talk*, and posts by David Leonhardt and Noah Smith frequently pointed me to ideas and sources I would otherwise not have discovered. Both Jim Rebitzer and Bob Kuttner encouraged me to write the book from its earliest days. These folks taught me a lot, but none of them endorses a word of this book – and a few may disavow it.

I owe a particular debt to Robert Reich, not only for his tireless writing and teaching on income inequality but for a risk he took as a freshly nominated US Secretary of Labor. Bob backed a high-risk plan for an entrepreneurial new agency, The Office of the American Workplace, in a Labor Department wired more for enforcement, grant-making, and data gathering than for local testing, learning, and teaching. Bob is a national treasure, the rare leader who manages to enjoy confrontation as much as education and emerge loved not only by his friends but frequently by his adversaries. Even and perhaps especially when I disagree with Bob, I admire the hell out of him.

Katie Weaver relentlessly but graciously edited my drafts into more readable form and Coralie Emberson proofed the book and built the index. Andy Meaden designed the book inside and out. Lisa Adams promoted a book that did not naturally stir the commercial hearts of most publishers. Thanks very much to each of you.

I dedicate the book to AnnaLee Saxenian and Steve Manley. Steve was my kid brother, killed fighting fire with the California Division of Forestry (now Cal Fire) shortly after his twenty-first birthday. Loggers, fishermen, miners, roofers, ironworkers, firefighters, powerline workers, cops, prison guards, and other men and sometimes women do work every day that can suddenly turn lethal. In most countries, including ours, work kills more people than war—between four and five thousand Americans each year—some 2.3 million workers worldwide. Initiatives and organizations devoted to workplace safety often bring out the best of employer, worker, and community organizations—as well they should.

Anno is my wisest, dearest, and most trusted critic and she raised Jamie and Robbie with her virtues. Regardless of how deep and confident the voice that expresses it, opinions unsupported by facts, logic, and empathy don't stand long here. There can be no power greater anywhere beneath the sun.

Martin Manley

For more a decade in the mid-1970s, Martin Manley organized unions and represented workers for Hotel and Restaurant Workers (now HERE), Hospital Workers (SEIU), and Machinists (IAM&AW). A journeyman machinist, Manley was elected the Political Director of the Silicon Valley AFL-CIO.

Convinced that labor needed to better understand corporate strategy, operations, and finance, he earned an honors degree from Harvard Business School and joined McKinsey & Co. In 1993, President Bill Clinton nominated Manley to create and lead a new federal agency, the Office of the American Workplace, as US Assistant Secretary of Labor.

As the Internet emerged in the late '90s, Manley co-founded e-commerce pioneer Alibris and served as its CEO for ten years. Manley has also held executive positions at Kaiser Permanente, RedLink, and Hult International Business School.

Marty lives in Oakland, California. Follow him on Twitter @martymanley.

Bibliography

Ackerman, Bruce, and Ian Ayres. *Voting with Dollars: A New Paradigm for Campaign Finance*. Yale University Press, 2008.

Anderson, Chris. *Makers: The New Industrial Revolution.* Crown Publishing Group, 2012.

Autor, David, David Dorn, Gordon Hanson, and Kaveh Majlesi. "Importing Political Polarization?" Massachusetts Institute of Technology Manuscript, 2016.

Autor, David, David Dorn, Lawrence F. Katz, Christina Patterson, and John Van Reenen. "Concentrating on the Fall of the Labor Share." American Economic Review 107, no. 5 (May 2017): 180–85.

Autor, David H. "Why Are There Still So Many Jobs? The History and Future of Workplace Automation †." Journal of Economic Perspectives 29, no. 3 (2015): 3–30.

Autor, David H., David Dorn, and Gordon H. Hanson. "The China Shock: Learning from Labor Market Adjustment to Large Changes in Trade." National Bureau of Economic Research, 2016.

Autor, David H., Alan Manning, and Christopher L. Smith. "The Contribution of the Minimum Wage to US Wage Inequality over Three Decades: A Reassessment." American Economic Journal: Applied Economics 8, no. 1 (January 2016): 58–99.

Azar, José, Ioana Marinescu, and Marshall I Steinbaum. "Labor Market Concentration." Working Paper. National Bureau of Economic Research, December 2017.

Baldwin, Richard. *The Great Convergence*. Harvard University Press, 2016.

Bardacke, Frank. Trampling Out the Vintage: Cesar Chavez and the Two Souls of the United Farm Workers. Verso, 2011.

Benkler, Yochai. The Wealth of Networks: How Social Production Transforms Markets and Freedom. Yale University Press, 2006.

Bennett, James T., and Bruce E. Kaufman, eds. *What Do Unions Do?: A Twenty-Year Perspective*. New Brunswick, N.J.: Transaction Publishers, 2007.

Bernstein, Irving. *The Lean Years: A History of the American Worker, 1920-1933.* Penguin Publishing Group, 1966.

Bessen, James. Learning by Doing: The Real Connection between Innovation, Wages, and Wealth. Yale University Press, 2015.

Blair, Peter Q., and Bobby W. Chung. "How Much of Barrier to Entry Is Occupational Licensing?" National Bureau of Economic Research, November 16, 2018.

Blanchflower, David G., and Alex Bryson. "The Union Wage Premium in the US and the UK." CEPDP 612 (February 2004).

"What Effect Do Unions Have on Wages Now and Would Freeman and Medoff Be Surprised?" Journal of Labor Research 25, no. 3 (September 1, 2004): 383–414.

Bock, Laszlo. Work Rules!: Insights from Inside Google That Will Transform How You Live and Lead. Hachette UK, 2015.

Bognanno, Mario F., and Morris M. Kleiner. "Introduction: Labor Market Institutions and the Future Role of Unions." Industrial Relations: A Journal of Economy and Society 31, no. 1 (1992): 1–12.

Bureau of Labor Statistics, US Department of Labor. "Contingent and Alternative Employment Arrangements," February 2005.

"Contingent and Alternative Employment Arrangements," USDL 18-0942, May 2017.

Caplan, Bryan. The Case against Education: Why the Education System Is a Waste of Time and Money. Princeton University Press, 2018.

Cappelli, Peter. Will College Pay Off?: A Guide to the Most Important Financial Decision You'll Ever Make. Public Affairs, 2015.

Card, David. "Is the New Immigration Really So Bad?" The Economic Journal 115, no. 507 (2005): F300–F323.

Card, David, and Alan B. Krueger. "Minimum Wages and Employment: A Case Study of the Fast Food Industry in New Jersey and Pennsylvania." National Bureau of Economic Research, 1993.

Myth and Measurement: The New Economics of the Minimum Wage. Twentieth-Anniversary edition. Princeton University Press, 2015.

Card, David, and John E. DiNardo. "Skill-Biased Technological Change and Rising Wage Inequality: Some Problems and Puzzles." Journal of Labor Economics 20, no. 4 (October 1, 2002): 733–83.

Caroline M. Hoxby. "The Dramatic Economics of the U.S. Market for Higher Education," 2016.

Chetty, Raj, John N. Friedman, Nathaniel Hilger, Emmanuel Saez, Diane Whitmore Schanzenbach, and Danny Yagan. "How Does Your Kindergarten Classroom Affect Your

Earnings? Evidence from Project STAR." Working Paper. National Bureau of Economic Research, September 2010.

Chetty, Raj, John N. Friedman, and Jonah E. Rockoff. "The Long-Term Impacts of Teachers: Teacher Value-Added and Student Outcomes in Adulthood." Working Paper. National Bureau of Economic Research, December 2011.

Chetty, Raj, David Grusky, Maximilian Hell, Nathaniel Hendren, Robert Manduca, and Jimmy Narang. "The Fading American Dream: Trends in Absolute Income Mobility since 1940." Science 356, no. 6336 (April 28, 2017): 398–406.

Cowen, Tyler. The Complacent Class: The Self-Defeating Quest for the American Dream. St. Martin's Press, 2017

David, Paul A. "The Dynamo and the Computer: An Historical Perspective on the Modern Productivity Paradox." The American Economic Review 80, no. 2 (1990): 355–61

De Loecker, Jan, and Jan Eeckhout. "The Rise of Market Power and the Macroeconomic Implications." National Bureau of Economic Research, 2017.

Donahue, John D. *The Warping of Government Work.* Cambridge, Mass: Harvard University Press, 2008.

Eberstadt, Nicholas. *Men Without Work: America's Invisible Crisis*. Templeton Press, 2016.

Edin, Kathryn J., and H. Luke Shaefer. *$2.00 a Day: Living on Almost Nothing in America*. Houghton Mifflin Harcourt, 2015.

Fallows, James, and Deborah Fallows. *Our Towns: A 100,000-Mile Journey into the Heart of America*. Knopf Doubleday Publishing Group, 2018.

Farber, Henry. "Union Organizing Decisions in a Deteriorating Environment: The Composition of Representation Elections and the Decline in Turnout." Working Paper, 2013.

———. "Union Success in Representation Elections: Why Does Unit Size Matter?" Princeton University Industrial Relations Section, no. Working Paper #420 (June 1999).

Farber, Henry S., Daniel Herbst, Ilyana Kuziemko, and Suresh Naidu. "Unions and Inequality Over the Twentieth-century: New Evidence from Survey Data." Princeton University Industrial Relations Section, no. 620 (May 2018): 94.

Ferguson, John-Paul. "The Eyes of the Needles: A Sequential Model of Union Organizing Drives, 1999–2004." ILR Review 62, no. 1 (October 1, 2008): 3–21.

Fleck, Susan, John Glaser, and Shawn Sprague. "The Compensation-Productivity Gap: A

Visual Essay." Monthly Labor Review, no. January (2011): 57–69.

Frandsen, Brigham R. "The Effects of Collective Bargaining Rights on Public Employee Compensation: Evidence from Teachers, Firefighters, and Police." ILR Review 69, no. 1. 2016.

Freeman, R. B., and James L. Medoff. *What Do Unions Do?* New York: Basic Books, 1986.

Freeman, Richard B. "Unionism and the Dispersion of Wages." Industrial & Labor Relations Review 34, no. 1 (1980): 3–23.

———. "What Can We Learn from the NLRA to Create Labor Law for the Twenty-First Century?" ABA Journal of Labor & Employment Law, 2011, 327–343.

Freeman, Richard B., and Casey Ichniowski. *When Public Sector Workers Unionize.* University of Chicago Press, 2007.

Ganong, Peter, and Daniel Shoag. "Why Has Regional Income Convergence in the US Declined?", 2013.

Garmaise, Mark J. "Ties That Truly Bind: Noncompetition Agreements, Executive Compensation, and Firm Investment." The Journal of Law, Economics, and Organization 27, no. 2 (2011): 376–425.

Goldin, Claudia Dale and Hugh Rockoff, eds. *Strategic Factors in Nineteenth Century American Economic History: A Volume to Honor Robert W. Fogel*, National Bureau of Economic Research Conference Report. Chicago: University of Chicago Press, 1992.

Gordon, Robert J. The Rise and Fall of American Growth: The U.S. Standard of Living since the Civil War. Princeton University Press, 2016.

Gordon, Robert J. "U.S. Productivity Growth: The Slowdown Has Returned After a Temporary Revival." International Productivity Monitor, no. 25 (2013): 7.

Guvenen, Fatih, Greg Kaplan, Jae Song, and Justin Weidner. "Lifetime Incomes in the United States over Six Decades." Working Paper. National Bureau of Economic Research, April 2017.

Hadfield, Gillian. Rules for a Flat World: Why Humans Invented Law and How to Reinvent It for a Complex Global Economy. Oxford University Press, 2016.

Hanushek, Eric A. "The Economic Value of Higher Teacher Quality," December 2010.

Hirsch, Barry T. "Reconsidering Union Wage Effects: Surveying New Evidence on an Old Topic." Journal of Labor Research 25, no. 2 (2004): 233–266.

———. "What Do Unions Do for Economic Performance?" Journal of Labor Research Volume XXV, no. Number 3 (Summer 2004).

Hirschl, Thomas A., and Mark R. Rank. "The Life Course Dynamics of Affluence." PLOS ONE 10, no. 1 (January 28, 2015): e0116370.

Hirschman, Albert O. *Exit, Voice, and Loyalty: Responses to Decline in Firms, Organizations, and States*. Cambridge, Mass: Harvard University Press, 1970.

Hlatshwayo, Sandile, and Michael Spence. "Demand and Defective Growth Patterns: The Role of the Tradable and Non-Tradable Sectors in an Open Economy." American Economic Review 104, no. 5 (May 2014): 272–77.

Ipeirotis, Panagiotis G. "Demographics of Mechanical Turk." SSRN Scholarly Paper. Rochester, NY: Social Science Research Network, March 1, 2010.

Jardim, Ekaterina, Mark C. Long, Robert Plotnick, Emma van Inwegen, Jacob Vigdor, and Hilary Wething. "Minimum Wage Increases and Individual Employment Trajectories." Working Paper. National Bureau of Economic Research, October 2018.

Jardim, Ekaterina, Mark C. Long, Robert Plotnick, Emma van Inwegen, Jacob Vigdor, and Hilary Wething. "Minimum Wage Increases, Wages, and Low-Wage Employment: Evidence from Seattle." National Bureau of Economic Research, 2017.

Karabarbounis, Loukas, and Brent Neiman. "The Global Decline of the Labor Share." Working Paper. National Bureau of Economic Research, June 2013.

Katz, Lawrence F., and Alan B. Krueger. "The Rise and Nature of Alternative Work Arrangements in the United States, 1995-2015," 2016.

Katz, Lawrence F., and Alan B. Krueger. "Understanding Trends in Alternative Work Arrangements in the United States." Working Paper. National Bureau of Economic Research, January 2019.

Keefe, J. "Are Public Employees Overpaid?" Labor Studies Journal 37, no. 1 (March 1, 2012): 104–26.

Kjellberg, Anders. "The Decline in Swedish Union Density since 2007." Nordic Journal of Working Life Studies 1, no. 1 (2011): 67–93.

Kleiner, Morris. "Intensity of Management Resistance: Understanding the Decline of Unionization in the Private Sector." Journal of Labor Research XXII, no. 3 (Summer 2001).

Kochan, Thomas A., Adrienne E. Eaton, Robert B. McKersie, and Paul S. Adler. *Healing Togeth er: The Labor-Management Partnership at Kaiser Permanente*. 1 edition. ILR Press, 2013.

Lee, David S., and Alexandre Mas. "Long-Run Impacts of Unions on Firms: New Evidence from Financial Markets, 1961–1999." The Quarterly Journal of Economics 127, no. 1 (February 1, 2012): 333–78.

Levitt, Steven D., "Using Repeat Challengers to Estimate the Effect of Campaign Spending on Election Outcomes in the US House." The Journal of Political Economy 102, no. 4 (August 1994): 777–98.

Lindsey, Brink, and Steven Teles. *The Captured Economy: How the Powerful Enrich Themselves, Slow Down Growth, and Increase Inequality*. 1 edition. New York, NY, United States of America: Oxford University Press, 2017.

Mangum, Garth L., and David E. McNabb. *Collective Bargaining in the Basic Steel Industry: The Rise, Fall and Replacement of Industry-Wide Bargaining*. 1 edition. Armonk, N.Y.: Routledge, 1997.

Martin, Lerone A. Preaching on Wax: The Phonograph and the Shaping of Modern African American Religion. NYU Press, 2014.

Milyo, Jeffrey. "What Do Candidates Maximize (and Why Should Anyone Care)?" Public Choice 109, no. 1–2 (2001): 119–39.

Milyo, Jeffrey, and Timothy Groseclose. "Electoral Effects of Incumbent Wealth, The." Journal of Law & Economics 42 (1999): 699.

Moretti, Enrico. "Real Wage Inequality." American Economic Journal: Applied Economics 5, no. 1 (January 2013): 65–103.

———. The New Geography of Jobs. Houghton Mifflin Harcourt, 2012.

Page, Joshua. *The Toughest Beat: Politics, Punishment, and the Prison Officers Union in California*. Reprint edition. Oxford; New York, N.Y.: Oxford University Press, 2013.

Piore, Michael J., and Andrew Schrank. *Root-Cause Regulation: Protecting Work and Workers in the Twenty-First Century*. Cambridge, Massachusetts: Harvard University Press, 2018.

Piore, Michael, and Charles Sabel. *The Second Industrial Divide: Possibilities For Prosperity*. Reprint edition. New York: Basic Books, 1986.

Rank, Mark R., and Thomas A. Hirschl. "The Likelihood of Experiencing Relative Poverty over the Life Course." PLOS ONE 10, no. 7 (July 22, 2015): e0133513

Redbird, Beth. "The New Closed Shop? The Economic and Structural Effects of Occupational Licensure." American Sociological Review 82(3) 600–624 (2017): 25.

Reid, Joseph, and Kurth, Michael M. "The Rise and Fall of Urban Political Patronage Machines." In Strategic Factors in Nineteenth Century American Economic History: A Volume to Honor Robert W. Fogel, edited by Claudia Dale Goldin and Hugh Rockoff. A National Bureau of Economic Research Conference Report. Chicago: University of Chicago Press, 1992.

Roberts, Russ. How Adam Smith Can Change Your Life: An Unexpected Guide to Human Nature and Happiness. Portfolio, 2014.

Rolf, David. *The Fight for Fifteen: The Right Wage for a Working America.* New York: The New Press, 2016.

Rosenfeld, Jake, and Meredith Kleykamp. "Organized Labor and Racial Wage Inequality in the United States." American Journal of Sociology 117, no. 5 (March 1, 2012): 1460–1502.

Saez, Emmanuel. "Striking It Richer: The Evolution of Top Incomes in the United States," March 2, 2012.

Saxenian, AnnaLee. *Regional Advantage: Culture and Competition in Silicon Valley and Route 128.* Harvard University Press, 1996.

Smith, Adam. *The Theory of Moral Sentiments.* Edited by Paul Boer. Excercere Cerebrum Publications, 2014.

———. *The Wealth of Nations*: Edited by Edwin Cannan. Modern Library, 2000.

Spence, Michael. "Job Market Signaling." The Quarterly Journal of Economics 87, no. 3 (August 1973): 355.

Staiger, Douglas O., and Jonah E. Rockoff. "Searching for Effective Teachers with Imperfect Information." Journal of Economic Perspectives 24, no. 3 (September 2010): 97–118.

Starr, Evan, J. J. Prescott, and Norman Bishara. "Non-competes in the U.S. Labor Force." SSRN Scholarly Paper. Rochester, NY: Social Science Research Network, January 12, 2019.

Starr, Kevin. *Embattled Dreams: California in War and Peace, 1940-1950.* Oxford University Press, USA, 2002.

Stern, Andy, and Lee Kravitz. Raising the Floor: How a Universal Basic Income Can Renew Our Economy and Rebuild the American Dream. Public Affairs, 2016.

Vestal, Stanley. *Sitting Bull: Champion of the Sioux*. University of Oklahoma Press, 2014.

Visser, Jelle. *Wage Bargaining Institutions from Crisis to Crisis*. Brussels: European. Comm., Directorate-General for Economic and Financial Affairs, 2013.

Williamson, Oliver (1968). "Wage Rates as a Barrier to Entry: The Pennington Case", The Quarterly Journal of Economics, 82(1): 815-116.

Winterhager, Henrik, Anja Heinze, and Alexander Spermann. "Deregulating Job Placement in Europe: A Microeconometric Evaluation of an Innovative Voucher Scheme in Germany." Labour Economics 13, no. 4 (2006): 505–517.

Notes

Introduction: Racing the Red Queen

1. Introduction: Racing the Red Queen. Paul Krugman. "Introducing This Blog: The Great Compression." Paul Krugman Blog (blog), September 18, 2007. https://krugman.blogs.nytimes.com/2007/09/18/introducing-this-blog/.

2. A welcome exception to this general rule is New Zealand, which formed a Fair Pay Working Group to recommend the design of a sector-level bargaining system, in order to establish minimum terms and conditions for all workers in an industry or occupation. They summarized their recommendations in a report "Fair Pay Agreements—Working Group Report," December 20, 2018, available at https://www.mbie.govt.nz/assets/695e21c9c3/working-group-report.pdf.

3. Leonhardt, David. "The American Dream, Quantified at Last." The New York Times, December 8, 2016. http://www.nytimes.com/2016/12/08/opinion/the-american-dream-quantified-at-last.html. These findings elaborated the conclusions of researchers at the San Francisco Federal Reserve that the ability of children to change their rank in the income distribution relative to their parents has declined. "U.S. Economic Mobility: The Dream and the Data." Federal Reserve Bank of San Francisco. http://www.frbsf.org/economic-research/publications/economic-letter/2013/march/us-economic-mobility-dream-data/.

4. Raj Chetty, et al. 2017.

5. Saez, 2012. Saez came up with 21 percent, Piketty 23 percent, and Pew 18 percent because they used different definitions of income. See https://www.theatlantic.com/business/archive/2016/03/brookings-1-percent/473478/.

6. Some economists have argued that consumption, not income, is the best way to measure equality. Bruce Meyer, an economist at the University of Chicago, has published a series of papers with James Sullivan arguing for measuring consumption, not income. Several other researchers have done the same. Meyer concludes that "The evidence from this literature is mixed. Some studies show little change in consumption inequality over the past few decades and others show a proportional rise equal to or exceeding that of incomes." He also notes, as have most researchers, that data quality declines with income and that important income sources for those at the bottom of the distribution are significantly underreported in surveys (and presumably tax returns). See Meyer, Bruce D., and

James X Sullivan. "Consumption and Income Inequality in the U.S. Since the 1960s." *National Bureau of Economic Research* Working Paper No. 23655 (August 2017). https://www.nber.org/papers/w23655.pdf.

7. Appelbaum, Binyamin, ed. "The Jobs Americans Do." *The New York Times*, February 23, 2017, sec. Magazine. https://www.nytimes.com/2017/02/23/magazine/the-new-working-class.html.

8. For a robust discussion of the value of absolute vs. relative economic mobility and an argument for using panel instead of time series census data to capture the state of US occupational mobility, see Roberts, Russ. "Do the Rich Capture All the Gains from Economic Growth?" Medium, October 23, 2018. https://medium.com/@russroberts/do-the-rich-capture-all-the-gains-from-economic-growth-c96d93101f9c.

Roberts argues that income polarization is over-reported and criticizes the use of tax-reported income, noting that wealthy families can more easily underreport income than families relying primarily on W2 and 1099 income. This is true, but would lead tax-based analysis to under-report income polarization.

9. Emmanuel Saez, and Gabriel Zucman. "Wealth Inequality in the United States since 1913: Evidence from Capitalized Income Tax Data." The Quarterly Journal of Economics 131, no. 2 (May 2016). https://eml.berkeley.edu/~saez/SaezZucman2016QJE.pdf.

10. Stewart, Matthew. "The 9.9 Percent Is the New American Aristocracy." *The Atlantic*, June 2018. https://www.theatlantic.com/magazine/archive/2018/06/the-birth-of-a-new-american-aristocracy/559130/.

11. Hirschl, and Rank, 2015. Guvenen, Fatih, Greg Kaplan, Jae Song, and Justin Weidner. "Lifetime Incomes in the United States over Six Decades." Working Paper. National Bureau of Economic Research, April 2017. https://doi.org/10.3386/w23371.

12. Rank and Hirschl, 2015.

13. Guvenen, Fatih, 2017.

14. The BLS publishes a useful explanation of the "Differences between the Consumer Price Index and the Personal Consumption Expenditures Price Index," at https://www.bls.gov/opub/btn/archive/differences-between-the-consumer-price-index-and-the-personal-consumption-expenditures-price-index.pdf.

15. Jason DeBacker, Bradley Heim, Vasia Panousi, and Ivan Vidangos. "Rising Inequality: Transitory or Permanent? New Evidence from a US Panel of Household Income 1987-2006." FRB: Finance and Economics Discussion Series, 2011. https://www.federalreserve.gov/PubS/feds/2011/201160/.

16. Miles Corak (2013), "Inequality from Generation to Generation: The United States in Comparison," in Robert Rycroft (editor), The Economics of Inequality, Poverty, and Discrimination in the 21st Century, ABC-CLIO.

17. Great Gatsby Curve updated with IGE data from Corak, Miles. "Inequality from Generation to Generation" Discussion Paper 9929 Institute for Study of Labor (IZA), Bonn, Germany. http://ftp.iza.org/dp9929.pdf and Gini coefficient estimates from the World Bank "GINI Index" https://data.worldbank.org/indicator/SI.POV.GINI?locations=SE.

18. Mickey Kaus, "The Most Important Chart," kausfiles.com (blog), May 17, 2017, http://www.kausfiles.com/2017/05/17/the-most-important-chart/. Chart from Economic Policy Institute, State of Working America Data Library, "Wage-Education Series," 2018 based on Current Population Survey Outgoing Rotation Group microdata.

19. Ibid.

20. An above-median (50th to 90th percentile) high-school-only grad took home between $35,000 and $73,000 in 2016. This is often more than low-earning bachelor's degree holders (10th to 50th percentile), who took home between $29,000 and $60,000. "Weekly Earnings by Educational Attainment in First Quarter 2016 : The Economics Daily: U.S. Bureau of Labor Statistics." https://www.bls.gov/opub/ted/2016/weekly-earnings-by-educational-attainment-in-first-quarter-2016.htm.

21. Auten, Gerald, and David Splinter. "Using Tax Data to Measure Long-Term Trends in US Income Inequality," (Draft manuscript) December 23, 2016. https://www.aeaweb.org/conference/2017/preliminary/paper/NkfkQ2ak.

22. Tyson, Alec, and Shiva Maniam. "Behind Trump's Victory: Divisions by Race, Gender, Education." Pew Research Center (blog), November 9, 2016. http://www.pewresearch.org/fact-tank/2016/11/09/behind-trumps-victory-divisions-by-race-gender-education.

23. Appelbaum, Binyamin, ed. "The Jobs Americans Do." *The New York Times*, February 23, 2017, sec. Magazine. https://www.nytimes.com/2017/02/23/magazine/the-new-working-class.html.

24. See Romei, Valentina. "US Statisticians Are in the Dark over the 20 Million Working-Age Americans Who Don't Want a Job." Financial Times, October 16, 2015. https://www.ft.com/content/d40d9120-5c13-3bc8-bca2-158d098e3667.

25. The US labor force participation rate has been shrinking since it peaked in the late 1990s and is now back to levels seen in the 1980s. Suggested reasons for the fall include

an aging population, illness or disability, family responsibilities, young people living longer at home or taking longer to graduate, changes in statistical methods, and an unfriendly working environment for mothers. None of these answers appear to be fully explanatory.

26. Guyot, Katherine and Richard V. Reeves. "College Friends Keep Getting Married? It's Bad News for Your Travel Budget… and Inequality." Brookings (blog), November 17, 2017. https://www.brookings.edu/blog/social-mobility-memos/2017/11/17/college-friends-keep-getting-married-its-bad-news-for-your-travel-budget-and-inequality/.

27. Eberstadt, 2016.

28. Wilkinson, Will. "Urbanization, Polarization, and Populist Backlash." Niskanen Center, 2019. https://niskanencenter.org/wp-content/uploads/2019/06/Wilkinson-Density-Divide-Final.pdf.

29. Census Bureau, "Americans Moving at Historically Low Rates, Census Bureau Reports."

30. Moretti, 2012 and Cowen, 2017.

31. Moretti, 2013.

32. Porter, Eduardo, and Guilbert Gates. "Why Workers Without College Degrees Are Fleeing Big Cities." *The New York Times*, May 21, 2019. https://www.nytimes.com/interactive/2019/05/21/business/economy/migration-big-cities.html.

33. Raven Molloy, Board of Governors of the Federal Reserve System, Christopher L. Smith, Board of Governors of the Federal Reserve System, Riccardo Trezzi, Board of Governors of the Federal Reserve System, and Abigail Wozniak, University of Notre Dame, NBER, and IZA. "Understanding Declining Fluidity in the US Labor Market," 2016. https://www.brookings.edu/wp-content/uploads/2016/03/MolloyEtAl_DecliningFluidityLaborMarket_ConferenceDraft.pdf.

34. Steuer, Eric "The Customer-Service Rep" *The New York Times*, February 23, 2017, sec. Magazine. https://www.nytimes.com/2017/02/23/magazine/the-new-working-class.html.

35. Solow, Robert M. "Thomas Piketty Is Absolutely Right. " *The New Republic*, April 22, 2014. https://newrepublic.com/article/117429/capital-twenty-first-century-thomas-piketty-reviewed.

36. A helpful summary at Smith, Noah. "Blame Monopolies for Short-Changing US Workers." Bloomberg View, January 26, 2017. https://www.bloomberg.com/view/articles/2017-01-26/blame-monopolies-for-short-changing-u-s-workers.

A commonly cited peer-reviewed analysis is Fleck, Glaser, Sprague, 2011.

The Economic Policy Institute research in labor share of income includes "Understanding the Historic Divergence Between Productivity and a Typical Worker's Pay: Why It Matters and Why It's Real." Economic Policy Institute and their related "State of Working America" research. See http://www.epi.org/publication/understanding-the-historic-divergence-between-productivity-and-a-typical-workers-pay-why-it-matters-and-why-its-real/.

Government sources include "2015 Economic Report of the President." The White House. https://obamawhitehouse.archives.gov/administration/eop/cea/economic-report-of-the-President/2015 and an analysis by the Federal Reserve Bank of Philadelphia, Armenter, Roc. "A Bit of a Miracle No More: The Decline of the Labor Share." Business Review 98, no. 3 (2015): 1–9.

A detailed breakdown of the NIPA accounts can be found at Emmanuel Saez and Gabriel Zucman. "Online Appendix of Wealth Inequality in the United States since 1913: Evidence from Capitalized Income Tax Data." http://gabriel-zucman.eu/files/SaezZucman2016QJEAppendix.pdf

37. Ostry, Jonathan, Prakash Loungani, and Davide Furceri. "Neoliberalism: Oversold?" Finance & Development, June 2016, cited in Rodrik, Dani. "Economics of the Populist Backlash." VoxEU.org, July 3, 2017. http://voxeu.org/article/economics-populist-backlash.

38. Karabarbounis and Neiman, 2013.

39. Rognlie, Matthew. "Deciphering the Fall and Rise in the Net Capital Share: Accumulation or Scarcity?" Brookings Papers on Economic Activity 2015, no. 1 (2016): 1–69. https://muse.jhu.edu/article/611902/summary. Gutiérrez and Piton used two National account databases to measure labor shares: sector and industry accounts and concluded that the non-housing share is stable, except in the US, where it has declined 6 percent. Gutiérrez, Germán, and Sophie Piton. "Revisiting the Global Decline of the (Non-Housing) Labor Share." https://drive.google.com/file/d/1RMTqNNJFUSxeMx9U-sObAgqUeb3HU2K8i/view. Importantly, however, even if housing has grown as a share of value-added, the consequence for below median income workers is likely to be grim, as their incomes are not likely to grow with rent or mortgage costs and the importance of inherited housing is likely to grow.

40. See Koh, Dongya, Raül Santaeulàlia-Llopis, and Yu Zheng. "Labor Share Decline and the Capitalization of Intellectual Property Products." Unpublished Paper, Washington University in St. Louis, 2015. http://r-santaeulalia.net/pdfs/IPP-and-USLaborShare-short.

pdf.

41. This debate goes back many years. See Cole, Alan. “A Walkthrough of Gross Domestic Income.” http://taxfoundation.org/article/walkthrough-gross-domestic-income and, for a more recent and careful treatment of pass-through income for top earners, see Smith, Matthew, Danny Yagan, Owen Zidar, and Eric Zwick. “Capitalists in the Twenty-First Century.” Pre-publication draft, June 10, 2019. http://www.ericzwick.com/capitalists/capitalists.pdf.

42 “Labor Share of Income: A New Look at the Decline in the United States”, McKinsey Global Institute Discussion Paper, May 2019. https://www.mckinsey.com/featured-insights/employment-and-growth/a-new-look-at-the-declining-labor-share-of-income-in-the-united-states.

43. Autor, Dorn, Katz, et al., 2017. De Loecker and Eeckhout, 2017 reached a similar conclusion using a different approach. “Labor Share of Income: A New Look at the Decline in the United States | McKinsey.” https://www.mckinsey.com/featured-insights/employment-and-growth/a-new-look-at-the-declining-labor-share-of-income-in-the-united-states.

44. James Manyika, Sree Ramaswamy, Jacques Bughin, Jonathan Woetzel, and Michael Birshan. “The Superstar Firms, Sectors, and Cities Leading the Global Economy | McKinsey.” https://www.mckinsey.com/featured-insights/innovation-and-growth/superstars-the-dynamics-of-firms-sectors-and-cities-leading-the-global-economy.

45. Manyika, James, Sree Ramaswamy, Somesh Khanna, Hugo Sarrazin, Gary Pinkus, Guru Sethupathy, and Andrew Yaffe. “Digital America: A Tale of the Haves and Have-Mores,” no. December (2015).

46. Ian Hathaway and Litan, Robert E. “Declining Business Dynamism in the United States: A Look at States and Metros.” Brookings (blog), November 30, 2001. https://www.brookings.edu/research/declining-business-dynamism-in-the-united-states-a-look-at-states-and-metros/.

47. Calvino, F., C. Criscuolo, and C. Menon (2016), “No Country for Young Firms?: Start-up Dynamics and National Policies”, OECD Science, Technology and Industry Policy Papers, No. 29, OECD Publishing, Paris. http://dx.doi.org/10.1787/5jm22p40c-8mw-en.

48. Europe. “How Stockholm Became a ‘Unicorn Factory.’” Knowledge@Wharton. http://knowledge.wharton.upenn.edu/article/how-stockholm-became-a-unicorn-factory/. Cited in “Why Does Sweden Have So Many Start-Ups? ” *The Atlantic*. https://www.theatlantic.com/business/archive/2017/09/sweden-startups/541413/.

49. These examples courtesy of Tyler Cowen and Alex Tabarrok's blog, Marginal Revolution.

1 The Productivity Seduction

50. Paul Krugman famously asserted that "Productivity isn't everything, but in the long run it is almost everything." Krugman, Paul R. The Age of Diminished Expectations: U.S. Economic Policy in the 1990s. MIT Press, 1997.

51. "The Productivity–Pay Gap." Economic Policy Institute (blog). http://www.epi.org/productivity-pay-gap/. Data are for average hourly compensation of production/nonsupervisory workers in the private sector and net productivity for the total economy. "Net productivity" is the growth of output of goods and services minus depreciation per hour worked.

EPI analysis of unpublished Total Economy Productivity data from Bureau of Labor Statistics (BLS) Labor Productivity and Costs program, wage data from the BLS Current Employment Statistics, BLS Employment Cost Trends, BLS Consumer Price Index, and Bureau of Economic Analysis National Income and Product Accounts.

Cited by Summers, Lawrence. "Productivity Still Matters for Median Worker's Pay." Financial Times, November 16, 2017. https://www.ft.com/content/a497331e-8fe8-31df-8aff-70ab584bf705.

52. Groshen, Erica. "How Are Wages Determined?" Federal Reserve Bank of Cleveland, February 15, 1990.

53. Azar, Marinescu, Steinbaum 2017.

54. Alexander, Scott, "Considerations On Cost Disease." Slate Star Codex, February 10, 2017. http://slatestarcodex.com/2017/02/09/considerations-on-cost-disease/.

55. Gordon, 2016.

56. Leonhardt, ibid.

57. "Apprenticeship Programs in a Changing Economic World | Eric A. Hanushek." http://hanushek.stanford.edu/publications/apprenticeship-programs-changing-economic-world.

58. Spence, 1973.

59. For a well-argued polemic that most of the gains from education are from signaling

and that neither signaling nor human capital returns justifies the level of current investment in education, see Caplan, 2018.

60. Economic Policy Institute, State of Working America Data Library, "Wage-Education Series," 2018 based on Current Population Survey Outgoing Rotation Group microdata analysis of wage and salary workers aged 18-64. Wages by education are the average hourly wages of workers disaggregated by the highest level of education attained.

61. "The Condition of Education - Participation in Education - Postsecondary - Undergraduate Enrollment - Indicator May (2016)." http://nces.ed.gov/programs/coe/indicator_cha.asp.

62. Raj Chetty and his colleagues have shown that parental income predicts whether a child goes to college even more strongly than parental college attainment. 90–95 percent of kids from high income families enroll in college, compared with 25–30 percent of children from bottom income families—and income matters more than attainment. Gregor Aisch, Amanda Cox, and Kevin Quealy. "You Draw It: How Family Income Predicts Children's College Chances." *The New York Times*, May 28, 2015. http://www.nytimes.com/interactive/2015/05/28/upshot/you-draw-it-how-family-income-affects-childrens-college-chances.html.

63. Dynarski, Susan. "For the Poor, the Graduation Gap Is Even Wider Than the Enrollment Gap." The New York Times, June 2, 2015. http://www.nytimes.com/2015/06/02/upshot/for-the-poor-the-graduation-gap-is-even-wider-than-the-enrollment-gap.html reporting on "The Condition of Education - Spotlights - 2015 Spotlights - Postsecondary Attainment: Differences by Socioeconomic Status - Indicator May (2015)." https://nces.ed.gov/programs/coe/indicator_tva.asp.

64. Caroline M. Hoxby. "The Dramatic Economics of the US Market for Higher Education," 2016. http://www.nber.org/feldstein_lecture_2016/hoxby_feldstein_lecture_27july2016.pdf. "2016number3.pdf." Full lecture available at http://www.nber.org/feldstein_lecture_2016/feldsteinlecture_2016.html.

65. Gordon, Grey, and Aaron Hedlund. "Accounting for the Rise in College Tuition." National Bureau of Economic Research, 2016. http://www.nber.org/papers/w21967.

66. OECD. Education at a Glance 2014. Education at a Glance. OECD Publishing, 2014. http://www.oecd-ilibrary.org/education/education-at-a-glance-2014_eag-2014-en.

67. Chart on Four Year College Wage Premium from Economic Policy Institute, State of Working America Data Library, "College Wage Premium" 2018. Wages are in 2017 dollars. The regression-based gap is based on average wages and controls for gender, race and ethnicity, education, age, and geographic division. The log of the hourly wage

is the dependent variable. From the Current Population Survey Outgoing Rotation Group microdata.

68. The 2014 report of the National Student Clearinghouse showed that in 2013, 81 percent of college-age adults from families in the top income quartile (income of $108,650 or more) enrolled in college. 77 percent earned at least bachelor's degrees by the time they turned 24. In contrast, 45 percent of 18- to 24-year-olds from the lowest income quartile (family income of $34,160 or less) enrolled in college in 2012. By the time they turn 24, only 9 percent had college degrees. In short, family income now predicts college graduation more strongly than it does college enrollment.

69. Cappelli, Peter. Will College Pay Off?: A Guide to the Most Important Financial Decision You'll Ever Make. Public Affairs, 2015.

70. James, Jonathan. "The College Wage Premium." Cleveland Fed, August 8, 2012. https://www.clevelandfed.org/newsroom-and-events/publications/economic-commentary/economic-commentary-archives/2012-economic-commentaries/ec-201210-the-college-wage-premium.aspx.

71. "Digest of Education Statistics, 2016." https://nces.ed.gov/programs/digest/d16/tables/dt16_222.85.asp.

72. Freedman, David H. "The War on Stupid People." *The Atlantic*, June 16, 2016. https://www.theatlantic.com/magazine/archive/2016/07/the-war-on-stupid-people/485618/.

73. "What Sitzfleisch Has To Do with Wages." https://www.stlouisfed.org/on-the-economy/2015/march/what-sitzfleisch-has-to-do-with-wages.

74. "Rate of Return of College Compared to Alternative Investments | The Hamilton Project." http://www.hamiltonproject.org/charts/rate_of_return_of_college_compared_to_alternative_investments.

75. Leonhardt, David. "A Simple Way to Send Poor Kids to Top Colleges." *The New York Times*, March 29, 2013. http://www.nytimes.com/2013/03/31/opinion/sunday/a-simple-way-to-send-poor-kids-to-top-colleges.html.

76. "U.S. Economic Mobility: The Dream and the Data." Federal Reserve Bank of San Francisco. http://www.frbsf.org/economic-research/publications/economic-letter/2013/march/us-economic-mobility-dream-data/.

77. Goodman, Joshua, Michael Hurwitz, Jonathan Smith, and others. College Access, Initial College Choice and Degree Completion. National Bureau of Economic Research, Cambridge, MA, 2015. https://www.hks.harvard.edu/publications/college-access-ini-

tial-college-choice-and-degree-completion.

78. Elon Musk: https://twitter.com/elonmusk/status/984882630947753984.

79. Anderson, Chris, 2012 (p. 16) and "Craig Venter's 'Digital-to-Biological Converter' Is Real." Motherboard. https://motherboard.vice.com/en_us/article/craig-venters-digital-to-biological-converter-is-real.

80. Murphy, Mike. "Amazon Is Opening a Grocery Store with No Cashiers and No Checkout Lines." Quartz. http://qz.com/853205/amazon-amzn-launches-a-new-grocery-store-called-amazon-go-that-could-mean-the-end-of-checkout-lines-and-millions-of-cashier-jobs/. Cashier data from http://www.bls.gov/opub/ted/2015/occupational-employment-wages-2014.htm. Wingfield, Nick. "Amazon Pushes Facial Recognition to Police. Critics See Surveillance Risk." *The New York Times*, May 23, 2018, sec. Technology. https://www.nytimes.com/2018/05/22/technology/amazon-facial-recognition.html.

81. http://www.latimes.com/business/autos/la-fi-hy-ihs-automotive-average-age-car-20140609-story.html and http://grist.org/cities/500-million-reasons-to-rethink-the-parking-lot/.

82. Table of employment that may be affected by self-driving cars. Author calculation.

Sector	Jobs	Average Income	Source
Heavy tractor trailer truck driver	1,678,280	$42,500	A
Light Truck or Delivery Service	826,510	$34,080	B
School bus drivers	505,600	$30,580	C
Rental car agencies	447,050	$28,210	D
Auto body repair	256,620	$43,000	E
Taxi Drivers and Chauffeurs	180,960	$26,070	F
Transit and Intercity bus drivers	168,620	$40,160	G
Uber drivers	160,000	$12,000	H
Parking lot attendants	144,150	$22,520	I
Meter maids	8,710	$38,280	J
	4,376,500	**$156 billion**	

Sources:

A: BLS OES 53302 at http://www.bls.gov/oes/current/oes533032.htm

B: BLS OES 533033 at http://www.bls.gov/oes/current/oes533033.htm

C: BLS OES 533022 at http://www.bls.gov/oes/current/oes533022.htm

D: BLS OES 412021 at http://www.bls.gov/oes/current/oes412021.htm

E: BLS NAICS at http://www.bls.gov/oes/current/naics5_811120.htm based on estimates of 90 percent fewer crashes with self-driving cars.

F: BLS OES 533041 at http://www.bls.gov/oes/current/oes533041.htm

G:BLS OES 533021 at http://www.bls.gov/oes/current/oes533021.htm

H: Jobs from http://www.wsj.com/articles/uber-touts-its-employment-opportunities-1422229862. Income estimated to account for large share of part-time drivers.

I: BLS OES 536021 at http://www.bls.gov/oes/current/oes536021.htm

J: BLS OES 333041 at http://www.bls.gov/oes/current/oes333041.htm

83. Martin, 2014.

84. Meyer, Gregory. "'A Good Living but a Rough Life': Trucker Shortage Holds US Economy Back." Financial Times, July 8, 2018. https://www.ft.com/content/cf42db68-755e-11e8-b6ad-3823e4384287.

85. Miller, Michael. "AI's Implications for Productivity, Wages, and Employment. Report on MIT Conference on AI and Future of Work." *PC Magazine*, November 20, 2017 https://www.pcmag.com/article/357490/ais-implications-for-productivity-wages-and-employment.

86. Autor, 2015.

87. "The Toll of a New Machine." Fast Company, May 1, 2004. https://www.fastcompany.com/49359/toll-new-machine.

88. "Tellers: Occupational Outlook Handbook: US Bureau of Labor Statistics." https://www.bls.gov/ooh/office-and-administrative-support/tellers.htm.

89. "The Toll of a New Machine", op. cit.

90. Markoff, John. "The End of Lawyers? Not So Fast." *The New York Times*, 2016.

91. Bessen, James. "The Automation Paradox." *The Atlantic*, January 19, 2016. http://www.theatlantic.com/business/archive/2016/01/automation-paradox/424437/.

92. Markoff, John. "Planes Without Pilots." *The New York Times*, April 6, 2015. http://www.nytimes.com/2015/04/07/science/planes-without-pilots.html.

93. Gordon, 2013.

94. Cited in Oren, op. cit.

95. Erik Brynjolfsson "The Key to Growth? Race with the Machines". TED Talk 2013, available at https://www.ted.com/talks/erik_brynjolfsson_the_key_to_growth_race_em_with_em_the_machines. See also, David, 1990.

96. "The Inescapable Trilemma of the World Economy." Dani Rodrik's blog. http://rodrik.typepad.com/dani_rodriks_weblog/2007/06/the-inescapable.html.

97. Rodrik, Dani. The Globalization Paradox: Democracy and the Future of the World Economy. W. W. Norton & Company, 2011.

98. "Globalisation Has Faltered - The Global List." https://www.economist.com/briefing/2019/01/24/globalisation-has-faltered.

99. World Trade Organization. "World Trade Statistical Review, 2016," 2016. https://www.wto.org/english/res_e/statis_e/wts2016_e/wts2016_e.pdf.

100. Seo, Sok-Min. "Number of International Migrants Reached 244 Million in 2015." United Nations Sustainable Development, January 12, 2016. http://www.un.org/sustainabledevelopment/blog/2016/01/244-million-international-migrants-living-abroad-worldwide-new-un-statistics-reveal/.

101. For an excellent summary of research on the impact of US trade deals on manufacturing employment, see DeLong, J. Bradford. "NAFTA and Other Trade Deals Have Not Gutted American Manufacturing — Period." Vox, January 24, 2017. http://www.vox.com/the-big-idea/2017/1/24/14363148/. As a Treasury official, DeLong helped sell NAFTA during the Clinton Administration. I promoted it from the Labor Department.

102. Blinder, Alan S. "Five Big Truths About Trade." *The Wall Street Journal*, April 21, 2016, sec. Opinion. http://www.wsj.com/articles/five-big-truths-about-trade-1461280205.

103. Porter, Eduardo. "The Danger From Low-Skilled Immigrants: Not Having Them." *The New York Times*, January 20, 2018. https://www.nytimes.com/2017/08/08/business/economy/immigrants-skills-economy-jobs.html and Appelbaum, Binyamin. "Lack of Workers, Not Work, Weighs on the Nation's Economy." The New York Times, December 22, 2017. https://www.nytimes.com/2017/05/21/us/politics/utah-economy-jobs.html.

104. Streep, Abe "The Meat Cutter" *The New York Times*, February 23, 2017, sec. Magazine. https://www.nytimes.com/2017/02/23/magazine/the-new-working-class.html.

105. "U.S. Unauthorized Immigration Total Lowest in a Decade | Pew Research Center," November 27, 2018. http://www.pewhispanic.org/2018/11/27/u-s-unauthorized-immigrant-total-dips-to-lowest-level-in-a-decade/.

106. Federal Reserve Bank of St. Louis, "Is US Manufacturing Really Declining?"

https://www.stlouisfed.org/on-the-economy/2017/april/us-manufacturing-really-declining.

107. Schuman, Michael. “Is China Stealing Jobs? It May Be Losing Them, Instead.” *The New York Times*, July 22, 2016, sec. International Business. https://www.nytimes.com/2016/07/23/business/international/china-jobs-donald-trump.html.

108. Autor, Dorn, Hanson, 2016.

109. Moretti, Enrico. “The Future of Jobs in America” National Agricultural & Rural Development Policy Center Policy Brief 31, June 2014.

110. Autor, Dorn, et al., 2016.

2 The Lure and the Limits of Mandated Pay

111. “Usual Weekly Earnings of Wage and Salary Workers Second Quarter 2018,” https://www.bls.gov/news.release/pdf/wkyeng.pdf.

112. Card, 2005 and “Estimates of the Elasticity of Employment with Respect to the Minimum Wage | Econbrowser.” http://econbrowser.com/archives/2015/03/23316 cited in Smith, Noah. “Noahpinion: An Econ Theory, Falsified.” Noahpinion, December 3, 2016. http://noahpinionblog.blogspot.com/2016/12/an-econ-theory-falsified.html. Also, Paul Krugman, “The Mutability of Wages” at https://krugman.blogs.nytimes.com/2015/06/11/the-mutability-of-wages/. Note that efficiency wage theory does not explain how a market can be simultaneously insensitive to both supply (immigration) and price (minimum wages).

113. “More Than One Million Walmart US Associates Receive Raises as Part of Largest Single-Day Pay Increase in the History of Corporate America.” http://news.walmart.com/_news_/news-archive/2016/01/20/more-than-one-million-walmart-associates-receive-pay-increase-in-2016.

114. Krueger, Alan B. “The Rigged Labor Market.” Milken Institute Review. http://www.milkenreview.org/articles/the-rigged-labor-market.

115. Google settled on a radical solution: a senior committee that never meets that candidate makes all hiring decisions, based upon detailed standardized reports and evaluations from those who do. This removes hiring and firing authority from managers, a process detailed in Bock, 2015.

116. Williamson, 1968.

117. Card, and Krueger, 1993.

118. Card, and Krueger, 2015. More recently, Godøy and Reich have tested the impact of higher wage minimums on counties where the new minimum would constitute 82 percent of the county median wage and found no negative effects. Anna Godøy and Michael Reich. (2019). "Minimum Wage Effects in Low-Wage Areas". IRLE Working Paper No. 106-19. http://irle.berkeley.edu/files/2019/07/Minimum-Wage-Effects-in-Low-Wage-Areas.pdf

119. "Characteristics of Minimum Wage Workers, 2016. BLS Reports: US Bureau of Labor Statistics." https://www.bls.gov/opub/reports/minimum-wage/2016/home.htm. This is CEPS data, a monthly survey of 60,000 households that the Census Bureau conducts for the Bureau of Labor Statistics. Because estimates of worker pay are based on reported hourly wages and don't include overtime, tips, or commissions, an even smaller share of workers are affected by the federal minimum wage. On the other hand, increases in the minimum wage "ripple" upwards and extend the wage floor by about half of the wage increase. Economist often figure that a $2 increase in the minimum wage to $10, for example, would increase the earnings of most workers earning less than $11 per hour.

120. Allegretto, Sylvia and Michael Reich 2018. "Are Local Minimum Wages Absorbed by Price Increases? Estimates from Internet-based Restaurant Menus." ILR Review 71, 1: 35-63. Brummund, Peter 2017. "How Do Restaurants Pay for the Minimum Wage?" conference.iza.org/conference_files/WoLabConf_2018/brummund_p6819.pdf. Cooper, Daniel, Maria Luengo-Prado and Jonathan Parker 2019. "The Aggregate Local Effects of Minimum Wages." NBER WP 25761.

121. Dube, Arindrajit, William Lester and Michael Reich 2016. "Minimum Wage Shocks, Employment Flows and Labor Market Frictions." Journal of Labor Economics 34, 3: 663–704. Azar, Jose, Emiliano Huet-Vaughn, Iona Marinescu, Bledi Taska and Till von Wachter 2019. "Labor Market Concentration and Minimum Wage Employment Effects." 2019 SOLE meetings, Arlington, VA, May 4.

122. Coviello, Decio, Erika Deserranno and Nicola Persico 2019. "Minimum Wage and Individual Worker Productivity: Evidence from a Large US Retailer." tintin.hec.ca/pages/decio.coviello/research_files/Draft_MinW.pdf. Cooper, Daniel, Maria Luengo-Prado and Jonathan Parker 2019. "The Aggregate Local Effects of Minimum Wages." NBER WP 25761.

123. Aaronson, Daniel and Brian Phelan 2019. "Wage Shocks and the Technological Substitution of Low-Wage Jobs." Economic Journal 129,617: 1–34. https://doi.org/10.1111/ecoj.12529

124. "What Is a $15 Wage Really Worth? Depends Where You Live." Pew Research Center (blog). http://www.pewresearch.org/fact-tank/2018/10/10/the-real-value-of-a-15-minimum-wage-depends-on-where-you-live/.

125. "Seattle's Minimum Wage Experience 2015-16." http://irle.berkeley.edu/seattles-minimum-wage-experience-2015-16/.

126. Jardim, Ekaterina, Mark C. Long, Robert Plotnick, Emma van Inwegen, Jacob Vigdor, and Hilary Wething. "Minimum Wage Increases, Wages, and Low-Wage Employment: Evidence from Seattle." National Bureau of Economic Research, 2017. http://www.nber.org/papers/w23532. See also, Luca, Dara Lee, and Michael Luca "Survival of the Fittest: The Impact of the Minimum Wage on Firm Exit": SSRN." https://papers.ssrn.com/sol3/papers.cfm?abstract_id=2951110, which shows that higher minimum wages in Bay Area restaurants forced the weakest operators to close but had no effect on high-quality restaurants.

127. Washington is one of only four states that collects earnings and hours data detailed enough to enable a more precise analysis of the impact of a minimum wage increase. The Washington data covers multiple sectors, whereas prior research focused on the restaurant industry exclusively (for technical reasons, the Washington study included franchises but excluded some of the region's largest employers). Ehrenfreund, Max. "A 'Very Credible' New Study on Seattle's $15 Minimum Wage Has Bad News for Liberals." *The Washington Post*, June 26, 2017, https://www.washingtonpost.com/news/wonk/wp/2017/06/26/new-study-casts-doubt-on-whether-a-15-minimum-wage-really-helps-workers/.

128. Distressed by these findings, the mayor of Seattle commissioned a competing study by a team at UC Berkeley, which disputed these conclusions for using a national rather than regional control group. Reich, Michael, Sylvia Allegretto, and Anna Godoey. "Seattle's Minimum Wage Experience 2015-16," 2017. http://murray.seattle.gov/wp-content/uploads/2017/06/Seattles-Minimum-Wage-Experiences-2015-16.pdf.

The scholars overseeing the team published their more segmented findings as Jardim, Long, Plotnick, et al., 2018.

129. Rolf, 2016.

130. A version of this approach was proposed by Dube, Arindrajit. "Proposal 13: Designing Thoughtful Minimum Wage Policy at the State and Local Levels." Policies to Address Poverty in America 137, no. 7 (2014). http://www.hamiltonproject.org/assets/files/policies_address_poverty_in_america_full_book.pdf#page=139. Rather than relying on county-level wage data (which are not routinely gathered by the BLS), Dube adjusts

his proposed minimums for differences in regional living costs.

131. Rampell, Catherine. "'Free Lunches' like the $15 Minimum Wage May Hurt the People They're Meant to Help." *The Washington Post*. August 7, 2017. https://www.washingtonpost.com/opinions/free-lunches-like-the-15-minimum-wage-may-hurt-the-people-theyre-meant-to-help/2017/08/07/d55e8476-7bad-11e7-9d08-b79f191668ed_story.html.

132. Ganong and Shoag, 2013.

133. Unlike Uber and Upwork, Mechanical Turk is under-researched, despite no shortage of vocal "Turkers." A welcome exception is Panos Ipeirotis, who conducted an early survey of Turk workers. Ipeirotis, 2010. He blogs regularly on the nature of online work at www.behind-the-enemy-lines.com and has argued that Mechanical Turk represents a "market for lemons" where sellers cannot evaluate the quality of the goods (workers, many of whom are spammers) and that this drives good workers from the marketplace. Given Mechanical Turk's failure to thrive, despite some innovative uses such as ProPublica's efforts to use it to detect false reporting, this explanation deserves research.

134. Bureau of Labor Statistics, US Department of Labor. "Contingent and Alternative Employment Arrangements," February 2005, 20. https://www.bls.gov/news.release/archives/conemp_07272005.pdf.

135. Katz and Krueger, 2016.

136. Will Rinehart and Ben Gitis, "Independent Contractors and the Emerging Gig Economy" (Research, American Action Forum, July 29, 2015).

137. Katz and Krueger, 2019.

138. See, for example, "Evaluating the Growth of the 1099 Workforce." Mercatus Center, December 10, 2015. https://www.mercatus.org/publication/evaluating-growth-1099-workforce.

139. BLS, op. cit. The BLS also surveyed contingent workers, including wage and salary workers who did not expect their jobs to last. The two groups are distinct: a worker in an alternative employment arrangement may or may not be a contingent worker and a contingent worker may or may not be in an alternative employment arrangement. The data cited here are from alternative employment relationships.

140. Stern and Kravitz, 2016.

141. "Celebrating Generation's 10,000th Graduate—McKinsey Social Initiative." https://www.generation.org/voices-news. Foroohar, Rana. "US Workforce: Paying Young

Americans to Learn the Right Skills." *Financial Times*, June 15, 2017. https://www.ft.com/content/b5ceec2a-50e4-11e7-a1f2-db19572361bb.

142. Winterhager, Heinze, and Spermann, 2006.

3 Does Income Bargaining Matter?

143. Cited in DiNardo and Card, 2002.

144 . Ibid.

145. Farber, Herbst, Kuziemko, and Naidu, 2018.

146. Autor, Manning, Smith, 2016.

147. Oppenheim, James (December 1911). American Magazine. Colver Publishing House. p. 214.

148. "Table 3. Union Affiliation of Employed Wage and Salary Workers by Occupation and Industry." https://www.bls.gov/news.release/union2.t03.htm.

4 The High Cost of Enterprise Bargaining

149. BLS data cited by Irving Bernstein in "Americans in Depression and War" at https://www.dol.gov/general/aboutdol/history/chapter5.

150. Cohen and DeLong, 2016.

151. Bernstein, 2014.

152. Bernstein, ibid.

153. Freeman and Medoff 1986, p. 190.

154. Blanchflower and Bryson, 2004.

155. Blanchflower and Bryson, Summer, 2004

156. Several scholars have attempted to measure the impact of unions on stock prices. Positive effects are rare, but these studies confront enormous data and methodological challenges. Lee and Mas, op. cit. describe these methodological challenges in detail. They looked at the impact of unionization on public companies and found that, on average, unions reduced the equity value of a firm by $40,500 per worker—but that a great deal depended on the magnitude of a union victory and that the stock market impact

of a narrow union win vs. a narrow union loss is vanishingly small.

157. Blanchflower and Bryson, 2004.

158. Blanchflower and Freeman, 1992. Reprinted in Bognanno and Kleiner, 1992, pp. 56–79.

159. Bennett and Kaufman, 2007 and Hirsch. Summer 2004.

160. Unions try to persuade the NLRB to approve smaller bargaining units of supporters. Employers argue for larger units, hoping to dilute union strength. The spectacle of federal officials debating which workers share common interests is Kafkaesque and the exact criteria used by the NLRB to delineate bargaining units is something of a dark art.

161. Kleiner, 2001.

162. Ibid.

163. Farber, 1999 and Farber, 2013.

164. "Loss at Volkswagen Plant Upends Union's Plan for US South." Reuters, February 15, 2014. https://www.reuters.com/article/us-autos-vw-election-idUSBREA1D-1DP20140215.

165. Bureau of National Affairs data cited in Warren, Dorian T. "Union Organizing In National Labor Relations Board Elections." Dorian T. Warren, October 7, 2015. http://rooseveltinstitute.org/wp-content/uploads/2015/10/Union-Organizing-In-National-Labor-Relations-Board-Elections.pdf.

166. Median bargaining unit size from NLRB at https://www.nlrb.gov/news-outreach/graphs-data/petitions-and-elections/median-size-bargaining-units-elections. Note that a handful of large elections each year brings the average bargaining unit size to roughly 40 employees. NLRB reports on RC petitions at https://www.nlrb.gov/news-outreach/graphs-data/petitions-and-elections/representation-petitions-rc.

167. Bargaining outcomes data cited in Freeman, 2011 and Ferguson, 2008. Estimate of 300-400,000 cited in Silverstein, Stuart. "Union Push Shows Scant Payoff for American Labor." *Los Angeles Times*, November 8, 1997. http://articles.latimes.com/1997/nov/08/news/mn-51453.

NLRB election data from https://www.nlrb.gov/news-outreach/graphs-data/petitions-and-elections/representation-petitions-rc.

168. NLRB annual summaries at https://www.nlrb.gov/reports-guidance/reports/election-reports.

169. NLRB annual summaries of RC elections available at https://www.nlrb.gov/reports-guidance/reports/election-reports.

5 The Hidden Cost of Exclusive Bargaining

170. The Wagner Act provided that a company could lawfully agree to any of four arrangements:

1) a closed shop, which requires that employees be members of a particular union as a condition of employment (meaning that a union could fire a worker by expelling them). The 1947 Taft-Hartley Act that modified the Wagner Act outlawed the closed shop.

2) a union shop, which requires that an employee join a union within a certain period of time after starting work,

3) an agency shop, in which employees pay the equivalent of dues but don't formally join the union, or

4) an open shop in which an employee cannot be compelled to either join or pay agency fees. A state with Right to Work laws permits only open shops.

171. Both "Right to Work" and "Fair Pay" are obviously rhetorical. "Union Members Summary." http://www.bls.gov/news.release/union2.nr0.htm. Table 5. Right to Work states for purposes of this calculation included Alabama, Arizona, Arkansas, Florida, Georgia, Idaho, Indiana, Iowa, Kansas, Kentucky, Louisiana, Michigan, Mississippi, Nebraska, Nevada, North Carolina, North Dakota, Oklahoma, South Carolina, South Dakota, Tennessee, Texas, Utah, Virginia, West Virginia, Wisconsin, and Wyoming. As of 2019, Right to Work laws are being litigated in West Virginia and the legality of a county declaring itself Right to Work is being litigated in Hardin County, Kentucky. Litigation over the possibility that counties or cities might enact Right-to-Work laws could force the entire question of the constitutionality of Right to Work to the Supreme Court, which isn't expected to be highly sympathetic to protecting the economic interests of labor unions in their current form.

172. State calculations by author based on monthly CPS data compiled using BLS standards by Hirsch, Barry T., and David A. Macpherson. "Union Membership and Coverage Database from the CPS." Unionstats.com, 2015. http://unionstats.com/. Calculations exclude Oklahoma, Indiana, and Michigan, which adopted Right to Work laws during the 1983–2015 period under review. Virginia, which became a Right to Work state in 2016, was counted as Fair Pay for purpose of this analysis.

173. "Right-to-Work Laws and Union Density: New Evidence from Micro Data - Springer." http://link.springer.com/article/10.1007%2FBF02685742 and "The Effects of Right-to-Work Laws: A Review of the Literature." http://ilr.sagepub.com/content/38/4/571.short.

174. Table of union coverage and membership from http://www.worker-participation.eu/National-Industrial-Relations/Compare-Countries. US data from BLS at https://www.bls.gov/cps/cpsaat40.xlsx.

175. Bardacke, 2011.

176. Bessen, 2015.

177. Ibid.

178. Frey, Carl Benedikt, and Michael A. Osborne. "The Future of Employment: How Susceptible Are Jobs to Computerisation. " https://www.oxfordmartin.ox.ac.uk/publications/the-future-of-employment/.

6 The AFL-CIO: Solidarity or Sedative?

179. The graph on labor density is cited at http://www.justfacts.com/unions.asp#membership and is constructed with data from the Union Sourcebook: Membership, Structure, Finance, Directory by Leo Troy and Neil Sheflin. IRDIS (Industrial Relations Data and Information Services), 1985 and US Department of Labor, Bureau of Labor Statistics from the CPS at http://www.bls.gov/webapps/legacy/cpslutab1.htm, Series Id: LUU0204899600.

180. The second measure of union strength is the contract coverage ratio: the portion of workers covered by a labor agreement. According to the Bureau of Labor Statistics, in 2015, 14.8 million (11.1 percent) of employed Americans were union members, but unions represented 16.4 million, or 12.3 percent of working Americans. BLS "Union Member Summary" at http://www.bls.gov/news.release/union2.nr0.htm.

181. Rosenfeld and Kleykamp, 2012.

182. Starr 2002 and Vander Meulen, Jacob. "West Coast Aircraft Labor and an American Military-Industrial Complex, 1935-194." Unpublished Manuscript. https://depts.washington.edu/pcls/documents/research/VanderMeulen_WestCoastAircraft.pdf.

183. Cited by Irving Bernstein in "Americans in Depression and War" at https://www.dol.gov/general/aboutdol/history/chapter5.

184. Discussions of Article Twenty began by the AFL in May of 1953 and were initially

opposed by most affiliates. In part, this reflected the nature of AFL craft union disputes, which related to jurisdiction. According to *The New York Times*, the Teamsters, Carpenters, and 30 unnamed unions all opposed Article Twenty as unnecessary. "Union Raiding Ban Drafted by AFL; Federation Due to Approve Council's Plan, Which Beck Refuses to Support. " August 14, 1954. https://www.nytimes.com/1954/08/14/archives/union-raiding-ban-drafted-by-a-f-l-federation-due-to-approve.html.

185. "NEA Convention: Less Than 3 Million Warm Bodies | Intercepts." http://www.eiaonline.com/intercepts/2013/07/03/nea-convention-less-than-3-million-warm-bodies. Union membership numbers are rarely exact because unions fog their membership numbers for a variety of reasons. Even the federally mandated LM reports don't always tally members consistently. With NEA, for example, part-time teachers are counted differently, as are "affiliate" and "agency fee" payers who are covered by labor agreements and pay the union but are not technically members.

7 The Challenge of Public Employee Unions

186. Examples of library innovation from Fallows and Fallows, 2018.

187. "Labor's Future", *The New York Times Magazine*, December 4, 1955. https://www.nytimes.com/1955/12/04/archives/meany-looks-into-labors-future-meany-looks-at-labors-future.html.

188. Reid, Joseph, and Kurth, Michael M. "The Rise and Fall of Urban Political Patronage Machines." In Goldin and Rockoff, 1992.

189. Reid and Kurth, ibid.

190. For reasons related to the federal structure of the US government and historic accident, federal, railroad, and a handful of other workers are covered by their own labor laws. Agricultural and home care workers only have organizing rights that have been granted by each state.

191. The graph on labor density is cited at http://www.justfacts.com/unions.asp#membership and is constructed with data derived from the Union Sourcebook: Membership, Structure, Finance, Directory by Leo Troy and Neil Sheflin. IRDIS (Industrial Relations Data and Information Services), 1985 and US Department of Labor, Bureau of Labor Statistics using CPS data http://www.bls.gov/webapps/legacy/cpslutab1.htm, Series Id: LUU0204922700.

192. "Employment by Major Industry Sector." http://www.bls.gov/emp/ep_table_201.htm.

193. The Center for Economic and Policy Research described the result.

"In four states—North Carolina, South Carolina, Tennessee, and Virginia– it is illegal for firefighters to bargain collectively. In these same states and Georgia, it is also illegal for police officers to bargain collectively. Five, mostly overlapping, states—Georgia, North Carolina, South Carolina, Virginia, plus Texas– don't allow collective bargaining for teachers. North Carolina, South Carolina, and Virginia have blanket statutes that prohibit collective bargaining for all public sector employees and don't make exceptions.

Texas and Georgia have state statutes banning collective bargaining in the public sector, but explicitly carve out exceptions for police and firefighters in the case of Texas … and firefighters in the case of Georgia... Georgia is the only state that singles out teachers in legislation in order to prevent them from bargaining collectively... In Tennessee, case law has ruled public sector collective bargaining to be illegal, but the state legislature passed a law that specifically permits collective bargaining for teachers."

"The Regulation of Public Sector Collective Bargaining in the States" at http://cepr.net/documents/state-public-cb-2014-03.pdf.

194. "Schools and Staffing Survey (SASS)." https://nces.ed.gov/surveys/sass/tables/sass0708_043_t1s.asp.

195. Munnell, op. cit.

196. Public Use Microdata Sample of the US Census for 1960, 1970, 1980, 1990, and 2000 and American Community Survey for 2010 (Ruggles et al. 2010) and NBER Collective Bargaining Law Data (Freeman and Valletta 1988). Table excerpted from Keefe, J. "Are Public Employees Overpaid?" Labor Studies Journal 37, no. 1 (March 1, 2012): 104–26. doi:10.1177/0160449X11429263.

197. Canada, which embraces exclusive representation, enterprise unions, and labor cartels, appears on the surface to stand in stark contrast to the American experience of union decline, since Canadian union density has remained at about 30 percent for decades. Union leaders frequently cite this fact in arguing for stricter enforcement of NLRB protections.

However, the underlying story illustrates the danger in aggregating public and private-sector density. Canadian private-sector density fell from 30 percent in 1970 to 15.2 percent today. (Statistics Canada https://www150.statcan.gc.ca/n1/pub/11-630-x/11-630-x2015005-eng.htm). Public sector density was the reverse, rising from 10 percent in the late seventies to 71.3 percent today. Rather than an exception, Canada is a poster child for a robust public sector union camouflaging the collapse of their private-sector counterparts.

198. US Office of Special Counsel. "Political Activity of the State and Local Employee." Summary of Hatch Act provisions. https://www.sheriffs.org/sites/default/files/tb/hatch_act.pdf.

199. Because public employees can request representation by any union and any union can represent public employees, the phrase "public employee union" is descriptive, not precise. AFSCME, NEA, and AFT have no significant private-sector membership. SEIU has 1.5 million members, of whom they commonly estimate about 1 million are government workers. More than twenty smaller unions appear to represent mostly public employees. Most major industrial unions, including the UAW and the Steelworkers, represent some public employees.

200. Silver, Nate. "The Effects of Union Membership on Democratic Voting." FiveThirtyEight (blog), February 26, 2011. https://fivethirtyeight.blogs.nytimes.com/2011/02/26/the-effects-of-union-membership-on-democratic-voting/.

201. "Top Organization Contributors | OpenSecrets." All cycles 1990–2018. Totals on this page reflect donations from employees of the organization, its PAC and in some cases its own treasury. These totals include all campaign contributions to federal candidates, parties, political action committees (including super PACs), federal 527 organizations, and Carey committees. This useful database has gaps and some visible errors. About 1.3 percent of all contributions were to neither Democrat/Liberal nor Republican/Conservative candidates. Moreover, in the case of ten contributing organizations, donations to conservative plus liberal organizations exceed total contributions. https://www.opensecrets.org/orgs/list.php?cycle=ALL.

202. Gallup, Inc. "Democrats Lead Ranks of Both Union and State Workers." Gallup.com. http://www.gallup.com/poll/146786/Democrats-Lead-Ranks-Union-State-Workers.aspx. Note that the raw results shown here are not controlled for demographic differences. See also https://www.opensecrets.org/orgs/list.php?cycle=ALL.

203. "Democrats Smash Watergate Record for House Popular Vote in Midterms." NBC News. https://www.nbcnews.com/politics/elections/democrats-smash-watergate-record-house-popular-vote-midterms-n940116. National Conference of State Legislatures, "State Partisan Composition." http://www.ncsl.org/research/about-state-legislatures/partisan-composition.aspx. There are 99 legislative bodies for 50 states because Nebraska has a unicameral legislature.

204. Seminal study is Levitt, 1994. A standard public choice study is Milyo, 2001. On the impact of wealth on candidates and elections, see Milyo and Groseclose, 1999.

205. "The Price of Prison Guard Unions—Capital Research Center." https://capitalre-

search.org/2011/10/the-price-of-prison-guard-unions-2/.

206. Ibid.

207. Page, 2013.

208. See, for example, Schwirtz, Michael, and Michael Winerip. "At Rikers Island, Union Chief's Clout Is a Roadblock to Reform." *The New York Times*, December 14, 2014. http://www.nytimes.com/2014/12/15/nyregion/at-rikers-a-roadblock-to-reform.html and Benjamin Weiser, Michael Schwirtz, and Michael Winerip. "U.S. Plans to Sue New York Over Rikers Island Conditions." *The New York Times*, December 18, 2014. http://www.nytimes.com/2014/12/19/nyregion/us-plans-to-sue-new-york-over-rikers-island-conditions.html.

209. "South Dakota Measure 22 — Revise Campaign Finance and Lobbying Laws — Results: Approved." http://www.nytimes.com/elections/results/south-dakota-ballot-measure-22-campaign-finance-overhaul. "'Democracy Vouchers' Win in Seattle; First in Country." *The Seattle Times*, November 3, 2015. http://www.seattletimes.com/seattle-news/politics/democracy-vouchers/. The South Dakota initiative is the subject of intense legal challenges.

210. Ackerman and Ayres, 2008.

211. Some legal scholars find the Court restrictions on both unions and elected officials to be inconsistent. Gely, Rafael, and Timothy D. Chandler. "Restricting Public Employees' Political Activities: Good Government or Partisan Politics." House. L. Rev. 37 (2000): 775.

212. Ibid. The National Conference of State Legislatures maintains a summary of the statutes from each state that govern public employee political activity at http://www.ncsl.org/research/ethics/50statetablestaffandpoliticalactivitystatutes.aspx.

213. "(Government) Workers of the World Unite!", January 6, 2011. http://www.economist.com/node/17849199 .

214. Freeman and Ichniowski, 2007.

215. Extensive research has found modest impacts of collective bargaining laws on public employee wages. Richard Freeman and Robert Valletta found that a state that moved from no bargaining provision to a duty to bargain increased wages by 6–8 percent in cross-sectional analysis, although the estimate was smaller in longitudinal analysis. They found an effect even when controlling for collective bargaining status, suggesting that collective bargaining laws have direct effects beyond their marginal impact on unionization or bargaining coverage. Ibid.

Frandsen, 2016, exploited differences in the timing of bargaining laws across states to estimate the impact of public sector collective bargaining rights on pay, benefits, and employment for teachers, fire fighters, and police. Surprisingly, he found little effect on teachers' pay, benefits, or employment, despite significantly growth in teachers unions. For fire fighters, he found that unions had a substantial positive effect on wages. For police, the wage effect was more modest but the workweek was significantly shortened.

216. Several progressive think tanks have concluded that public and private employee pay is comparable by averaging compensation over a large number of workers. Since the composition of public and private employees is fundamentally different however, determining pay comparability requires that pay and benefits for similar positions be compared in each sector.

217. According to the Bureau of Labor Statistics, the average annual salary for the roughly 330,000 office clerks who work in government was almost $27,000 in 2005, while the 2.7 million in the private sector received an average pay of just under $23,000. Nationwide, among the 108,000 janitors who work in government, the average salary was $23,700. The average salary of the 2 million janitors working in the private sector, meanwhile, was $19,800.

218. On the tendency for unions to reduce the polarization of average wages across industries, so that on net unionism reduces rather than increases wage dispersion in the United States, see Freeman, 1980.

219. The PEW Charitable Trust. "The State Pensions Funding Gap: Challenges Persist," July 2015. http://www.pewtrusts.org/~/media/assets/2015/07/pewstates_statepension-debtbrief_final.pdf.

220. Walsh, Mary Williams. "Dallas Stares Down a Texas-Size Threat of Bankruptcy." *The New York Times*, November 20, 2016. http://www.nytimes.com/2016/11/21/business/dealbook/dallas-pension-debt-threat-of-bankruptcy.html. Unfunded retiree health insurance obligations are a more manageable problem because, unlike pensions, they are rarely backed by explicit constitutional guarantees or protected by case law. States, cities, and counties are free to make benefits less generous, require higher co-pays or insist that employees or retirees pay a greater share of the premium—and as health care costs have continued to rise, they have done all of these things.

221. Private sector comparison from Munnell, Alicia H., Jean-Pierre Aubry, Josh Hurwitz, Laura Quinby, and others. "Unions and Public Pension Benefits." Issue Brief, Washington, DC: Center for State and Local Excellence (July), 2011. http://dlib.bc.edu/islandora/object/bc-ir:104206/datastream/PDF/download/citation.pdf.

222 . Donahue, John D. The Warping of Government Work. Cambridge, Mass: Harvard

University Press, 2008.

223. Bureau of Labor Statistics, "Job Opening and Labor Turnover (JOLT) Report for June, 2016", released August 10, 2016. Table IV: Quit Levels and Rates at http://www.bls.gov/news.release/pdf/jolts.pdf.

224. "Police Chiefs Are Often Forced to Put Officers Fired for Misconduct Back on the Streets." *The Washington Post*. https://www.washingtonpost.com/graphics/2017/investigations/police-fired-rehired/.

225. Campaign Zero Planning Team. "Police Union Contracts and Police Bill of Rights Analysis," June 29, 2016. http://static1.squarespace.com/static/559fbf2be4b08ef197467542/t/5773f695f7e0abbdfe28a1f0/1467217560243/Campaign+Zero+Police+Union+Contract+Report.pdf.

Campaign Zero both overstates and understates the barriers to police accountability. Police with no union contract or state bill of rights have qualified immunity under the law. This protects officers from civil claims or monetary damages if the courts deem that they have not violated a citizen's constitutional or statutory rights and so long as a "reasonable person" would conclude that the officer's conduct was within the law. Qualified immunity has historically been protection enough. Campaign Zero does not consider the impact of qualified immunity in evaluating police accountability. Also, they undercount the level of protection conferred by statutes. They show officers in Miami as lacking protections in their labor agreement for example, even though that the state's police bill of rights confers these same protections.

226. Tribune, Chicago. "Cops Traded Away Pay for Protection in Police Contracts." Chicagotribune.com. http://www.chicagotribune.com/news/local/breaking/ct-chicago-police-contracts-fop-20160520-story.html.

227. Campaign Zero Planning Team. "Police Union Contracts and Police Bill of Rights Analysis," June 29, 2016. http://static1.squarespace.com/static/559fbf2be4b08ef197467542/t/5773f695f7e0abbdfe28a1f0/1467217560243/Campaign+Zero+Police+Union+Contract+Report.pdf.

228. Washington Post, op. cit.

229. On the impact of good teachers, see Chetty, Raj, John Friedman, and Jonah Rockoff. "The Long-Term Impacts of Teachers: Teacher Value-Added and Student Outcomes in Adulthood." NBER Working Paper 17699. http://www.nber.org/papers/w17699 and Hanushek, Eric A. "The Economic Value of Higher Teacher Quality," December 2010. http://www.nber.org/papers/w16606.

230. "The Rubber Room." The New Yorker. August 8, 2009 http://www.newyorker.com/

magazine/2009/08/31/the-rubber-room.

231. The literature on the impact of teachers on future income is vast and well summarized by Raj Chetty. Chetty, Friedman, and Rockoff, 2011.

232. Hanushek, 2010.

233. Although confidence in teacher value-added measures has grown significantly over the past two decades, all measurements of teacher value-added remain controversial with teachers unions, as might be expected. For an interesting history on the statistical techniques used in measuring teachers, see Carey, Kevin. "The Little-Known Statistician Who Taught Us to Measure Teachers." *The New York Times*, May 19, 2017, sec. The Upshot. https://www.nytimes.com/2017/05/19/upshot/the-little-known-statistician-who-transformed-education.html.

234. Chetty, Friedman, Hilger, Saez, et al. 2010. For a critique, see Bryan Caplan, "Teachers and Income: What Did the Kindergarten Study Really Find?" Library of Economics and Liberty http://econlog.econlib.org/archives/2011/10/teachers_and_in.html.

235. Freddie. "Why Selection Bias Is the Most Powerful Force in Education." The ANOVA, March 30, 2017. https://fredrikdeboer.com/2017/03/29/why-selection-bias-is-the-most-powerful-force-in-education/.

236. Data regarding teacher value-added is summarized from "Rewarding and Employing Teachers Based on Their Value-Added." Education Next, March 10, 2014. http://educationnext.org/rewarding-and-employing-teachers-based-on-their-value-added/.

237. Staiger and Rockoff, 2010.

238. "Digest of Education Statistics, 2013." https://nces.ed.gov/programs/digest/d13/tables/dt13_211.60.asp.

239. "How Much Can a Dentist Expect to Get Paid?" https://money.usnews.com/careers/best-jobs/dentist/salary.

240. "Here's the News: The Annual Report on the Economic Status of the Profession, 2012-13 AAUP," https://www.aaup.org/article/heres-news-annual-report-economic-status-profession-2012-13#.W51cT5NKjUK.

241. McKenna, Laura. "The College President-to-Adjunct Pay Ratio." *The Atlantic*, September 24, 2015. http://www.theatlantic.com/education/archive/2015/09/income-inequality-in-higher-education-the-college-president-to-adjunct-pay-ratio/407029/.

242. The Education Reform Act 1988 is available at http://www.legislation.gov.uk/ukpga/1988/40/contents.

243. The database is available at http://www.ecs.org/teacher-tenure-continuing-contract-policies/.

244. "Boiling frog." Wikipedia, the Free Encyclopedia, https://en.wikipedia.org/wiki/Boiling_frog.

8 Bosses of the World, Unite!

245. Austen, Ben "The Fast-Food Worker" *The New York Times*, February 23, 2017, sec. Magazine. https://www.nytimes.com/2017/02/23/magazine/the-new-working-class.html.

246. 3F Labor agreement covering McDonald's workers is available at https://www.3f.dk/fagforening/fag/mcdonalds-medarbejder.

247. Alderman, Liz, and Steven Greenhouse. "Living Wages, Rarity for US Fast-Food Workers, Served Up in Denmark." *The New York Times*, October 27, 2014. http://www.nytimes.com/2014/10/28/business/international/living-wages-served-in-denmark-fast-food-restaurants.html. Note that the *NYT* asserts that Danish workers earn $20 per hour, a figure derived by converting wages from kroner to dollars using exchange rates (others have reported even higher rates using this method). To standardize for differences in purchasing power, it is preferable to convert the minimum monthly salary in the labor agreement to dollars using purchasing power parity based on OECD.stat indexes at http://stats.oecd.org/Index.aspx.

248. According to the 2015 census, the Detroit Combined Statistical Area, including Warren, Ann Arbor, Flint, and Monroe, is home to 5.3m residents. Like the Atlanta CSA with 6.3m inhabitants, it hosts 62 McDonald's outlets. Denmark had 5.6m residents in 2013 and 89 McDonald's locations.

249. Financial information about McDonald's Denmark disclosed at http://www.mcdonalds.dk/content/dam/Denmark/Downloads/Filer/%C3%98konomi/%C3%85rsrapport2015_McDonald%27s%20Danmark%20ApS.pdf. It reveals gross margins in Denmark of 60 percent and pretax margins of 20 percent . US franchise accounting and McDonald's corporate, especially real estate, activities make direct comparisons tricky, but these results appear no worse than those experienced by US franchisees as reported by Bloomberg at http://www.bloomberg.com/features/2015-mcdonalds-franchises/.

250. The US no longer sees much industry bargaining, although both formal, de jure industry bargaining and de facto pattern bargaining were once common in oligopoly industries. The Steel Workers' Organizing Committee, later the United Steel Workers of America, bargained a basic steel agreement in 1937 between the leader of the industry

oligopoly, US Steel that forced competitors to adhere to the agreement. Industry bargaining prevailed in the US steel industry through the early 1980s, when changes in both product markets and technologies reduced the commonality of employer interest. Since companies were unable to divide into smaller groups that reflected mutual interest, the union bargained single company agreements, which were initially highly concessionary. Mangum, Garth L., and David E. McNabb. *Collective Bargaining in the Basic Steel Industry: The Rise, Fall and Replacement of Industry-Wide Bargaining*. First edition. Armonk, N.Y: Routledge, 1997.

251. Fortini, Amanda. "The Hotel Cleaner" *The New York Times*, February 23, 2017, sec. Magazine. https://www.nytimes.com/2017/02/23/magazine/the-new-working-class.html.

252. Hlatshwayo, Sandile, and Michael Spence. "Demand and Defective Growth Patterns: The Role of the Tradable and Non-Tradable Sectors in an Open Economy." American Economic Review 104, no. 5 (May 2014): 272–77. doi:10.1257/aer.104.5.272.

253. Smith, Adam. *The Wealth of Nations* Book 1, Chapter 8 "Of the Wages of Labour."

254. Internal Revenue Service Tables at "Statistics for Tax Returns with EITC | EITC & Other Refundable Credits." https://www.eitc.irs.gov/eitc-central/statistics-for-tax-returns-with-eitc/statistics-for-tax-returns-with-eitc.

255. Oren Cass. "The Case for the Wage Subsidy." *National Review*, November 16, 2018. https://www.nationalreview.com/2018/11/case-for-wage-subsidy-government-spending-book-excerpt/.

256 . Cochrane, John H. "The Grumpy Economist: A Progressive VAT." The Grumpy Economist, April 26, 2017. http://johnhcochrane.blogspot.com/2017/04/a-progressive-vat.html. Alan Auerbach at Berkeley has proposed what amounts to a VAT with a wage subsidy, which he terms a Destination Based Cash Flow Tax. This achieves much the same thing, except that as structured may be deemed a Border Adjustment Tax in violation of WTO provisions. See Auerbach, Alan. "Demystifying the Destination-Based Cash-Flow Tax," 2017. https://eml.berkeley.edu/~auerbach/Demystifying%20the%20DBCFT%209%2020%2017.pdf.

257. Boeri, Tito, Andrea Ichino, Enrico Moretti, and Johanna Posch. "Wage Equalization and Regional Misallocation: Evidence from Italian and German Provinces." Working Paper. National Bureau of Economic Research, February 2019. https://doi.org/10.3386/w25612.

258. MWPVL International. "Amazon Distribution Network Strategy." Amazon Global Fulfillment Center Network, http://www.mwpvl.com/html/amazon_com.html. Note that Amazon is approaching 100 million square feet of distribution capability in the US alone, but operates 145 additional facilities around the world. The underlying complexity of

these operations defies description.

259. Visser, Jelle. *Wage Bargaining Institutions from Crisis to Crisis*. Brussels: Europe. Comm., Directorate-General for Economic and Financial Affairs, 2013. http://dx.doi.org/10.2765/42942 and International Labour Office. Negotiating the Crisis? *Collective Bargaining in Europe during the Economic Downturn.* Geneva: ILO, 2010.

9 Organizing Employers to Strengthen Labor Markets

260. Krueger, Alan B., and Eric A. Posner. "A Proposal for Protecting LowIncome Workers from Monopsony and Collusion," February 2018, 22. Quote from Krueger, Alan B., and Eric Posner. "Corporate America Is Suppressing Wages for Many Workers." The New York Times, February 28, 2018, Opinion. https://www.nytimes.com/2018/02/28/opinion/corporate-america-suppressing-wages.html.

261. 2. Starr, Evan P. and Bishara, Norman, and Prescott, J.J., "Non-competes in the US Labor Force" (August 29, 2016). Available at SSRN: https://ssrn.com/abstract=2625714.

262. Saxenian, 1996.

263. Krueger, Alan B. "The Rigged Labor Market." Milken Institute Review. http://www.milkenreview.org/articles/the-rigged-labor-market.

264. Lobel, Orly. "The New Cognitive Property: Human Capital Law and the Reach of Intellectual Property." https://www.law.berkeley.edu/files/Lobel_Orly_IPSC_paper_2014.pdf.

265. Garmaise, Mark J. "Ties That Truly Bind: Noncompetition Agreements, Executive Compensation, and Firm Investment." The Journal of Law, Economics, and Organization 27, no. 2 (2011): 376–425.

266. Morris M. Kleiner. *Licensing Occupations: Ensuring Quality or Restricting Competition?* Kalamazoo, MI: W.E. Upjohn Institute for Employment Research, 2006. https://doi.org/10.17848/9781429454865.

267. Hughes, Jazmine. "The Hair Braider" *The New York Times*, February 23, 2017, sec. Magazine. https://www.nytimes.com/2017/02/23/magazine/the-new-working-class.html.

268. Redbird, Beth. "The New Closed Shop? The Economic and Structural Effects of Occupational Licensure." American Sociological Review 82(3) 600–624 (2017): 25. https://doi.org/10.1177/0003122417706463.

269. The White House. "Occupational Licensing: A Framework for Policymakers," July

2015. https://obamawhitehouse.archives.gov/sites/default/files/docs/licensing_report_final_nonembargo.pdf.

270. Kleiner, Morris M. "Reforming Occupational Licensing Policies." The Hamilton Project, 2015. http://www.hamiltonproject.org/assets/legacy/files/downloads_and_links/reform_occupational_licensing_policies_kleiner_v4.pdf. Andy Koenig. "It Takes 890 Days to Become a Barber in Nevada." The Agenda. http://politi.co/1RXtdIH.

271. Salam, Reihan, and Miz Cracker. "The Upper Middle Class Is Ruining America." Slate, January 30, 2015. http://www.slate.com/articles/news_and_politics/politics/2015/01/the_upper_middle_class_is_ruining_all_that_is_great_about_america.single.html#return.

272. Blair, Peter Q., and Bobby W. Chung. "How Much of Barrier to Entry Is Occupational Licensing?" National Bureau of Economic Research, November 16, 2018. https://www.nber.org/papers/w25262.pdf.

273. Redbird, ibid.

274. Carpenter, Dick M., Lisa Knepper, Angela C. Erikson, and John K. Ross. "License to Work: A National Study of Burdens from Occupational Licensing." Institute of Justice, May 2012. http://ij.org/wp-content/uploads/2015/04/licensetowork1.pdf.

275. Four problems with licensing from "Four Ways Occupational Licensing Damages Social Mobility | Brookings Institution." Brookings, November 30, 2001. https://www.brookings.edu/blog/social-mobility-memos/2016/02/24/four-ways-occupational-licensing-damages-social-mobility/.

276. "Beth Redbird on Licensing | EconTalk | Library of Economics and Liberty." March 19, 2018. http://www.econtalk.org/archives/2018/03/beth_redbird_on.html.

277. Allensworth, Rebecca Haw. "Foxes at the Henhouse: Occupational Licensing Boards Up Close." California Law Review 105, no. 6 (2017): 1567–1610. https://doi.org/10.15779/z38cj87k75.

278. Craig, Ryan (2015-03-10). College Disrupted: The Great Unbundling of Higher Education. St. Martin's Press.

279. Analysis of BLS data at "Demand to Fill Cybersecurity Jobs Booming." Peninsula Press, March 31, 2015. http://peninsulapress.com/2015/03/31/cybersecurity-jobs-growth/.

280. Scheiber, Noam. "Creating a Pastry Chef From Scratch." *The New York Times*, October 13, 2016. http://www.nytimes.com/2016/10/14/business/economy/pastry-work-

ers-restaurant-job-training.html.

281. Conference Board. "Help Wanted: What Looming Labor Shortages Mean for Your Business, " 2016. http://www.conferenceboard.org/.

282. Sigelman, Matthew. "Half of Supervisors Now Need a College Degree: Are You Getting Better Service?" Burning Glass Technologies, August 30, 2016. https://www.burning-glass.com/blog/half-of-supervisors-now-need-a-college-degree-are-you-getting-better-service/.

283. Bessen, James. *Learning by Doing,* op. cit.

284. Miller, Claire Cain, and Quoctrung Bui. "Switching Careers Doesn't Have to Be Hard: Charting Jobs That Are Similar to Yours." *The New York Times*, July 27, 2017, sec. The Upshot. https://www.nytimes.com/2017/07/27/upshot/switching-careers-is-hard-it-doesnt-have-to-be.html.

285. Opportunity@Work. http://www.opportunityatwork.org/. "Skillful." https://www.skillful.com/. The Labor Department Employment and Training Administration has experimented with an Occupational Information Network ("O*Net") that maintains a taxonomy of job characteristics, experience requirements, worker characteristics, and occupation-specific information. Both Google and LinkedIn appear to have built richer taxonomies algorithmically.

286. Lohr, Steve. "Data Could Be the Next Tech Hot Button for Regulators." *The New York Times*, January 8, 2017. https://www.nytimes.com/2017/01/08/technology/data-regulators-google-facebook-monopoly.html.

287. Manyika, James, Susan Lund, Byron Auguste, and Sreenivas Ramaswamy. "Help Wanted: The Future of Work in Advanced Economies Discussion Paper," 2012. http://www.mckinsey.com/insights/employment_and_growth/future_of_work_in_advanced_economies.

288. "Siemens in Charlotte Welcomes Its Largest-Ever Class of Incoming Apprentices | Siemens USA Newsroom." https://news.usa.siemens.biz/press-release/siemens-usa/siemens-charlotte-welcomes-its-largest-ever-class-incoming-apprentices.

289. Quinton, Sophie. "How Did These Kids Score Good Jobs Right Out of High School?" *The Atlantic*, March 5, 2013. https://www.theatlantic.com/business/archive/2013/03/how-did-these-kids-score-good-jobs-right-out-of-high-school/425715/.

290. "Shaping the Future Workforce—Dennis Dio Parker | FAME-USA." http://fame-usa.com/shaping-the-future-workforce-dennis-dio-parker/.

291. In their landmark report, Symonds, Schwartz, and Ferguson cite several "Models

of 21st Century Technical Education". All are school-centric; none involve employers centrally. None have grown large. Op. cit., p27.

292. "Multiple Employment and Training Programs: Providing Information on Co-locating Services and Consolidating Administrative Structures Could Promote Efficiencies". Government Accountability Office Report January, 2011. GA)-11-92

293. North America's Building Trades Unions Research Department Survey - Survey of Building Trades Training Centers for Interactive Training Center Map, cited at "Building-Trades-Training-Capacity-Talking-Points-11-23-16.Pdf," https://nabtu.org/wp-content/uploads/2017/03/Building-Trades-Training-Capacity-Talking-Points-11-23-16.pdf. Note that in the building trades, it is very common for skilled journeymen to become building contractors, and even to work both a craft and as a contractor. This vastly simplifies the challenge of employer involvement.

294. "Careers and Apprenticeships | AFL-CIO." https://aflcio.org/about-us/careers-and-apprenticeships.

295. Rotella, Carlo. "The Pipe Fitter" *The New York Times*, February 23, 2017, sec. Magazine. https://www.nytimes.com/2017/02/23/magazine/the-new-working-class.html.

10 A Market for Worker Representation

296. Here a "labor co-op" is a voluntary labor organization with proportional, not exclusive, rights to bargain with industry-based employer associations. The term is meant to contrast with conventional industrial unions with involuntary membership, exclusive bargaining rights, and an enterprise focus. It should not be confused with a "worker co-op", which describes collective ownership and operation of a business. I am painfully aware, however, that other authors, including Oren Cass, Trebor Scholz, and Katherine Stone, have used the term "labor co-op" differently than I use it here—sometimes to refer to an enterprise-based advisory council.

297. Richard Freeman, and Joel Rogers. "Open Source Unionism: Beyond Exclusive Collective Bargaining." Working USA 5, no. Spring 2002. https://www.cows.org/_data/documents/1007.pdf.

298. Mayer, Gerald. "Union Membership Trends in the United States." Congressional Research Service Report for Congress, August 31, 2004. http://digitalcommons.ilr.cornell.edu/cgi/viewcontent.cgi?article=1176&context=key_workplace.

299. Most professional associations do not bargain income, but those that do function

as craft unions for people with college degrees. As a result, the distinction between craft unions and professional associations is neither perfect nor important.

300. Union revenue taken from DOL LM reports and NLRB reports, which are not completely inclusive. $8 billion is both a lot of money and less than total US spending on coffee, romance novels ($11 billion each), or chocolate ($16 billion).

301. Younger, Jay. "Comparative Dues Study ACS Industry Benchmarking Program," June 17, 2011. http://www.mckinley-advisors.com/wp-content/uploads/2010/08/Participants-Report-Dues-Benchmarking-Study.pdf.

US union dues vary widely. Generally, AFL unions pay a much higher rate of dues, regardless of member earnings. Unions like the Steelworkers collect nominal dues from retirees that reduce their average.

Data from the Labor Management Reporting and Disclosure Act (LMRDA) provide an incomplete picture of union dues. Reporting requirements make it harder to identify special assessments and local dues variations. (I approved these revisions while at the Labor Department and today wish I had not.) Also, many public employee unions do not report income to the Department of Labor.

LM Reports for most years show unions collecting roughly $8.5 billion in dues. If state and local unions exempt from DOL reporting account for another $1 billion and the US has 14.5 million union members, the average member pays $655 annually with a substantial dispersion around this mean.

302. "Data: Membership Dues Aren't the Only Revenue Stream." ASAE. https://www.asaecenter.org:443/en/resources/articles/an_magazine/2016/november-december/data-membership-dues-arent-the-only-revenue-stream.

303. Manyika, James, Susan Lund, Kelsey Robinson, John Valentino, and Richard Dobbs. "Connecting Talent with Opportunity in the Digital Age | McKinsey & Company." http://www.mckinsey.com/global-themes/employment-and-growth/connecting-talent-with-opportunity-in-the-digital-age.

304. "A Decade On, Freelancers Union Founder Sara Horowitz Takes Her Fight Mainstream." https://www.villagevoice.com/2013/02/13/a-decade-on-freelancers-union-founder-sara-horowitz-takes-her-fight-mainstream/.

305. Tankersley, Jim, and Alan Rappeport. "1.5 Million Retirees Await Congressional Fix for a Pension Time Bomb." *The New York Times*, February 18, 2018, sec. Business Day. https://www.nytimes.com/2018/02/18/business/multiemployer-pension-crisis.html.

306. Rolf, David, Shelby Clark, and Corrie Watterson Bryant. "Portable Benefits in the

21st Century." Aspen Institute Future of Work Initiative, 2016. https://assets.aspeninstitute.org/content/uploads/files/content/upload/Portable_Benefits_final2.pdf.

307. See for example Kjellberg, Anders. "The Decline in Swedish Union Density since 2007." Nordic Journal of Working Life Studies 1, no. 1 (2011): 67–93.

308. David Rolf has proposed a specific approach. He advocates a system of worker ratings to create a company's WorkScore. Oddly, I founded Reputation Networks in 2007 to do just this. Unbeknownst to Rolf, the company called its product WorkScore and beta tested it extensively. The idea is not without business and technical challenges, but can plainly be made to work. Rolf, David. "Toward a 21st-Century Labor Movement." The American Prospect, April 18, 2016. http://prospect.org/article/toward-21st-century-labor-movement.

309. "Resolution No. 27 - Worker Ownership and Workers Capital." United Steelworkers. http://www.usw.org/convention/resolutions/resolution-no-27-worker-ownership-and-workers-capital.

310. Benkler, Yochai. The Wealth of Networks: How Social Production Transforms Markets and Freedom. Yale University Press, 2006.

311. Like lottery tickets, stock options are an all-or-nothing proposition. As Bill Gates put it, "...the variation in the value of an option is just too great. I can imagine an employee going home at night and considering two wildly different possibilities with his compensation program. Either he can buy six summer homes or no summer homes." For this reason and others, technology companies increasingly award workers restricted stock units. RSUs are a commitment to a future payment based on a specific number of the company's shares, typically after vesting. RSUs pay more reliably and do not require that a worker pay to exercise shares as do stock options. On the other hand, employees must pay taxes on RSUs as they appreciate.

312. Strom, Stephanie. "At Chobani, Now It's Not Just the Yogurt That's Rich." *The New York Times*, April 26, 2016, sec. Business Day. https://www.nytimes.com/2016/04/27/business/a-windfall-for-chobani-employees-stakes-in-the-company.html.

313. Some companies, famously Polaroid, have tried to use ESOPs as poison pills to protect management from a corporate takeover. The Labor Department now discourages this.

314. Amazon is testing an interesting variant. Underperforming workers can take a severance package, agree to a performance improvement plan called a Pivot, or appeal to a jury of Amazonian peers. The jury votes for workers about 30 percent of the time, and those who lose do not forfeit the other two options. See Bill Murphy. "You Don't

Just Get Fired at Amazon. What Happens Instead Is Brilliant. (Or Maybe Insane. Your Choice).” Inc.com, June 26, 2018. https://www.inc.com/bill-murphy-jr/you-dont-just-get-fired-at-amazon-what-happens-instead-is-brilliant-or-maybe-insane-your-choice.html.

315. Membership numbers cited by “Kaiser Permanente Labor Management Partnership” at https://www.lmpartnership.org/about/how-partnership-works/what-is-partnership.

316. For a relentlessly positive and sanguine account of Kaiser’s effort, see Kochan, Thomas A., Adrienne E. Eaton, Robert B. McKersie, and Paul S. Adler. *Healing Together: The Labor-Management Partnership at Kaiser Permanente*. ILR Press, 2013.

For an update of the landmark 1995 research by Richard Freeman on workplace voice, see Kochan, Thomas A., Kimball, William T., Yang, Duanyi, and Kelly, Erin. “Voice Gaps at Work, Options for Closing Them and Challenges for Future Action and Research.” Forthcoming in ILR Review, 2019. https://gcgj.mit.edu/sites/default/files/imce/resource-uploads/Kochan%20et%20al.%20Worker%20Voice%20Survey%20Paper%20June%202018.pdf.

317. “History of the LMP.” October 23, 2016. http://www.lmpartnership.org/about/how-partnership-works/history-lmp.

318. Johnson, Stefanie K., and Juan M. Madera. “Sexual Harassment Is Pervasive in the Restaurant Industry. Here’s What Needs to Change.” *Harvard Business Review*, January 18, 2018. https://hbr.org/2018/01/sexual-harassment-is-pervasive-in-the-restaurant-industry-heres-what-needs-to-change.

319. Phillips, Matt. “Germany’s Bizarre Version of Capitalism—Where Bosses and Workers Actually Cooperate—Is Winning.” Quartz. http://qz.com/452076/this-just-in-german-capitalism-has-won/.

11 Rules, Rights, and Information.

320. “FY 2017 Congressional Budget Justification, Wage and Hour Division.” https://www.dol.gov/sites/default/files/documents/general/budget/2016/CBJ-2016-V2-09.pdf and “Commonly Used Statistics.” https://www.osha.gov/oshstats/commonstats.html.

321. Piore, Michael J., and Andrew Schrank. Root-Cause Regulation: Protecting Work and Workers in the Twenty-First Century. Cambridge, Massachusetts: Harvard University Press, 2018.

322. United States Department of Labor, OSHA Commonly Used Statistics https://www.osha.gov/oshstats/commonstats.html.

323. United States Department of Labor, Wage and Hour Division, Fiscal Year Data https://www.dol.gov/whd/data/datatables.htm#panel1.

324. Making standardized ratios like this public is warranted because CEO compensation is high relative to the compensation of a typical worker or even that of a wealthy earner in the top 0.1 percent. CEO pay has grown much faster than stock prices or corporate profits. Including stock options realized, salary, bonuses, restricted stock grants, and long-term incentive payouts, the CEO-to-worker compensation ratio was 271-to-1 in 2016. It was 299-to-1 in 2014 and 286-to-1 in 2015. It is far higher than the 20-to-1 ratio during the Great Compression in 1965. Mishel, Lawrence, and Jessica Schieder. "CEO Pay Remains High Relative to the Pay of Typical Workers and High-Wage Earners," Economic Policy Institute, July 20, 2017, p. 25. http://epi.org/130354.

325. The literature on agency theory is rich and diverse. An influential early paper that extends agency costs into a theory of the firm is Michael C. Jensen, and William H. Meckling. "Theory of the Firm: Managerial Behavior, Agency Costs and Ownership Structure." Journal of Financial Economics 3, no. 4 (October 1976): 305–60.

326. Hill, Steven. "Benefits for the Rest of Us." *The Washington Monthly*, February 2016. http://www.washingtonmonthly.com/magazine/januaryfebruary_2016/features/benefits_for_the_rest_of_us059188.php

327. Harris, Seth, and Alan Krueger. "A Proposal for Modernizing Labor Laws for Twenty-First-Century Work: The 'Independent Worker.'" Brookings Institution, December 2015. http://www.hamiltonproject.org/assets/files/modernizing_labor_laws_for_twenty_first_century_work_krueger_harris.pdf.

328. Today the both the Fair Labor Standards Act establishes multiple criteria to determine whether a worker is an employee or a contractor at https://www.dol.gov/whd/regs/compliance/whdfs13.pdf. The IRS distinguishes between independent contractors, common law employees, statutory employees, statutory non-employees, and government workers at https://www.irs.gov/businesses/small-businesses-self-employed/independent-contractor-self-employed-or-employee. These rules map poorly onto workplace reality and reliably drive employers nuts.

329. Goldhill, Olivia. "In Norway, You Can Browse Everyone's Tax Returns, but There's a Good Reason You Might Not Want To." Quartz. http://qz.com/784186/in-norway-you-can-browse-everyones-tax-returns-but-theres-a-good-reason-you-might-not-want-to/.

330. Author calculations from "County Employment and Wages, " First Quarter 2016. http://www.bls.gov/news.release/pdf/cewqtr.pdf.

331. Metz, Cade. "Tech Giants Are Paying Huge Salaries for Scarce A.I. Talent."

The New York Times, October 22, 2017, sec. Technology. https://www.nytimes.com/2017/10/22/technology/artificial-intelligence-experts-salaries.html.

332. Hirschman, Albert O. Exit, Voice, and Loyalty: Responses to Decline in Firms, Organizations, and States. Cambridge, Mass: Harvard University Press, 1970.

333. "Table 1. Work Stoppages Involving 1,000 or More Workers, 1947-2017." http://www.bls.gov/news.release/wkstp.t01.htm.

Conclusion

334. Spence, Michael. "The Inequality of Nations | by Michael Spence." Project Syndicate, August 1, 2019. https://www.project-syndicate.org/commentary/market-power-encroaching-on-politics-by-michael-spence-2019-08.

335. Klein, Ezra. "The Forgotten Economic Idea Democrats Need to Rediscover." Vox, May 17, 2019. https://www.vox.com/policy-and-politics/2019/5/17/18626801/2020-democrats-sanders-warren-buttigieg-power-socialism.

336. "Opinion | Ian Bremmer: Is Democracy Essential? Alarmingly, Millennials Aren't so Sure." NBC News. https://www.nbcnews.com/think/opinion/democracy-essential-millennials-increasingly-aren-t-sure-should-concern-us-ncna847476.

337 . Brink Lindsey, Will Wilkinson, Steven Teles, and Samuel Hammond of the Niskanen Center published "The Center Can Hold: Public Policy for an Age of Extremes". https://niskanencenter.org/wp-content/uploads/2018/12/Niskanen-vision-paper-final-PDF.pdf.

338 . Caruso, Anthony. "Statistics of US Businesses Employment and Payroll Summary: 2012. " US Department of Commerce, Economics and Statistics Administration, US Census Bureau, 2015.

339 . Since they would never stoop to a pun, credit the portmanteau to Brink Lindsey and Steven Teles. *The Captured Economy: How the Powerful Enrich Themselves, Slow Down Growth, and Increase Inequality*. 1st edition. New York, NY, United States of America: Oxford University Press, 2017.

340 . On the Fraser Institute Index of Economic Freedom, see https://www.fraserinstitute.org/economic-freedom/history-of-free-the-world.

341 . This is a rapidly advancing field of research in both economics and psychology. A strong recent contribution is Mercier, Hugo, and Dan Sperber. *The Enigma of Reason.*

Cambridge, Massachusetts: Harvard University Press, 2017.

334. Spence, Michael. "The Inequality of Nations | by Michael Spence." Project Syndicate, August 1, 2019. https://www.project-syndicate.org/commentary/market-power-encroaching-on-politics-by-michael-spence-2019-08.

335. Klein, Ezra. "The Forgotten Economic Idea Democrats Need to Rediscover." Vox, May 17, 2019. https://www.vox.com/policy-and-politics/2019/5/17/18626801/2020-democrats-sanders-warren-buttigieg-power-socialism.

335. "Opinion | Ian Bremmer: Is Democracy Essential? Alarmingly, Millennials Aren't so Sure." NBC News. https://www.nbcnews.com/think/opinion/democracy-essential-millennials-increasingly-aren-t-sure-should-concern-us-ncna847476.

336. Brink Lindsey, Will Wilkinson, Steven Teles, and Samuel Hammond of the Niskanen Center published "The Center Can Hold: Public Policy for an Age of Extremes". https://niskanencenter.org/wp-content/uploads/2018/12/Niskanen-vision-paper-final-PDF.pdf.

337. Caruso, Anthony. "Statistics of US Businesses Employment and Payroll Summary: 2012. " US Department of Commerce, Economics and Statistics Administration, US Census Bureau, 2015.

338. Since they would never stoop to a pun, credit the portmanteau to Brink Lindsey and Steven Teles. *The Captured Economy: How the Powerful Enrich Themselves, Slow Down Growth, and Increase Inequality*. 1st edition. New York, NY, United States of America: Oxford University Press, 2017.

338. On the Fraser Institute Index of Economic Freedom, see https://www.fraserinstitute.org/economic-freedom/history-of-free-the-world.

339. This is a rapidly advancing field of research in both economics and psychology. A strong recent contribution is Mercier, Hugo, and Dan Sperber. *The Enigma of Reason*. Cambridge, Massachusetts: Harvard University Press, 2017.

Index

Printed in the USA
CPSIA information can be obtained
at www.ICGtesting.com
LVHW042014191124
797081LV00002B/240

* 9 7 8 1 7 3 3 3 1 5 5 1 7 *